Pennies
from Vietnam

Pennies from Vietnam

*A Sister at Home,
a Brother at War*

TRACY SMITH
with LARRY RAY SMITH

McFarland & Company, Inc., Publishers
Jefferson, North Carolina

The content of this book can be emotionally challenging, and it is with the utmost respect that a warning is offered. This book contains images and depictions from war, trauma, traumatic incidents, and other content that could be triggering to some readers. Within you will find graphic language, substance abuse, profanity, racist language/slurs, and violence. Larry's words have been presented unedited for cultural and historical reference.

LIBRARY OF CONGRESS CATALOGING-IN-PUBLICATION DATA

Names: Smith, Tracy, 1962– author. | Smith, Larry Ray, 1948–2000, author.
Title: Pennies from Vietnam : a sister at home, a brother at war / Tracy Smith, with Larry Ray Smith.
Other titles: Sister at home, a brother at war
Description: Jefferson, North Carolina : McFarland & Company, Inc., Publishers, 2024 | Includes index.
Identifiers: LCCN 2024013795 | ISBN 9781476694634 (print) ∞
ISBN 9781476652559 (ebook)
Subjects: LCSH: Smith, Larry Ray, 1948–2000—Correspondence. | Smith, Larry Ray, 1948–2000—Family. | Smith, Tracy, 1962– | United States. Army. Field Artillery, 20th—Biography. | Vietnam War, 1961–1975—Personal narratives, American. | Vietnam War, 1961–1975—Aerial operations, American. | Soldiers—United States—Correspondence. | Soldiers—Family relationships—United States. | Siblings—New Jersey—Kendall Park—Biography. | Kendall Park (N.J.)—Biography.
Classification: LCC DS559.5 .S543 2024 | DDC 959.704/10922—dc23/eng/20240425
LC record available at https://lccn.loc.gov/2024013795

BRITISH LIBRARY CATALOGUING DATA ARE AVAILABLE

ISBN (print) 978-1-4766-9463-4
ISBN (ebook) 978-1-4766-5255-9

© 2024 Tracy Smith. All rights reserved

No part of this book may be reproduced or transmitted in any form or by any means, electronic or mechanical, including photocopying or recording, or by any information storage and retrieval system, without permission in writing from the publisher.

Front cover images: *clockwise from left* Tracy, age 2, on Larry's shoulders as sister Peggy looks on with father Kenneth in the background, Elizabeth, New Jersey, circa 1964 (Smith family photograph); Larry poses with a UH-1 Huey, October 1967; Larry receives Air Medal in newspaper article; *background* Vietnam jungle © Rick van Leeuwen/Shutterstock

Printed in the United States of America

McFarland & Company, Inc., Publishers
Box 611, Jefferson, North Carolina 28640
www.mcfarlandpub.com

To the memory
of my brother and superhero,
Larry, for his precious words
and endless love

Table of Contents

Acknowledgments	ix
Preface	1

Part One
1. "I Grew a Mushstash"	6
2. "Open Up with My M-60"	23
3. I SEE YOU	37

Part Two
4. "Things I Don't Want to Talk About"	42
5. "War Is Hell, but the Girls Are Nice"	78
6. I HEAR YOU	84

Part Three
7. "Charlie Don't Play Games"	86
8. "Still Here Raising Hell"	97
9. I FEEL YOU	107

Part Four
10. "I Get Pills"	112
11. "Have I Really Gone Crazy All the Way?"	123
12. I GOT YOU	132

Part Five
13. "Thought I was a Gonner"	136
14. "Got Shot Down"	149
15. I BEG YOU	171

Table of Contents

Part Six

16. "We Go Where the War Is" — 176
17. "Shove the Mini-Gun" — 189
18. "I Blew It by Extending" — 202
19. I PROMISE YOU — 209

Part Seven

20. "Still Have a Long Way to Go" — 212
21. In Memory of Charlie — 215
22. Love Always, Tracy — 225

Index — 231

Acknowledgments

To every man and woman who has worn a military uniform for our country and allies, thank you for your service. To every veteran of the Vietnam War, welcome home. To their families, thank you for your sacrifice and love for your warrior in support of their mission. Americans owe our freedom to each of you.

Several contributors to this book served with Larry on the front lines. Each of them offered independent and personal experiences that contributed to the heart of the story, which I could never have captured on my own.

Richard Passer was named in Larry's letters, and my search for him took years. One day in 2018 he replied and admitted that he had been searching for Larry for 48 years. Rich confirmed that I had the right "best friend" when he wrote, "We were the wild ones." Rich revealed stories that illustrate the spirit of my brother in wartime. I will forever be grateful for his contribution to my brother's life and story.

Barry Brady, another crew chief and one of the soldiers rescued alongside Larry, provided a priceless video interview with his wife, Sara Brady, and his brother Ron. In our meeting on Zoom, Barry proudly showed me his uniform, donned his First Cavalry Stetson, and shared several funny moments full of sarcasm and genuine love that brought his version of the stories to life. Rest in peace, Blue Max warrior. Sara is now a friend and huge support.

John Stewart, one of the "Scrufty Dozen" crew chiefs, has sent Larry's widow a Christmas card every year since Larry's death. John's memory is vivid, and his photos and stories provided firsthand knowledge of the living conditions and the company-wide search for

Acknowledgments

Larry. John fondly recalls Larry and Barry attending his wedding in the summer of 1968, days before Larry's second deployment.

Jane Jayroe Gamble, Miss America 1967, provided a unique perspective about the active combat zone where Larry was stationed. When she shared words from her personal diary, we realized my brother wrote about Miss America on the same calendar date she wrote about his bravado, but Larry and Jane never met. I will forever be appreciative of the joy she brought our troops, and the support she has been in telling this bittersweet part of the story.

Tom Stroud, who commandeered the Happy Valley rescue, offered frontline memories of the volatile events. Captain Stroud, the heroic Air Force Skyraider pilot, orchestrated an incredible collaboration with multiple military units in Larry's rescue effort and revisited the day's actions with incredible detail. Tom Stroud is the hero that Larry never met. Tom led the team effort between multiple Army and Air Force aircraft units with impressive tenacity to successfully complete the rescue against all odds.

Richard Leroue, like Barry and Larry, experienced the rescue as a (volunteer) door gunner. Richard shared personal stories from firsthand optics of the challenging conditions in the Au Shau and Happy Valleys. I am grateful for his perspective of being lost in a jungle and being lifted to safety with moments to spare.

Greg Bronder kept in touch with John Stewart, and John introduced us in 2022. Greg served many roles in Larry's unit, one of which was working with the company clerk. This provided him a close interaction with pilot Charles Alvarez. Greg shared his memories with me in an interview and in his memoir ("My Vietnam Story"), complete with colorful tales including the Happy Valley rescue and his respectful memories of Alvarez.

Carla Oberdier, widow of Lyn Oberdier, the Skyraider pilot who served with Tom Stroud during the search and rescue in Happy Valley, shared the personal story of her loss. Carla accepted Lyn's posthumously awarded Medal of Honor for his part in my brother's rescue. Carla posted on Lyn's "Wall of Faces" page: "A dedicated soldier, husband, father, and Christian. His death forever made a difference and left a void in my life and the lives of our two small children."

Acknowledgments

Holly Tureen left her email address on Alvarez's "Wall of Faces" page. By locating her, I was introduced to her beloved friend Charlie Alvarez and found his brother, Eddie. Without Holly, I wouldn't know about or be able to honor the sacrifice that Charlie Alvarez made for my brother.

Eddie Alvarez showed grace for the tragic connection between our brothers from our first discussion. Eddie told me many childhood stories and blessed sharing the difficult details of his brother's death, in honor of Charlie's service and sacrifice. The Alvarez family is a true example of an American military family that has made many sacrifices and suffered great losses in service to our country.

I am thankful to my beta readers, all of whom read Larry's letters and several draft versions of the manuscript and provided priceless feedback that kept me moving forward. They include:

The late Michael R. Schoenenberger, a Vietnam veteran who wrote, "Reading your brother's letters was a mind-blowing experience"; Colonel Russ Olson, who helped me understand military jargon and culture, and who was reminded of the brotherhood he continues to embrace and honor; other veterans including Bill Tucker, who served in seven tours of duty including three in Vietnam, who validated that Larry's experiences were meaningful and described lessons from military service as "timeless."

Ricky Gore, who always looked up to his cousin Larry and thinks of him with every passing helicopter, provided insightful sentiments about my brother's choice of words; and my cousin Diane's husband Roger Scarbrough, who said, "Larry's is the voice of every soldier" after reading the book in one weekend despite his lasting PTSD from the war, encouraging me to proceed with publication. My writer friend Sara's husband Russ, while on a Navy ship in foreign waters, read my book and left priceless words of inspiration, including "Know that Larry's story of silent pain is echoed in service members today and the only way to fix it is by stories like his, being told. Thank you for telling his story so eloquently."

Acknowledgments

There are many veterans and veteran agencies who contributed to my research. They include Kenneth Caughron, a 96-year-old Air Force colonel who wrote the commendation on Tom Stroud; Jack Watkins, who left a comment on the internet that helped me find him and locate Barry Brady; Jesse Hobby, with the Aerial Rocket Association (ARA), who helped me locate the origin of images contributed by John Stewart; Allen Norris, former president of the First Cavalry Association, and his wife Cathy, who welcomed me to the annual Veterans Day event as the keynote speaker and toured the White House with me, enhancing the historical importance of Larry's letters; Byron Hukee with the Air Force Skyraiders who located Tom Stroud for me.

Countless others gave me the resilience to keep researching and the fortitude to complete my own mission. They include Bob Rushing's family, and Kenneth Fields, Larry Russell, Russ Warriner, Ron Frawley, Ralph Norman, Clovis Jones, Joseph Galloway, and Jay Tolson, son of General Tolson. I must also thank my dear friend Bonnie Gell, whose father Jack Gell died in the Ia Drang battle, for introducing me to Joe Galloway and his lovely wife Grace, who permitted me to use Joe's quote after his passing.

Other military groups and individuals associated with them have been a huge support, including the First Cavalry Association, several chapters of the Daughters of the American Revolution (DAR), Aerial Rocket Association (ARA), Quilts of Valor (QOV), Veterans Helping Veterans, American Legion, VFW, Jessica Fickenscher, General Chuck Swannack, and Speedway Motorsports, Inc.

Kate DiZio took the lead on creative planning with graphic designs for branding, website design, logo, and touch/business cards. Kate provides endless inspiration and ideas for marketing and promotion as the project manager of the book's launch team. Kate is a big proponent of emotional healing with extensive PTSD knowledge, and a personal cheerleader for me and this book.

Caitlyn Francisca Johnson, with Caitlyn Tucker Photography, provided early influence for branding and web design with her generous offer to photograph letters and mementos. Her creative eye inspired the original book cover and branding elements.

Acknowledgments

Fellow authors, editors, and writer groups have been priceless cheerleaders for this cause: Amy Rupertus Peacock ("Old Breed General"), Steve Grossman ("Palimony"), Christine Guidry Law ("Hometown Coward"); Liz Giertz, my first gem of an editor who fostered a richer narrative; Jennifer Kaufman, a volunteer editor for the final draft who assured me it was a "beautifully written heroic tragedy"; Pitch to Published (P2P) founder Kathy Ver Eecke for her query letter expertise and for introducing me to a tribe of passionate, supportive writers, many of whom offered great advice and feedback on the final manuscript drafts, query letter and book proposal.

To my literary agent, Marisa Zeppieri, along with partner Laura Strachan of Strachan Literary Agency, who believed in my story and helped me navigate the murky publishing waters, and to McFarland & Company, Inc., Publishers and editor Charlie Perdue who championed the story from submission to completion, and honored my brother's words and story with the dignity they deserve.

Last but certainly not least are many family members and dear friends who provided memories, feedback, and heartfelt support as I lived through the toughest years of my life while writing this book. In heartfelt gratitude, I am thankful for my late son Nathan Himes who attended my first speaking engagement, where he expressed immense pride that gave me the courage to keep sharing hard topics. I'm also immensely thankful to my son Adam who offers inspiration to be my best me, and reason to encourage future generations to learn from past mistakes of senseless wars. I wouldn't have had either of my precious sons without Jeff Himes, my husband of twenty years who helped me raise two loving humans in the middle of the storms of life.

I'm grateful for my sister-in-law Marlene Smith who loved my brother like nobody else. Marlene has been a true sister and heartfelt support my entire life. I am thankful for my sisters Joanna Turner and Peggy Deak (may she rest in peace), who both validated my memories and offered powerful recall along with their blessings for this book. I appreciate them both for a lifetime of love and for the support to share our personal family stories. To my niece Michele Smith who inherited Larry's big heart and stunning blue eyes, preserved his

Acknowledgments

memorabilia, and worked so hard on Larry's behalf in the final chapters of his life to honor her father: know that your father and I are so proud of you. I appreciate your work ethic, love of family, and devotion to Larry's memory.

    To my childhood best friend, Betty McGuigan, and her entire family who treated me like their own and modeled a loving family unit in a way that shaped me into who I am today. I am blessed to have had you as an influence in my early life. To my cousin Cathy who emanates the strength of our family core, along with her mad photography skills and priceless support, I am grateful to have you as my person. To my college roommate and heart and soul friend Melinda Anderson who reacted to Larry's initial letters with, "I was riveted. I've never cared about war stories, but this story is about Larry. He just happens to be in a war."

Preface

> There is no greater agony than bearing
> an untold story inside you.
> —Maya Angelou

 This book will take you on a journey through the height of the Vietnam War, drawn from the innocent words of a teenage boy and memories from the family he wrote letters to almost daily in 1967 and 1968. In the year 2000, I was handed a box that contained his well-preserved letters from his days in the Army. I knew his stories were much larger than the ink on the page. The letters from his younger self were then 35 years old and told of tales I had never heard. The letters, 99 in total, held the heavy weight of a boy growing up in war. I felt responsible to protect them, absorb them and resolve the mysteries inside. My brother Larry's words had been so few and filtered my entire adult life that this immense volume of private words was a rare gem.

 The letters shocked me. I ran my fingers along the edges of the envelopes as if they contained broken glass. As I read them, the transformation of my hero unfolded on the pages, following Larry from his first days in basic training to his last days in hard combat. Like the paper itself, everything changed as time went on, starting with Army insignia stationery with matching letterhead, some with Army cartoons, to rice paper, to plain lined paper. His job changed, his hair changed, his voice changed, and his letters changed. My big brother aged on those pages, growing wiser than the rest of us in a single season. But one thing didn't change and became clear after reading them over and over. He truly loved me, worried about me and all of us, ending each letter with "Love Always, Larry."

Preface

I became obsessed with each proper noun in each letter and his place in the war, forcing myself to learn maps, study details of battles, and memorize military jargon and acronyms. I immersed myself in research, chronicled the letters, studied the details of battles, found his military records and medals, and searched the depths of the internet looking for Larry's buddies. After years of research, finding and interviewing his closest friends and many who served with him, I found my broken and battered hero. He was a boy I didn't recognize.

In the same breath, Larry could be fearful, and fearless. His letters showed me a side of him I didn't remember, a side that the war took away. On the receiving end of his letters was our patriotic family wincing at some of his word choices, searching for a purpose for his actions and praying for his return. When I shared my brother's words with Vietnam veterans, they wanted to know more about the people on the receiving end of the letters. The dual-perspective approach was born from that request. Unlike other Vietnam memoirs, *Pennies from Vietnam* humanizes the controversial war through the eyes of a family, thus closing the gap between the frontlines and the home front. The parallel memoir invites much-needed conversations among military circles that are long overdue.

Larry survived the war, but it took a toll on the rest of his life. And therefore, it took a toll on all our lives. Larry's tragic death years after the war is woven into the story in the final chapter of each part. The trauma of his death illustrates a literal example of the lasting effect of post-traumatic stress far beyond wartime. In the making of this book, I have cried a lifetime of tears. Because of my own PTSD from Larry's death, it has been therapeutic for me to express those tragic moments at the end of his suffering. I never intended to share these painful details, but they came through as a side effect of discovering his whole truth. Revealing can be quite healing.

Scattered among the pages of my brother's misspellings and bad grammar are his true words with no modifications in over 70 letters in total. None of his words have been changed, and few have been omitted or edited for clarity. Opinions of the war and military operations expressed in this book are based on personal reflection, fading

Preface

memories, and secondhand knowledge, from countless resources and interviews. Timelines have been compressed for effectiveness, but the facts in this book are all based on truth. My truth and Larry's truth.

It took years of research, heartache and edits to arrive at a final product worthy of my brother's story. My prayer is that this book will serve other military service members and their families struggling with active service challenges, whether past or present. It is an honor to serve our country directly or indirectly, but it is rarely an easy road.

In the end I realized that our family found love inside that war full of hate, received and given in different ways. But the love of family and the love of country conflicted with one another at the time. It didn't matter that we were in Kendall Park, New Jersey, in 1967 and 1968. Vietnam invaded us all.

Part One

1

"I Grew a Mushstash"

"I do solemnly swear that I will support and defend the Constitution of the United States against all enemies, foreign and domestic; that I will bear true faith and allegiance to the same; and that I will obey the orders of the President of the United States and the orders of the officers appointed over me, according to regulations and the uniform code of military justice. So help me God."
—Larry Ray Smith, January 1967

There was a war going on in Vietnam. At four years old, thousands of miles away from the conflict, I couldn't escape the war. The sights and sounds of battle infiltrated my earliest memories and repeated themselves in the soundtrack of my younger years, well into third grade. My family, neighbors and the heads on television talked about it all the time. They called it the Vietnam War. Vietnamese people called it the American War. I called it Larry's war.

The invasion of my big brother's new world changed us all, back in New Jersey. Mama took up smoking, Daddy grew monster tummy ulcers, and my sisters turned against each other like enemies in their own combat zone. Larry left home and went far, far away to a land that was more foreign than foreign, and everything changed. For him, and for us. Larry was just 17 when he joined the Army, and 18 when he landed in South Asia as a First Cavalry soldier.

A strong, inbred sense of patriotism provided a common thread that united my family in the early days. We were filled with pride to be Americans and all ages started each school day paying respect to the flag with our hands on our hearts. We were happy for our young soldier when he put on the uniform and left home to serve his

1. "I Grew a Mushstash"

country. Our anticipation of his letters kept our spirits strong. Larry's words were our glimpse into his new normal and not only delivered daily war news but also gave us the assurance we needed that he was alive and well. I am not sure how any of us would have survived without those letters or the mere promise of their arrival.

The metal mailbox hung beside the front door, filling with presents for our family every day. The swinging lid opened with a squeak and slammed tight with a loud clank, signaling the mail delivery by a nice postal man who walked house to house with a wave for each of us. Many of Larry's letters arrived in red, white, and blue striped envelopes, easy to spot among the other plain white mail. By the time letters arrived with his words "free postage" written on the front, I could reach the mailbox without help. I stepped up on the doorstep with my left foot, balanced on the milk box with my right, and leaned back enough to open the box and dig for the treasures. Directly beneath the mailbox, the beat-up silver container housed grade A pasteurized milk in glass quarts, delivered every Monday. It was my job to take the empties out and bring in the mail, but Mama would be first to open any letters. She read them first to herself, in a room alone. When she finished, she emerged to read us the family-friendly version.

I desperately wanted more than his words. I squeezed each envelope in hopes of finding pennies inside them like my brother had promised to send for my coin collection. Larry wanted me to save for a college education, but I hadn't even mastered Farm Life Nursery School. Mama bought me a pink piggy bank with white polka dots after Larry told me to get ready for lots of pennies. My sister Peggy mocked my coin collection when Mama was out of sight. She tossed around the ceramic pig pretending to drop it, shrugged, and snorted a snarky challenge: "It takes a hundred of those pennies to make a dollar, you know? You'll never get that fat pig filled up."

I became determined to prove her wrong, and a dollar was a lot of money to me so if it took a hundred, I would find a hundred. Pennies had been taped in several of Larry's letters during basic training, from Fort Dix, New Jersey, and more from Advanced Training in Fort Rucker, Alabama. I cherished them all. My penny collection took on a life of its own.

Part One

When he left home to go to Vietnam, Larry made another promise. He told Mama he would write often to let us know that he was "okay." He followed through on his promise. He wrote more letters than his friends, more letters than we sent him combined, and more in one day than most soldiers managed to send home in a month of Sundays. Mama beamed as she bragged, "Glory be! That boy is writing more than I ever wrote my whole life."

My brother shared his dreams for a bright future, getting married, and starting his own business. He confessed simple pleasures that helped him survive, lots of talk of beer, pretty girls, and fast cars. In each letter, he slipped in crazy stories about war stuff. Way more than Mama ever wanted to know.

As for me, Larry sent me plenty of advice, like a typical big brother. In the middle of his chaotic world, he worried more about us inside the safe haven of our suburban sprawl than he did about himself flying over those dark jungles. He lost friends, he professed his loss of sanity, and he lost track of time. He didn't falter on one thing though, the number of days to come home. He started counting as soon as he arrived in Vietnam.

* * *

5-Aug-67
Sat.
Dear Mom and Dad,
  Hope everything is fine at home. I am O.K. but could be better. I would have wrote sooner but I just got my address. We can't mail letters over here without a return address.
  I got to Ft. Lewis about 5:00 Monday morning. At 5:00 Monday afternoon we left for here {Quan Kay}. It took around 19 hours to get here. We stopped in Japan to refuel but we couldn't go anyplace. We landed in Cam Rahn Bay around 3:00 Wed. morning. I left Cam Rahn Bay at 4:00 Thursday morning and came here to Quan Kay. I stayed in a replacement co. all day Thursday and half of Friday. Then I went to my unit.
  I am in the 2d Bn 20th arty. 1st Cav. Div. The first Cav. loses more men and helicopters than any other div. It is also one of the roughest outfits over here.
  In the morning I start my 4 days of jungle training. 1½ days of the 4 we stay out in the jungle. They only started this about five months ago and they say only around six guys have been killed.
  After my jungle training, I am going out in the field. I will be there most or all of my year. That's when I start worrying about the V.C. {Viet Cong}. At night

1. "I Grew a Mushstash"

you can hear them fighting on the other side of the mountains. It don't sound too good.

So far, I like it over here. The country is real nice looking. Everywhere you look, all you can see is mountains. The weather where I am now is nice. It gets up to 85 and 90 degrees and there is a nice breeze blowing just about all day. In Cam Rahn Bay it was hot as hell and there was nothing there but sand. The place over here looks just like the places you see on TV, in them war stories.

I got all of my combat stuff yesterday. I get my M-16 rifle today. I got two pair of jungle boots and 5 sets of jungle clothes, plus all my field stuff. The rainy season starts next month and that is when it will be rough, because I will be in the field.

Tell everyone I said hi. I guess I will see you in a year or so. I only have 362 days to go. I won't be home this X-mas but at least you can buy everyone a nice present for me. I just found out there were only two Smiths in this company before. One was a crew chief and the other a door gunner. They were both killed. Everyone is telling me to be careful. It kind of worries me a little.

Well, I had better get my rifle and clean it and pack all my stuff for that jungle training.... So, write soon.

Love Always, Larry

* * *

The Army flew my brother far away from our spot on the map in New Jersey. We followed his journey across my desktop globe, and I went with him, in my dreams. Daddy put a finger on each spot as we routed out Larry's path from our home directly to the left with the first stop at Washington State. The globe needed to rotate a good bit to find Japan, then Vietnam. I imagined flying with him, through the clouds, over large bodies of water that filled much of the world according to my condensed version of planet Earth.

My brother's new land was ten times bigger than our state, on the edge of another ocean directly opposite the sphere from Mama and me, the two people he needed most. Larry had never been anywhere except up and down the East Coast. None of us had. Now, we had giant oceans between us.

Daddy made sure I understood the conflict when I questioned him. "Who is Larry fighting, Daddy? Who is the bad guy and what does he want?"

"They all want freedom. Your brother is fighting against North

Part One

Vietnam, the bad guys. But he is supporting South Vietnam, the good guys. Don't worry, Larry is on the right side."

Even in my confusion, I knew it was an important distinction, North versus South. Confusion appeared to spread to adults, too, and Mama started pacing the floors within days after Larry's first few letters. That's also when the whispers started. My little ears were not big enough to pick up many words as I leaned around corners listening for answers. I knew the whispers were not for me. I wasn't sure I wanted to hear them, but I longed to, anyway.

* * *

Cam Rahn Bay was said to be one of the finest harbors in all the world, and it would have impressed Larry if he had arrived in daylight. Haze gray warships and wooden barracks dotted the earth throughout the massive military base and stood opposed to the color surrounding them. Deep inlet waters danced around the 20-mile-long peninsula with stunning blues and greens in perpetual art formation. The beckoning of creamy sands along the shoreline served as a doormat to the fuzz-covered dark green mounds that filled the land in every other direction. The hills lie dormant over a dark, triple-canopy jungle my brother had heard about and seen only in the war movies and news programs. Perhaps the midnight arrival time was intentional, to soften a soldier's anxiety about the doomed fate awaiting them beneath those soft blankets of plush comfort.

The same oceanside port that welcomed soldiers from around the world would be the coveted exit door when the time came, typically 12 months later. Cam Rahn Bay was where innocent, eager young boys went in. Where hardened, exhausted men came out. The lucky ones. First, though, they had to survive the jungle. And all the rest.

* * *

9-Aug-67
Wednesday
Dear Mom and Dad,
   Hi, hope things are fine at home. I am still doing okay. Today was the last day of my jungle training and I am glad.

1. "I Grew a Mushstash"

The first day of jungle training we had classes on stuff about Vietnam. In the afternoon we had to slide down a rope off a 40-foot tower. We had to do it twice and it was a lot of fun. The only bad part was climbing up the rope type ladder.

The second day we had more classes, and, in the afternoon, we had to go through the gas chamber. That, I didn't like at all.

The third day we left early in the morning and marched out into the jungle. We fired our rifles and then we had to hold a LZ (landing zone). We all split up and got a bunker to stand guard in. We stayed there all night.

That was one of the worst nights I ever had. It rained and was cold. The LZ was on top of a small mountain. I didn't have a blanket or anything to cover up with and I was wet all over.

Then in the morning we went on patrol through the jungle. I have never seen any woods so thick in my life. We walked through elephant grass that was over 9 feet tall. I hadn't had a shower or shave for four days and all we had to eat was C rations. We didn't even see a V.C.

Now I am back in my unit. I just came home from the E.M. [Enlisted Men's] club. I had a few beers. Today was the first day I had a hot meal and something cold to drink since I started that training. Now I am going back into the field. I am leaving tomorrow. I don't know how long I will be there this time.

I haven't got much more to say except that I miss everyone at home and wish I was there. So, write often and tell everyone I said hi. My base camp is AN KHE. It is spelled right this time. And don't let anyone tell you it don't get cold over here. I froze last night. In South Vietnam it is hot. Well, I am going to go for now so write soon.

Love always, Larry

* * *

Larry knew if he got picked for the draft, he would end up in the infantry, marching through the jungle. He was eager to skip the last year of high school and fly around in something fast. He wanted to fight over the war and planned to become a "polit." He couldn't spell pilot no matter how many times he wrote it. It drove Mama crazy.

Raised between a handful of women, among tobacco farms and mill houses down south (when Mama couldn't handle him by herself), and the streets of Jersey in his teenage years, dodging high school and homework (while also dodging Mama), Larry grew up independently and craved adventure. He believed that a change of scenery would do him good, help him grow into a man, and make his parents proud by volunteering to fight the war.

Larry had to buzz cut his thick black hair to look like the other recruits. He was issued a couple of starched uniforms and learned

Part One

how to shoot guns and climb ropes while wearing them. My curious nature provided endless questions for Mama. "Where is Larry today, Mama? What do you think he does it when it rains? Does he have any pets? When will he come home again? Why did he leave?" She skirted most questions. "He wants to find his place in the world," Mama told me, and added, "He's searching for his own peace. Peace of mind."

My big brother was assigned to the First Cavalry Airmobile Division and joined the Aerial Rocket Artillery "Blue Max" crew. Sky troopers. Larry's job as a helicopter crew chief doubled as a door gunner, where he joined the backseat boys in the air. He didn't care that his seat was in the rear instead of at the front controls; he was happy if he got to fly, and he embraced the bravado behind his personal machine gun operation.

The helicopter could be good for my brother because he wasn't so big in that jungle. The two-story elephant grass and three-story high trees dwarfed his 5'8" height. With his new jungle boots and field clothes in hand, he joined the ranks of the First Cavalry weighing in at a buck fifty, at best. Barely a legal adult, eager to fight, he embraced the challenge to join U.S. forces and allies in the action, just not in the trenches. He remained hopeful that he would soon leave the ground and be in the air.

Mama had strong opinions and wasn't afraid to make them known. "I swear, Larry will not like that jungle one bit, and doesn't deserve to go anywhere near it. Being over it is not going to be much better. Maybe they will send him to Germany soon. He didn't start that stupid war and he shouldn't have to fight to end it. Nobody wins in a war like that. It's been going on for years."

She was still sore about the fact that he volunteered instead of taking his chances with the draft call, along with the nagging reminder that she signed the papers to get him there. Larry knew Daddy would sign the underage permission slip. However, it would take some strategy to convince Mama. He cleared the air one night as the family finished eating, even before the dishes were in the sink.

"Mom, Dad, there's something I gotta ask you." He didn't need to beat around the bush. He wasn't asking permission, so he continued

1. "I Grew a Mushstash"

with a mature clearing of his throat. "Umm, well, I want to join the Army. My country needs me. I know I may have to go to Vietnam, but I may not have to, and I'm willing either way."

Mama's head and shoulders froze. She managed a sideways roll of the eyes toward Daddy. She figured her husband and son had already discussed this, leaving her the odd one out. Mama did not like surprises. Her left eyebrow lifted, Daddy's cue to stay neutral. He started the annoying clicking sound in the back of his throat that drove Mama out of her ever-loving-mind, until she snapped her neck at him, and he stopped.

Larry spoke faster than normal, wanting this part over as soon as possible. "In just a couple months I will be 18 years old and will probably get drafted as soon as I register. There ain't no reason to wait. South Brunswick High is ready to kick me out anyway. Can I get your permission on this paper?" He didn't look her in the eyes, just slid the papers over to her on the table with a slow blink.

Mama pursed her lips. She was not often without words. This request took her voice away, knowing if she spoke, she would cry. This was a battle she couldn't win. If she didn't agree, her son would wait a few months and enlist himself, or he would be drafted. Signing that paper felt like giving him permission to die. She couldn't do it. Nor could she argue her position against it with the lump stuck in her throat.

Larry engaged his strategy. "This way, I can avoid being in the infantry. If I get drafted, I'll spend all my time walking through the swamps with the jungle rats and snakes."

He paused, as Mama shuddered, and then added, "If I enlist, I get to choose where I go. I'd like to fly a plane, maybe even become a pilot. That is a much better place to be and much safer than being in the infantry on the ground. I think I'd do good as a pilot." Larry played on the one anxiety she couldn't keep to herself. Snakes terrified Mama. She broke out in shivers and body chills any time they were mentioned, and especially when they showed them on the television screen.

Our Mama, Bernice Mae Herring Smith, may have had a petite frame, but everything else about her was large. Her dominant

Part One

personality matched her well-endowed upper body, and her thick, black bouffant hairdo awarded her a good bit of authority and added a half a foot to her height. Normally, she took charge of everything. With Daddy's blessing, she made most of the family decisions, paid the bills, planned, and executed our family trips to either Washington, D.C., or the Jersey shore. She did the decorating, hosting, and shopping with pleasure. She bought the finest brands. On holidays, or even a trip to the bank, she reveled in dressing us girls up. Every spring promised fashionable, matching Easter dresses with long gloves and fancy purses used for the semi-annual Polaroid moments when no hairs were out of place. We were prim, proper, and well-dressed children when she needed us to be. Coifed is what we were. Perfect through the lens of the world, like the porcelain dolls displayed on my shelves.

Mama could be difficult to figure out; she loved hard when she loved you. She would give the shirt off her back to a person in need. She didn't like change unless it was her idea and planned well in advance. Her dark eyes could cut or create tension in the room. She didn't have to say much since her shoulder shrugs and hip swings spoke volumes. She could easily flip and turn a cold shoulder into a warm welcome, becoming the kindest mother on the block when you least expected it. Most people didn't know that she carried heavy burdens, concealed by a lifetime of secrets, many of which she would take to her grave.

When Larry and Daddy cornered her for an answer on Larry joining the military, it may have broken Mama's heart. She felt conflicted. The logic of her deeply rooted patriotism should rule her decision. But too many neighborhood boys didn't make it home. How could she let him go?

She wouldn't show her tears to anyone, ever. Mama stomped out of the kitchen, swept the jet-black hair out of her wet eyes as she twirled around, and managed an audible "humph." She knew Ken would sign the papers and she had no choice but to sign. The men swapped smiles, knowing her exit signaled a complete surrender.

Daddy supported Larry's decision and was proud of his son's presentation to his mother on the matter. He left home as a young

1. "I Grew a Mushstash"

man to serve his country, too, so he considered military service an honor and patriotic privilege. However, Daddy never enjoyed his days at sea or anything about his Naval experience, and agreed the Army would probably be best for his son. Daddy nodded, as if to say, "give me the papers." Mama's silent ending on the topic handed him the reins, which he accepted without boast. He knew how to satisfy his spunky wife and keep peace in the family, by allowing her unquestioned space when needed and a safe place to rule the rest of the time. Daddy knew all too well that when Mama was happy, the rest of us were, too.

The next day, Mama conceded, adding her signature to the Army papers beside Daddy's name. Her concession allowed Larry to immediately drop out of school and enlist in the United States Armed Forces. She bore the weight of that decision every day, but his letters delivered her temporary sighs of relief.

It had been one year earlier when Mama had taught Larry to drive a stick shift, about the same time he grew his hair long and discovered his first whiskers. She shared her car with him. She was proud of herself for guiding him through these rites of passage. I'm pretty sure Larry had Mama wrapped around his little finger. She knew he skipped school to hang with his buddies and felt him growing restless with high school. As her first child and only son, he could do no wrong in her eyes. He spent less time lately at home, and more time anywhere else, except school.

His closest friends, Butch Daley and Billy Robbins, dreamed of serving together in the military. Billy joined the Marines while Larry and Butch decided it best to join the Army and stay together by entering on the buddy system. The friendly recruiter nudged the boys to visit him in the recruitment office, reminding Larry how disappointing his latest test grades must be for his parents.

The heaviness of his decision weighed hard even while he couldn't contain his excitement. Having grown up on a steady diet of war flicks with the good guys ending victorious, he embraced the chance to fight and win. Larry believed he had a bigger purpose to fulfill. Like most patriotic young men willing to put on the military uniform, his head was likely filled with all the mantras—I will

Part One

protect America. Fight for freedom. Make my parents proud and serve the country that I love. Uncle Sam wants me.

Among the rhetoric circling Larry's thoughts, in the days leading up to his decision he had all the right reasons to join the Army and convinced himself it was the best path forward. He laid the foundation for his return, checked all the boxes at home and make a pact with his buddies. While envisioning the fun experiences and secure future the recruiter painted, his decision was easy. His bags were packed before his voluntary enlistment became official.

In a few short months, the Army sent him to South Asia and dropped him off in the jungle. His life of adventure would begin with a jump start in Vietnam and never slow down. He experienced on-the-job training and more adventure than any of us knew existed outside of novels and movies. We tried to keep up with his location, but it was hard because he never stopped moving around. In all his travels, though, I'm not sure he ever located a single bit of that peace Mama said he needed to find.

* * *

11-Aug-67
Sat.

Dear Mom and Dad,

   Hi, hope everything is fine at home. I am still doing fine. I am in the field now. It is a lot different than base camp.
   The weather here is a lot different too. It gets up to 110° out here, and there ain't too much of a breeze. I don't have no bed or anything. So, I put four ammo boxes on the ground and put my air mattress on top of them. Plus, I am sleeping in a tent.
   I am going to be out here till around 15 of September. Then we go back to base camp for a rest period. Then we go back into the field around December.
   I have guard tonight so I don't guess I will get much sleep. I grew a mush-stash—spelling?–(hair on upper lip) but I had to shave it off because it ain't on my ID card. I am going to grow another one and then have my ID changed.
   I bought me a radio yesterday, but I am so far out in nowhere I can hardly pick up anything. Well, it is time to eat so I will go for now. I sure hope to hear from you soon. I know I will feel a lot better when I start getting some mail. So, write when you can. Tell everyone I said hi, and tell Tracy to be good.

Love always, Larry

* * *

1. "I Grew a Mushstash"

He kept reminding me to be good, like I needed to be told. He sent lots of updates and details on his adventures. Larry's words came to us in neat handwriting, sometimes on matching stationery with comics, and sometimes on unlined paper he scratched on late at night by the light of his Army-issued flashlight. Almost every time, he asked us to "write soon" as if our words were basic needs like food and water. Mail from loved ones provided the fuel he required to keep fighting another day, vital to his survival.

Three words framed the end of every letter and because we never used the "L word" in our family, it must have been difficult for him to write it each time. That didn't stop him; he didn't miss a single beat in his closing sentiments: *"Love Always, Larry."*

Along with his opinions, we got front-row tickets to the fighting. Between his stories and the CBS Evening News with Walter Cronkite, along with the local newspaper and constant neighborhood chatter, we got reports on the Vietnam War from all angles. There was no escaping the sounds of combat under the low ceilings and small rooms of our one-level starter home. Rocket explosions, bombs, smoke, and fires were all part of the backdrop of our dinner hour. Like clockwork when the big hand was straight up and the little hand was straight down, our home was invaded by Larry's war.

I recognized the vibrations of battle and memorized the difference between gunfire noises and aircraft types in one summer. Jets were higher pitched and lasted less time than the rhythm of the whop, whop, whop of helicopter blades that filled the skies. The firing of a machine gun soothed me with long-lasting, even sounds, bdddddddddd, bddddddddd. Somehow coming together for dinner with explosions in our living room, limited to the safety of our black and white RCA television, brought us all comfort. As if we were visiting Larry's new home, we were all ears and eyes on his war on the news while we filled our bellies with homemade meals that couldn't take his place but did make us feel better.

We waited to hear news of the war ending. Instead, Killed in Action (KIA) counts mounted, triggering Mama to wear out the floor in that first week of August. The year was 1967; her son had been home for less than 30 days since the Army took him in January. She

Part One

wouldn't rest until his next letter from Vietnam arrived. Then she still wouldn't rest for long.

Daddy drank most all the milk for his growing ulcers and spent more time on the couch, watching television between naps. He taught me to play games with casino playing cards. "Teach me to shuffle, Daddy, just like you do."

There was an arch involved that Daddy called the "bridge," and my little hands couldn't manage the reach without cards going in every direction. We played Rummy, Go Fish and War. War seemed the simplest. I wondered aloud if Larry enjoyed it as much as we did, which made Daddy laugh. We loved to play with those cards, and he taught me how to stack them in tower form to make a delicate high rise on the dining room table. Like my pennies, those cards became my obsession. Jacks were my favorite, especially after I heard Daddy mumble a subtle warning one day.

"Those one-eyed jacks, watch out for them. Sometimes they're wild," he chuckled, then added, "Kind of like your brother. Boys will be boys. Stay away from them all when you get older." I knew he was teasing me, but I wondered about the magic of those one-eyed wild boys in my future.

Talk of the war took up all the grown-ups' time in our house. When Daddy was asked about the conflict, he answered "It's a corrupt war for political gain," whatever that meant. Mama would answer, "It's a worthless war. No sense about it."

I kept asking Mama, "Who is winning Larry's war today?" "I don't know. Stupid war." Her pat answer. Both sides lost and both sides suffered, yet depending on who you asked, both sides were also winning the war. I was full of questions. Mama hated the whole subject of war now that her child was in the middle of it.

Despite her new distrust for the Army, Mama morphed into a military action figure and went on a mission of her own. She bought a long cord for the wall phone so she could reach the entire length of the galley kitchen, with the family room on one end where she could see the television, and the back patio on the other. With a folding metal chair perched outside the sliding glass door, Mama sat to talk on the phone with the cord lodged in the door crack. All we could see

1. "I Grew a Mushstash"

were her tapping shoes, or a pumping leg, from the one crossed over the other. It was like she put herself in time-out, to be alone until she calmed down. After all, unlike me, she never promised to be good, and this war business tested all her patience.

Mama's popularity grew as her worry circle multiplied. The mailman became her best friend. The bridge club ladies stopped playing cards on Thursdays, gathering instead to read letters from Larry or swap news clips from the newspaper or magazines. Sometimes they worked on their S&H Green Stamp collections and let me help stick the stamps and place them in the outlines inside the coveted books. We earned stamps with every visit to the A&P. When the 24-page book filled up, we had 1,200 points and Mama had her eye on the electric ice cream maker. It would mean more ice cream for me and save Daddy from wearing out his arm by turning the handle for hours. Even though we took turns cranking, homemade ice cream required bags of dry ice and half a day to make it creamy enough. Daddy smiled big when he saw our new appliance with the "start" button. We saved green stamps for a year to get that ice cream maker and all of us agreed on one thing. Homemade ice cream made every lick worth the work and tasted a whole lot better than green stamps.

※ ※ ※

13-Aug-67
Sunday
Dear Mom and Dad,

    Well, here I am again writing. I have some time left before I go on guard. I have been out on the flight line working all day. And I am dead tired. I did the same thing I did yesterday. I had to inspect two engines plus today I also had to do the tail boom and tail rotor. It may not sound like much, but it took me 7½ hours and I didn't stop once. I stopped for half an hour for lunch but I ain't counting that.

    It is a lot more than just looking at it. You have to take parts off and clean them and check them close, then when you put them back on you have to safety wire them. My hands are already tore up.

    I haven't got my own ship to crew yet. From what I have heard I might take over somebody's in the morning for a few days. My boss said they don't want to let me crew, because of the other Smiths getting killed. But I am about the only guy left that is a qualified crew chief. So, they will have to let me crew if they need a crew chief.

Part One

I was going swimming or into town today, but we had too much work to do. Maybe I will be able to go tomorrow. I hope so.

Friday night was the first time I have been scared since I've been here. I had guard that night and word came down there were V.C. 2000 meters to the south of us. I didn't worry about it then, but later a trip flare went off. I grabbed the machine gun, but I didn't see anything.

There is a little village right behind us and they come out at all hours of the night to use the bathroom and they mess around with our fence. So I guess it must've been one of them. The only bad thing is we can't shoot at anyone unless they are between our two main fences. So, if the VC do come, they can stand on the outside of the fence, and we can't shoot them. That is because of the village. But if they get between our fences, they are free game.

The place I am in now ain't the safest place in the world. The V.C. have been trying to get in but they have been stopped so far. They have tried every side but ours, so we expect them any night. Today I saw two Air Force planes dropping 750 bombs. Plus, two of our ARA ships and two gunships. They were tearing up someplace not too far from here.

Well, I have to go for now so tell everyone I said hi. I will see you sometime in the future. Only 352 more days to go. So, write when you can.

Love always, Larry

* * *

One of Larry's concerns before he enlisted was his sweetheart, Maryanne. They had dated for several months, but he was smitten with the redhead and didn't want to lose her like so many others who came home from war with a "Dear John" letter. She asked Larry not to enlist, advising him to take his chances with the draft call.

"They may not even pick you! If you escape the draft, then we can go to the prom next year. You can graduate from South Brunswick with me. You need to stay away from all that danger." Her words fell on deaf ears. She saw his determination grow in the days to follow. They talked it over and he admitted how much he wanted to enlist. They both made promises.

"I will wait for you, Larry. I will stay true to you, I promise. I will write you letters and send you pictures, so you won't forget me." As a good Catholic girl, she meant it, and continued, "Our family prays for the troops every day, so I know you will be okay, but here is something I got for you." She handed him a silver chain with a charm on the end that Larry didn't recognize.

1. "I Grew a Mushstash"

"This is Saint Christopher, the Patron Saint of Travelers. He will keep you safe on your journey. I hope you like it." She handed him the necklace, and their eyes met as he took it from her. He believed her. He knew he would come home from the war. Now he had divine help.

"I promise you, I will be back soon. I will keep your Saint around my neck if they let me. Thank you." Larry didn't have anything to give his girl or anything else to promise.

As for my promises, the pennies stopped coming as soon as he got to Vietnam. With every letter came my obvious disappointment, and I constantly quizzed Mama. "Do you think Larry sent pennies and the mailman lost them? Do you think he will find some this week? Will I ever get any more?" I'm certain I annoyed her, not knowing she didn't have the actual answers. Her answer was always, "Just wait and see."

After a while, I stopped asking about pennies. I knew the answer. That didn't stop me from wishing more would show up, but I hid my disappointment. Larry told me I could always count on his promises, and I believed him. But finding pennies in a foreign land would prove impossible, and while Larry had the best intentions by telling me to prepare a large piggy bank, he didn't know how difficult that promise would be to keep. He had admitted in Alabama that he wasted money on 50-cent "girl shows" and then complained about having no money. After spending my pennies on cigarettes, he promised he would replace my stash when he got "payed." Larry couldn't spell to save his life, Mama said. But at least he was honest.

Mama preached honesty as the best policy. However, when it came to her childhood, she gave herself a free pass. She never talked about her abusive father whom for some reason she named me after, or the mother who abandoned her, or her sister who disappeared as a young girl. She never spoke about the entire chapter of her life with Larry's biological father. For someone who could always be found with her nose in a novel, she herself was a closed book.

I counted and recounted the pennies, bringing them to life on the dining room table, where they marched across the grains of wood like seasoned troops. Mama read the years with her spectacles in place, cursing her aging eyes. I lined up each one on the seam of the

Part One

table, facing the same way with Lincoln's head looking right, toward the front of our house. The copper coins became their own force in my young mind, protecting our family as well as my brother and his friends. The back side reminded us of our nation's motto, with "E Pluribus Unum," meaning "out of many, one."

I liked the shiny pennies best because "In God we Trust" was visible and they brightened the collection. I knew the dull ones needed me, though. Those were tarnished with age, too damaged to see which side was which. Some of Lincoln's faces were worn off. The troops, both shiny and old, would stick together like my brother and his Army buddies.

Mama found solace playing around with the pennies, too, but the letters from Vietnam didn't do much to help Mama's nerves. Her only son was in a jungle, with mere basics for survival, no solid training, while living on "a wing and a prayer," as Daddy used to say before Mama shot him that look. We all knew that look.

2

"Open Up with My M-60"

We all missed Larry the moment he left. His first day in uniform was the last day we saw him, before the Army changed him. Mama was not happy that entire day and the days leading up to it. At the gates of Fort Dix, where he promised to send me treats if I was good, we each posed for pictures with him. He looked so handsome in his new uniform and short haircut. We were proud of those instant Polaroids the minute Daddy waved them in the air to dry and put them on top of the trunk for us to see. Mama hated her picture being taken and didn't crack a smile. She allowed Daddy to take a single picture, the only picture she ever took with her son in uniform. When the Rambler pulled away from the Army base, Mama grunted at Daddy, spoke no words, and we rode in hushed tones all the way home as she smoked her L&M cigarettes with the windows rolled up tight. I dared not complain and knew better than to ask questions.

We went weeks without contact during Larry's busy basic training days. Then, we started getting letters almost daily from Alabama. My taped pennies would grace the inside of the luckiest letters. I wore that little pig out in no time, even before Larry's deployment to Vietnam would begin. The money slot on the pig's back would get a chip in it, but nobody knew how. Masking tape replaced the pig's belly and kept the coins from falling out after the plastic plug went missing. Mama told me I would lose my head if it wasn't screwed on tight, and I had to keep checking the tape because it was my job to keep each coin safe. They needed me and I needed them.

Larry had looked forward to Vietnam, after his experience in Advanced Training. Heat and humidity, the kind that comes from

Part One

the depths of the southern corner of the state of Alabama, added to his misery of those early Army days. A large amount of cold beer was in order to tolerate Fort Rucker and all that it offered. The only thing bigger than the giant black bugs in his life were the textbooks. He looked forward to getting out of the books and into the action.

> "We got our books this morning, and you wouldn't believe how many we got and how thick and heavy they are. Some of them are about 8 inches thick."

Larry was told he was lucky to be in one of the best and fastest-growing fields in the Army. His future looked bright, the leaders assured him. Once pilot training was off the table due to low test grades, he predicted he would be a mechanic's helper and get on-the-job training while in Vietnam, which would qualify him to be a mechanic when he got out of the Army. He had no clue what the lessons ahead would cost him.

He learned the basics of electricity and drew current, voltage, and resistance symbols in a P.S. message. He tried harder than he ever had in high school and wrote home with the challenges he faced.

> "Right now, we are learning to run up aircraft engines and tell what is wrong with it when something happens. We have one engine called the R 985. It has 9 cylinders in a circle. It's max. is 26 g—and when it gets there it will rattle your brains out. Ask dad if he can figure this out. The R 985 has only 1 connecting rod. It is called the master rod. How are the other pistons connected? Don't forget they are in a circle. Also, ask him if he knows what kind of cam it has in it."

Larry tried to school Daddy and impress Mama with his new knowledge. Beyond schoolwork, much of his time in Fort Rucker he spent serving "KP," Kitchen Patrol. There, he washed dishes and mopped floors as punishment for dress code violations, mostly because he didn't shine his boots, or for not shaving close enough, or for being late for formations. A locker full of empty beer cans didn't help his case with the sergeants. Daddy said he was learning a lot of hard lessons. Mama perfected her eye rolls.

Larry missed his friends right away and blamed the military's poor management skills. Butch got the wrong orders in Fort Dix and ended up in Texas, then reunited in Alabama with Larry, but not for long. When Larry went to Huey School, Butch went to Choctaw

2. "Open Up with My M-60"

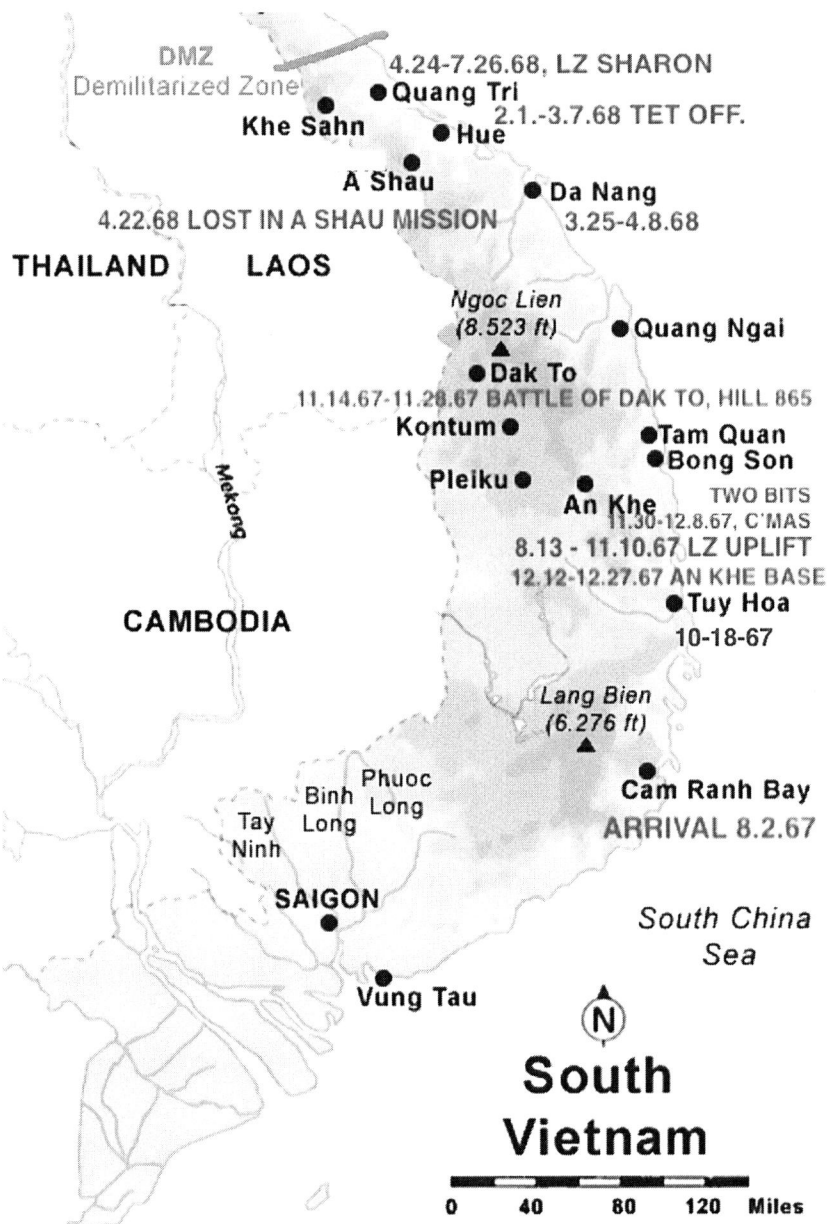

South Vietnam map with Larry's approximate locations and dates.

Part One

Larry and Tracy saying goodbye at Army Training Center, Fort Dix, New Jersey, 2-26-67.

Siblings farewell photograph, left to right: Peggy, Larry, Joanna, with Tracy in front. Fort Dix, New Jersey, 2-26-67.

2. "Open Up with My M-60"

Larry posing with his mother, Fort Dix, New Jersey, 2-26-67.

school, and they got separated for a long time. Larry lost touch with Billy, too, and didn't know how to find him. More than once, he asked Mama to find his location or address and let him know so he could write him a letter.

The Fort Rucker, Alabama, training fort ("Mother Rucker" with some slang additions) held a swift reputation for chewing up young, healthy boys and spitting out bitter young men, especially those that didn't graduate with honors. Larry was no exception.

> "I heard today if I don't do good in school, I will end up a machine gunner on a helicopter. And if I do real good, I will learn how to fly one."

His dreams of becoming a pilot had been crushed. With marginal grades, sub-par eyesight, and a few questionable behavior infractions on his record, Larry would never make it to the coveted flight school. He complained about pilots and expressed many grievances in the days to come. Pilots relied on their crew chief when the ship needed something, causing tension between the tandem positions and an ego struggle my brother had no patience for. Larry would be tested at keeping his opinions to himself.

Part One

Barely a week in Vietnam and Larry witnessed a shower of bombs drop from above, a signal to the power of the airmobile war he now faced. His new unit leaders welcomed him, warned him how dangerous it was to claim the name of Smith, strapped a machine gun to his young body, and handed him the keys to his first Huey.

* * *

17-Aug-67
Thursday
Dear Mom and Dad,

Hi, Hope everything is fine. Things are sort of bad right now. The V.C. are all around this place.

I was crewing my own ship for three days. Then it went back to base camp for a PE and hat end inspection. I flew nine missions and one mortar patrol. I flew five missions in one day and they were rough. We flew way up north and had all five of them up there. That is where most of the fighting is.

On one mission I shot 1400 to 1500 rounds from my machine gun. I was mad because they were shooting back at us.

Mr. Blackman, my polit, got a case of the ass because they didn't send me back to base camp with my ship. I really love flying them missions. I sit half in and half out of the door with my machine gun and when he quits firing the rockets I open up with my M-60. I always wondered what it felt like to kill somebody and now I know. It don't even bother me.

I thought I would be scared flying the missions because they are shooting at you, but I think it is a lot of fun. Last night I was walking across the flight line, and I heard shots. I turned around and I saw a tracer going over my head. I still haven't found out who was firing.

So far, I've been taking this war as a joke, but I think I had better start taking it serious. I need around 15 more hours of flying time and I will get my air medal. I might sit in for this guy this afternoon and fly a few missions. I sure hope so.

It is now 7 o'clock and I just got off of work. Now I have to go get ready for guard. I didn't get to fly any missions. I rode into town to take some empty rocket containers to the people. I don't know what they use them for, but they use them.

You should see how these people live. I really felt sorry for them. I gave some of the kids some candy and you should've seen how happy they were. They were talking to me, but I don't know what all they were saying. I know how to say a few things to them, but most of what I know, you only say it to the girls.

So, write when you can, and I will see you when I come home again.

Love always, Larry

* * *

2. "Open Up with My M-60"

Strapped in the backseat of a Huey that my brother called his ship, Larry enjoyed his new role in the skies, with some trepidation. Mama complained that he had next to no flight experience, even less training with machine guns, and had no business going so far away from his home and being dumped in the middle of some dumb war that made no sense to begin with. Daddy seemed prouder than ever. I thought my brother's new life was a dream come true, since his days appeared to be full of playing games with rockets in a giant ship flying over clouds.

The entire war effort relied on the Army Huey helicopter for many crucial reasons. Larry played an important role in the Airmobile strategies and took full responsibility for doing his best. If his ship flew, he flew. He was the "keeper of the copter," Daddy would say. Mama had little to say on the matter, except to brag about her son's bravery and shake her head. She feared heights and any talk of flying and didn't feel any bit of Daddy's humor when she read the line Larry wrote, "I never had a new car, but I do have a *65* UH-1C Helicopter."

Our family remained proud to be Americans, while patriotic lamps, upholstered furniture, and matching curtains full of liberty bells proved our devotion to Old Glory and served as daily symbols to remind us of our country's freedom. Mama grew up in Washington, D.C., where they had a lot to say about the flag and where we visited regularly. My nursery school started each day with the Pledge of Allegiance, and I had long ago memorized it but had a hard time pronouncing the letter R. I wouldn't start speech therapy until kindergarten, so I called my brother "Lawwy" and pledged my early days of allegiance to the "United States of Amewica."

I recognized the American flag as sacred, not to be touched. Seeing early images of stars and stripes draped over boxes like a blanket confused me more. I didn't know why anyone wanted to fight, why the flag would be involved, or when my brother's war would be over so things could return to normal. I did know that people had little else to talk about and nobody was happy about any of it.

* * *

Part One

20-Aug-67
Sunday

Dear Mom and Dad,

   Well, here I am again writing. Hope everything is fine at home. I am still doing ok.

   I am just sitting around again this morning. Haven't got any work to do yet, but we will have some to do soon. I got a letter from you yesterday. I sure was glad to hear from you. Sorry to hear you ain't feeling too good. If anything happens and you or anyone else has to go to the hospital for an operation or anything bad, have Dad get in touch with the Red Cross and tell them what's wrong. They will have me sent home to be with you.

   The place my base camp is in, is AN KHE. What I mean by being out in the field is, we find someplace in a valley or on top of a mountain and clear it out and make camp there. The camp I am in is right outside Bong Son. I have the spelling right this time.

   I went into town yesterday. I walked around looking at all the stores. I stopped and had a few cold beers and then I went off with some girl. I saw a lot of nice things in town I would like to buy and send home but I ain't got the money right now.

   When I get married are you paying for the wedding? If so, start saving now. I am thinking about getting married when I come home, and it <u>ain't</u> going to be any girl over here. I will let you know more about it later.

   I got another letter and a package from Mary Anne. I wear the St. Christopher medal with our names on the back of it that she got me. It is really nice. I go to church services every time the chaplain comes out here and I carry a Bible in my pocket all the time. It makes me feel a lot better.

   Sorry my pet is so much trouble. If you want to get rid of him, go ahead. I don't blame anyone for not wanting to pick it up. I still have a mark on my finger where he bit me.

   Well, I had better go for now. I am sorry to hear someone was taking money from Tracy's bank. I know it wasn't me. I have grown up a little bit and I don't think I could do anything like that.

   So, tell everyone I said hi and write when you can.

Love always, Larry

* * *

   That pet that caused us trouble would be one of my brother's final gifts, a few days before his deployment. It would ensure his sarcastic pleasure at our expense for a short time. Larry brought home our "special gift" and presented it to the family at dinnertime. Mama had made her famous spaghetti dish, with those fat sausages that I avoided, covered in peppers, onions, and the red sauce I also avoided (spaghetti dinner for me was noodles and butter). Larry was late for

2. "Open Up with My M-60"

dinner, so Mama was approaching irritated when he slipped into the kitchen with a big grin on his face and a glass bowl in his hand.

"Look, y'all, I got a pet for you," not asking permission or forgiveness, he placed it on the table. Mama gasped. Under any other circumstances, she would have never permitted any reptile in our house. She couldn't tell him no, and he knew it. And once he added, "This little guy will make sure you don't forget me," she knew the baby alligator would be ours to keep, against every grain of sensibility in her body.

The gator took a bite out of his hand before he left, so he was understanding when weeks later, the alligator went missing. Mama didn't tell him until he asked about it, months later. None of us liked the little gator enough to name it. It grew large enough to jump out of the goldfish bowl, and it escaped one day when Peggy was cleaning the bowl in the backyard. Nobody cared to chase it, so evidently, the nameless creature made his way to a city sewer somewhere to grow up without us.

That was the one pet I couldn't love. Mama's disdain of alligators and snakes and all creepy things seeped into my own fears. Two of Larry's letters from Alabama had set the stage for our combined terror and may have been his best training for the swamps of Vietnam.

> *Saturday, I went down to a creek in the woods with six other guys. We were swimming and a water moccasin (snake) crawled in with us. One of the guys grabbed it and threw it on the bank. Then he hits it in the head with a rock. It was about 5½ feet long. After that, we went snake hunting. We killed two rattlesnakes and two other kinds.*
>
> *They told us there were 254 [types of] snakes in Vietnam and 253 of them were poisonous and the other one would squeeze you to death.*

Once he got to Vietnam, snakes were never mentioned in Larry's letters. Along with giant rats, deadly mosquitos, and evil scorpions that lived in bunkers and grew as big as me, creepy crawlies took a back seat to the combat he faced daily. Perhaps Mama asked him to leave out all talk of South Asian creatures. Perhaps he fought those kinds of enemies, too, but spared us the bloody details. Daddy always said everything is relative.

* * *

Part One

Sunday night
20-Aug-67

Dear Mom and Dad,

I received another letter from you this afternoon. You just don't know how much better it makes a guy over here feel to get mail. I also got another one from Mary Anne. I am glad to hear you're feeling better, and it is nothing real bad.

You're right about the war being a bad thing, but from TV and books they don't tell you the half of it. The war ain't like the last two or three. Over here you don't know who you are really fighting. You can't tell who your friends are and who ain't. It's just like a game of guess who.

I wish I could look out my tent and see houses and nice yards, but all I see is a war-torn area. I don't think you're stupid for thinking them things. I think about them too. I can't say I don't like it over here, but I had much rather be back home with you and everyone else. I have only seen and been in real combat nine times. This may sound crazy, but I liked it and thought it was fun. But I guess after a while I will begin to face this war like I should.

I can't really say I am safe because nobody is safe anyplace over here. I usually have my rifle with me most of the time and I always have plenty of ammo with it.

I am in South Vietnam. You should see the South China Sea from the air. It is really nice. It ain't but around 20 miles or so from here (Bong Son).

Well, it is getting dark and I want to write Butch a few lines before it gets too dark to see. Tell everyone I said hi again and tell Tracy I miss her a lot. I saw a jacket in town with a map of Vietnam on it and some other things. It had some writing on it which said something like this: "For I have walked through the valley of death and if I die, I know I will go to Heaven for I know I have already been through hell."

Then under it is a map of Vietnam with Vietnam wrote on it. I'm going to get Tracy one when I get paid. So, tell me what size she wears. So, write often and take care of yourself. Don't worry about me, because I am alright, and you can bet every penny you have I will be home again safe and sound.

Love always, Larry SNUFFY—That's what I am called now.

P.S. Here is 50 P's or 50 cents to put in Tracy's bank. I doubt if you can spend it, but if you ever come over here you will have it. Tell Jo and Peggy to write when they have time.

* * *

Piasters ["P's"] were the 50 coins Larry sent me, a new addition to the penny collection that I cherished and the first gifts I got from him from Vietnam. It didn't matter that they were worthless in America, they were worth everything to me.

I didn't know the game of guess who, and it seemed as though my

2. "Open Up with My M-60"

brother had to figure it out all alone. Daddy assured me it was complicated and not a game for kids to worry about. The enemy in Larry's war was the biggest mystery. I heard Mama and Daddy talking about them. They wore a variety of clothing that looked like pajamas. The faces of the enemy looked like the faces of the good guys. Nobody could explain these things to me. They called them gooks, guerrillas, zipperheads, dinks, V.C., short for Viet Cong, or Victor Charlie, a radio signal which got shortened to Charlie, plus a few other terms whispered under grown-up breaths. Without a true frame of reference other than the *Jungle Book* story, I imagined giant apes, like the ones at the Washington Zoo, wrestling my brother while he marched through a dark jungle and wrestled back to escape. Larry was fighting gorillas and fighting bad guys, too. I wasn't far off. Those enemies were ruthless and came in all shapes and sizes. No wonder Mama started fidgeting; if she wasn't biting her nails, she was twisting her rings or picking her cuticles.

Larry—now apparently called Snuffy—had been away from home all spring and summer, missing our favorite seasons to play outside. He used to love games like I did and played Red Rover with me in the front yard and let me dance on his feet when Daddy was away. I was the only one who fit on his shoulders and folded backward in his arms. We played fetch with our mutt, Smitty, in the backyard. We wrestled on the braided rug where Larry let me win if I put up a fight worthy of a rising kindergartener. I felt his absence when it came time to play, and none of the girls had any interest. The energy of the house moved like molasses on Daddy's Sunday waffles, slow and sticky. Things changed in every room.

We ditched old rituals, leaving the kitchen table for breakfast and lunch. The formal dining room table became used for storage of our pennies, photographs and newspaper clippings. Dinners were served on wooden folding trays, one for each of us as we crowded into the family room, Mama and Daddy in their respective recliners, and us three girls lined up on the couch. There were three channels to manually select from, ABC, CBS, and NBC, and all of them were filled with news during dinner time, 90 percent dedicated to the war. News coverage had recently expanded from 15 to a full 30 minutes,

Part One

helping the journalists who went to war feed the public appetite for seeing violence up close. Mama's affection for Walter Cronkite shifted as the nightly numbers of war statistics grew. His soothing voice may have helped deliver the news tactfully at first—where our boys were, which were missing, wounded, coming home even if wrapped in bandages—but provided little justice for the families who shared the names of those on the screen. Then, the acronyms. KIA. POW. MIA. Some neighbors waited for letters and lived in uncertainty for weeks and months. Some got really bad news. Each piece of mail brought a collective sigh of relief to our household. Some days, like August 20, we got two letters.

Our nightly updates would have been quality time together if it wasn't such a sore spot for Mama as a constant reminder of Larry's new dangerous job. The evening symphony of helicopter blades serenaded us with the sounds of Larry's war. I was growing up right alongside my soldier brother, Daddy said, when he showed me how to adjust the rabbit ear antennas to get a better picture on the console television. Tinfoil helped, too.

The noisy war on TV started to make Mama jump. In my attempt to ignore the loud background noise and talk from the boring heads, I dug shallow moats in my mashed potatoes and gravy or piled up sweet peas into a large fortress. Nobody cared about my creative vegetable designs, and they kept me preoccupied enough to avoid studying the black and white images. I looked forward to the 7:00 hour when I could be entertained by the magic of *Bewitched*, *I Dream of Jeannie*, or Ellie Mae Clampett and her hillbillies. The Clampetts reminded me of Daddy's family, the way they talked and dressed, and Samantha and Tabitha's powers and Jeannie's talents gave me the promise of magic with a wiggle of a little button nose or a nod with crossed arms.

Daddy used every television show, every meal, every everything as a lesson, feeding my perpetual quest for answers. He had an affection for history and the makings of the military, yet he distrusted authority much like his son. He taught me a mature perspective on matters that most preschoolers did not have. I soaked up Daddy's lessons and looked at the war with a healthy curiosity but never grew fond of the gunshots and bomb blasts.

2. "Open Up with My M-60"

Both men spoiled me differently than Mama, by treating me like an adult. They took me places Mama would never be caught dead in. They loved to have fun, played for hours in the summer during pool season, and in winter they sleighed on the snow and skated on icy ponds with my sisters and me. They loved country music like me, especially Charlie Pride, Hank Williams, and Loretta Lynn. My sisters listened to Motown and rock-n-roll, and Mama, well she liked to stay inside, and dry, and liked music if the volume was turned down low enough so she couldn't hear it.

The two men under our roof shared an affection for cars and anything with an engine. Daddy and Larry could usually be found tinkering in the garage on some greasy car part. Sometimes the entire engine adorned our otherwise pristine formal living area. When they used Mama's good towels to protect the floor, the weekend hobby became a form of contention in the atmosphere. The men could care less about fancy furniture and appearances, yet Mama cared enough for all of us. It was all so confusing, to know who was right and who was wrong. Kind of like the war.

When it came to my sisters, I never knew which side to take, either. They loved to disagree, and fight about the color of lipstick, or some boy, or the weather forecast. Mostly they fought with words and flying objects. With two pillows pulled over my ears, I could muffle their screams. Tucked under the covers, my humming echoed through my head, trying to mute the verbal war or diffuse the thumps from high heels slamming against their bedroom door, right next to mine. I memorized several tunes from *The Sound of Music* that brought me comfort as I dreamed of packages tied up with strings and repeated songs to myself in a self-preserving tent of pale pink cotton linens. "Doe, a deer, a female deer. Way, a dwop of golden sun. Me, a name I call myself, faw, a long, long way to wun."

Larry grew sick of the conflict in the house, too. As bookends to our middle sisters, Larry was the oldest and I was the baby, much younger than all of them. When someone had to talk to the police, Larry stepped up when Daddy was away (and bad things only happened when Daddy was away), assuring the officers that he would

Part One

Left: **Bernice Mae Smith, Larry's mother, circa 1955.** *Right:* **Kenneth Vestal Smith, Larry's father, in Navy uniform, circa 1955.**

calm everyone down. And he did. I'm convinced that he left home searching for quiet time.

"Why are Jo and Peggy mad, Mama?" I asked on a regular basis.

"Remember I told you they are in their troubled teen years? Give 'em time. They will work it out." She never provided any better reasoning behind their verbal combat. Time seemed to be the answer to everything. Waiting became my nemesis.

I think Mama taught my sisters how to do that yelling, and she did a good job at it. My sisters practiced a lot, and since Mama yelled loud, they had to yell louder. But Mama didn't yell at me. Or at Larry.

3

I SEE YOU

His eyes are open. That's all.

Nobody adds any caveat. Nobody prepares you for the truth. You enter the room with anticipation, a healthy mix of pent-up hope and optimism ready to let loose and celebrate with him. For him. You don't want to wish too hard, but *his eyes are open*. Months of your specific prayers have been answered, and your brother is awake.

Your footsteps offer little sound to the stale air as they cross shiny speckled tiles to reach the end of the bed. You see his look shift, as his eyes move in a jerky motion, sweeping the room to meet you. The gaze you have longed for pierces the thick hospital air as your eyes merge. Deep in your soul, you feel him come alive. A gasp escapes from deep in your throat. It's been so long. He's here. He has so much to say. And so much you need to hear.

You wait to see what he will do next. The room gets heavier with every moment of silence. The rhythm of the rise and fall of his chest fills the room with a thick blanket of desperation. His chest remains open after all these months, in preparation for another bypass if needed. He glares at you with a hateful look, not a look you've seen before, and not at all what you expect. You have never seen him disappointed in you, angry at you, or scared. Now he looks like all of those combined. His look doesn't bring the comfort you yearned for and your heart sinks.

The sounds of medical equipment interrupt your thoughts and a putrid mixture of scents strike your senses—ammonia from the floor cleaner, blood, urine, latex and body odor. The sights and smells of sickness alone justify the *Intensive* in Intensive Care Unit. *Do the nurses see what you see? Do they hear his eyes? Are those baby blues screaming for anyone else?*

Part One

The corners of the room darken, despite the stark fluorescent lighting overhead. Medical uniforms come and go, seemingly indifferent to his look, or silence. Is this silence a normal transition? This is what you asked for, open his eyes, open his eyes, God let him open his eyes. You prayed for his old eyes, not these. You crave that recognition. You step to his side and take his swollen hand in yours, noticing it is soft, much too soft. Missing are his calloused palms, embedded with lines of mechanic grease stains. Harley riders don't have soft hands. He wouldn't like this one bit.

You lean closer and bravely meet his gaze. Instant comfort comes from the inner layers of his eyes. Brilliant, bright blues overlap and weave together the hues of your youthful ties. Carolina-sky blue, Tarheel-powder blue, deep-water Jersey shore blue. Bordered by a weathered outline of Periwinkle blue and light grays, like the furniture he stained for your 3-piece matching bedroom set.

In the middle of all that blue, you find deep, deep black pupils, smaller than normal, laser-focused on your own. Neither of you blinks, and your eyes start to water. He's back. His eyes are open, and he's back. He's in there.

Words try to spit from his eyes, with all the stored up energy of his immobile body. Your brother's baby blues dart from person to person, never landing on inanimate objects. He is seeking answers. His optic lenses speak to you with a silent but manic plea. *Get me out of here.*

The comfort of seeing his eyes, seeing him fully awake, is replaced by the disappointment of what is missing in him. Gone are the bloodshot eyes framed by tired and droopy lids that tell their own story of a life lived hard, fast, and fun. Gone are his endearing smirks and sarcastic responses. Gone are the whispered promises to be better, do better. Gone is the wild pony ride all the way to the moon and back on his shoulders.

You release an audible sigh, realizing your breath has been shallow. You look around the room and feel a stillness in the air, even amid the commotion around you. His broken body stays spotlighted and motionless. Overhead lighting makes a sick body look sicker by showcasing every physical flaw, and the tube-shaped bulbs reflect off

3. I SEE YOU

each braided vein inside the white of his eyes. His long brown lashes form a natural shadow on his sunken cheeks the few times he blinks his eyes. He blinks slow, much too slow. In the crowded ICU pod, you test him.

"Blink for me, Larry. Can you do that? Just one blink, please," you ask him in a loud voice, sweat rolling down your back. How can he not blink on command? Why isn't anyone doing tests on him or poking him for a response? Nobody talks. The beeps and bells generated from tangled wires and tubes, flashing lights and devices he never wanted, take up space, sucking the air from any possible peace of mind left in the room. The distractions annoy you, serving as constant visual and audible reminders that he is not breathing on his own.

Larry would shudder from the noise in this place and hate all the attention. You feel his anger, and wish he would ball his fist, wrinkle his eyebrows, or scream to the heavens for Christ's sake. After several attempts to get a reaction, the nurses see your struggle.

"I wouldn't worry, honey. Your brother has been asleep so long and it will take awhile for things to get moving again inside his body. It will be a long recovery. Give it time. Be patient. Keep talking to him."

It's the same elusive advice you've received for months. It's not enough.

Racking up a lifetime of hard farewells, this is by far the hardest yet. You leave him silent, and still. And you leave him with a promise.

"I know this is your worst nightmare, Larry. I'm not sure what happened, but I promise you I will not let you stay this way." You squeeze his hand, and he stares back at you. As you lower his hand to the bed and your tears well up, you remember how much he hated to see you cry and you break the gaze and turn away. As you leave his bedside, you realize that for once, he is awake without his legs and hands shaking.

Part Two

4.

"Things I Don't Want to Talk About"

> No event in American history is more
> misunderstood than the Vietnam War.
> It was misreported then, and it is misremembered now.
> Rarely have so many people been so wrong about so much.
> Never have the consequences of their misunderstanding been so tragic.
> —President Richard Nixon

I'm not sure who they hated the most—each other, our mother, or themselves. My sisters' differences defined the way they fought and may explain why they bothered to fight at all since there was no clear motive or reason for their animosity. Jo was the oldest, 18 months younger than Larry, tall, slender, and perfectly poised with good posture and a pleasant smile. She intended to ruffle no feathers, avoid attention, and fly under the radar in all settings. More attention usually meant more chores. She helped take care of me when Mama was working, and she did so without complaint. Jo couldn't get away with talking back, not like Peggy could.

Peggy was the loudest one, and you could count on her emotions to announce her arrival and shower the room with volatility. Her drama could be fabulous, or tragic, and it would be a lot. She should have become an actress, for the award-winning shows she could produce on a moment's notice. Her thick brown, pixy-cut hair swiveled side to side as she shook her head in defiance, by habit. She had mastered the art of headbanging as a toddler when she fake-fainted and pounded the floor during her infamous tantrums.

Until I came, Peggy was the baby. She was not particularly fond of me when she was nine years old, and I took her place as the

4. "Things I Don't Want to Talk About"

youngest. Not that she treated me badly (other than letting me fall off the bed that first week), but when all the attention turned toward me, and away from her, she had to resent my presence. She fought hard for years to reclaim some of that attention.

When they were not home, I jumped on my sisters' beds in the room they shared and selected my favorite 45 records off the walls, where each one hung on an individual nail. Peggy's boredom got her in trouble more than once, and one night resulted in a redesign. She filled the room with vinyl records on every wall. She claimed she needed somewhere to put the music collection and had no other options. I suspect Mama grounded her.

I had to return them to the right place, or they would realize I had "borrowed" their records without asking. I knew that Elvis Presley and Beatles records were completely off limits. My record player with the retractable needle got worn out on the song "Daddy's Home" by Shep & The Limelites, while I pined for my Daddy to get back from his latest long-distance truck driving route. The song became a constant reminder to Mama that she couldn't compete for the piece of my heart that Daddy held so tight.

Daddy was the light in our home, and we were all a little sad until he got back from his long road trips. Including Mama. Daddy wrote her a note one month after they got married, that professed his love, where he wrote in large letters, "Only 49 more years and 11 months to our 50th wedding anniversary." He was an easy man to love. Even neighbors, strangers at the store, and my teachers felt his genuine charm and were drawn to his childhood stories of living on a farm in North Carolina. Everything quieted down the minute Daddy pulled into the driveway. I would run to jump in his arms first, intoxicated by the comforting smell of diesel fuel inside his warm hug.

Once Larry left home, we suffered from Daddy's road trips even more. Peggy got in trouble more and more and packed a suitcase and ran away from home at least weekly there for a while. Mama predicted she would be back every time. She was right. Usually, we found her on the curb out front by dinner time. Jo continued to live in the shadows of Peggy and Mama, despite being the oldest child in the house. And she did the cooking and housework since Peggy

Part Two

argued her way out of it. It might explain why Jo played second fiddle and stayed in a bad mood. Or why she eventually escaped to join the traveling carnival.

Everybody wanted peace. Our family didn't know how to find it or what it looked like. My sisters hung giant posters on their bedroom doors with groovy two-finger peace symbols and stuck "Make Love Not War" stickers on all the mirrors, yet they still argued over peace like they did everything else. The news did not help when they talked about Americans in favor of peace, and then showed violent riots in the city streets ignited by anti-war protestors. My brother yearned for peace in his own world and in ours back home. He wanted everyone to get along and find common ground. While he cherished his family, he did not miss the theatrics of arguing females. I learned to stay out of the drama and enjoy the days when my sisters got along, even though they were covered in Dippity Do and too much hairspray.

I never got grounded, but my sisters sure did make up for my good behavior. They took turns making Mama angry. Their group of friends, specifically Chris and Irene, were often mentioned in arguments. Mama called them trouble and trouble, and I wondered if they had anything to do with my missing pennies.

* * *

25-Aug-67
Sunday
Dear Mom and Dad,
   Sorry I haven't wrote in the last few days, but I have been very busy.
   Well—I am back in the air again. My ship came back the other night. It sure feels good to be flying again. Remember when I told you I would get to fly the ship myself? Well, I did. It sure is fun. I never had a new car, but I do have a *65*UH–IC helicopter.
   Today I only flew two missions. It wasn't nothing much. We put on a show for "Miss America" today. She is over LZ up lift. All we did was 4 of our ships shot our rockets at the side of some mountain.
   You think it rained a lot at home, you should be over here. The monsoon season is starting, and it don't just rain, it pours. I have to sleep in my ship now because I slept in my tent last night and I got soaking wet. I won't be going back to base camp in September. My platoon is going to someplace by the shore for 90 days in September. When I ain't working I will be down at the beach. The place we are going to is an R & R center.

4. "Things I Don't Want to Talk About"

I am still doing fine. I was sick last night but I feel better today. How is everything at home? I hope everyone is fine. Well, I am going to go for now. So, write when you can and don't worry about me. I am alright. Tell Tracy I said to be good. What are you going to do about my car? Well, I am going.

Love always, Larry

* * *

Twenty days after arriving in Vietnam, my flirtatious brother used his gunship's firepower in a show of protection for the prettiest girl in America. He never met her. He didn't know that Miss America 1967 wrote about him on the same day he wrote about her. He never knew how much he impressed her.

Jane Jayroe was the first beauty queen to wear the crown and travel to a war zone. As a young lady from Oklahoma, she stumbled into beauty contests. She never aspired to win for the purpose of wearing the crown and sash. Jane came from a military family and her cousin Mike was currently deployed to Vietnam, and she wanted nothing more than to sing and dance for the troops. When her college audition failed to land her dream job with a performing USO group, she turned to her other avenue, beauty pageants, which proved fruitful with her talent for singing and entertaining. In very short order she won local, regional, and national titles to her own surprise. The popular platforms of Miss Oklahoma, then Miss America, gave her the opportunity to travel to Vietnam in August 1967 and perform for the soldiers. With five other beauty queens in white cocktail dresses, Jane arrived with a television crew in hand and brought a few moments of diversion to the war.

A visit from American girls offered a ray of brilliance in a wet and dreary monsoon season, and the boys welcomed them with open arms. But the first stage show didn't go as expected. The ladies came on stage with baggy fatigues and muddy boots, as a sign of unity they thought would be appreciated. However, the boys didn't come for patriotic reasons and made it clear with their grunts and boos. The ladies scrapped the fatigues, so the rest of the show's wardrobe consisted of beautiful short dresses and high heels. They saved the Army attire for traveling by helicopter and walking around in the mud, and graciously delivered what the troops wanted. Pretty ladies with pretty legs showing.

Miss America wrote in her private diary at the end of each day. In one entry, she mentioned the rocket show Larry put on, a deliberate act of prowess intended by the First Cavalry Division, to make her and the other ladies feel safe while in the country:

> "What a day! We flew out of Da Nang on a Caribou. Monsoon Day. Constant downpour. They wouldn't stop at Dak To. The First Cavalry took over completely and wouldn't let Frank (the Officer accompanying the ladies) have any authority. Wouldn't even let him talk to us (because he was so mad). And they took us into areas which were not secure enough. We landed in LZ English. Met everyone there. Went to Blackhorse. Mud! Sad. Nothing but tents. Ate lunch here. Countryside was really shot up. Lunch, hospital, very primitive tent, like an old-timey movie. Then they fired into a nearby mountain. What a sight. Helicopter missiles flew back to LZ English for a show. Our show. But it was raining so hard, our equipment wouldn't work. So, we sang a few numbers then shook hands with everyone. The guys were so nice. They stood in the rain for so long. They made us some cookies."

As promised, the First Cavalry kept the ladies well protected even while the Viet Cong amped up mortar attacks and the monsoons rained havoc. Monsoon rain, Daddy explained, was the rain that fell in buckets and for days on end. Monsoon rain fell so loud you would have to yell at the guy beside you to hear anything and fell from the sky so long you forgot what the sun looked like. The ground in Vietnam stayed saturated for an entire season, where raindrops didn't even get the chance to hit the ground once the rains started. A constant pool of water kept a soldier's feet soaked, and high humidity added to the rancid smells of burning feces mixed with soot, smoke, and human decay.

Larry flew border patrol the night Miss America slept in the base camp, so he spent hours protecting her. He completed a successful mission and returned to his own camp across the valley. Ground troops moved the ladies out the next day when they realized the area was not safe enough for civilians. Jane never felt in danger or realized how combative the region had become in the war. The First Cavalry officers assured her of their protection and proved their firepower with a show of their Aerial Rocket Artillery (ARA) forces, compliments of my brother's unit. She never knew that enemy forces

4. "Things I Don't Want to Talk About"

mortared her camp throughout the night. She heard the bombing and didn't realize it was incoming fire. From the comfort of the General's quarters where they moved the ladies, it sounded like background target practice.

> "We dressed in a tent and finished off the white dresses (so much rain that they were ruined). We saw some V.C. weapons, some prisoners. Old men. Flew over to headquarters and met General Tolson at Two Bits. Back to LZ English. Rain. Yuck. And finally made it to Qui Nhon.... Stayed in the General's quarters, very nice."

Each time the boys from LZ Uplift went on an air mission for the weeks following Jane's visit, they named spots on the ridge where Larry shot the mountainside. They named it "Miss America Ridge" and the ridge included six landing zones, named for Jane and her friends, Angie, Barbara, Carole, Ellen, Lucille, and Sharon. LZ Sharon would become an integral landing zone for Larry's unit at the height of the conflict ahead. It would be a long time before the smiles left behind by the talents of those lovely ladies would fade from the faces of the weary warriors they entertained.

Jane received a hand-drawn map and a letter explaining the importance of "Miss America Ridge" and expressing the gratitude of the First Cav Soldiers she visited. The letter reads:

HQ, 2nd Bn, 1st Cav Div
APO 96490
LZ Uplift, 26 Sep 67

Dear Jane:

Enclosed is an accurate overlay of our Command Post area and the surrounding prominent terrain features. Colonel Karmons departs in a few days, and I asked him to authenticate this copy for you.

The 2nd brigade enjoyed your visit, and we have continued to have fun by naming The Ridge and the Landing Zones (LZ) on top. Each time during the following days that we made an air assault there, the LZ was named for one of your party. In the bunkers on the perimeter defense, there is a copy of this overlay. The soldier can use it in a very practical way, i.e., "Give me illumination over Sharon," or perhaps, "Request direct fire on Miss America below Jane." Duster Hill is named for the M 42 guns we have there; Morriss Hill, for Sgt Morriss of Co "C," 2nd Bn, 12th Cav, KIA on 21 Aug 67—he was a member of The Infantry Company you met.

My wife wrote that the Pageant people were a little annoyed that your trip cut into rehearsal time for the 1968 pageant. If so, I believe they are not fully aware of the good will and appreciation that your visit created among the

PART TWO

Top: Miss America 1967, Ms. Jane Jayroe, far right, arrives in Vietnam during monsoon season, August 1967 with fellow contestants. *Bottom:* Miss America traveled to active war landing zones in fatigues and army boots, August 1967 (both photographs courtesy Jane Jayroe Gamble).

4. "Things I Don't Want to Talk About"

74th Aviation Company welcomes Miss America with her cousin Mike, August 1967 (courtesy Jane Jayroe Gamble).

> American soldiers in Vietnam. Your idea was a fine, patriotic, and unselfish one, and it meant a lot to the men here. Thanks again.
>
> Best wishes for your future happiness,
>
> Sincerely,
> J.B. Love
> Lt. Colonel, Infantry
> Deputy Commander

PART TWO

MISS AMERICA RIDGE

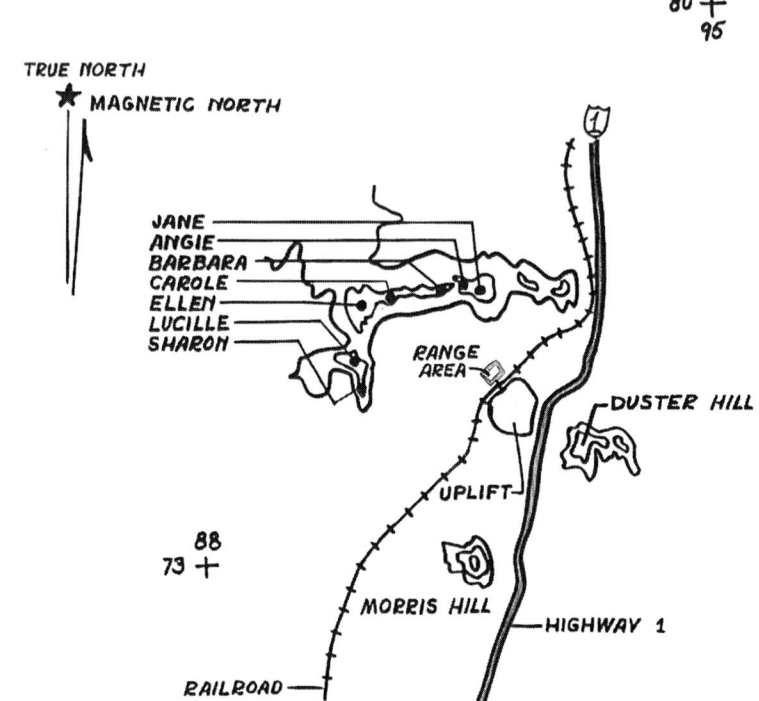

Authentic hand-drawn "Miss America Ridge" map marks named landing zones to honor each beauty queen: Jane, Angie, Barbara, Carole, Ellen, and Lucille (credit Jane Jayroe Gamble).

Jane Jayroe was the pride of Western Oklahoma and etched in the dreams of many young Americans. She returned to the United States after several days in Vietnam with her friends and camera crew on a plane full of U.S. soldiers. When they entered the plane, loud applause welcomed them, and soldiers stood up and cheered. The ladies humbly returned the honor and applause, feeling lucky to be among the uniformed men and women that represented our

4. "Things I Don't Want to Talk About"

nation's finest patriots. Soldiers were greeted at the airport by no family or friends, only to face the second part of their battles—the American backlash.

The ladies didn't realize how lucky they were to escape the war zone unscathed. Yet some of those battle scars followed them home, too.

* * *

28-Aug-67

Dear Mom and Dad,

    I have a little free time, so I thought I would write. I have really been busy lately. I have been up the last three nights and will be up again tonight.

    Things have been hot around here lately. Remember that night we put on a show for Miss America over at LZ uplift area? Well, they got mortared that night. I was over by there on a plane mission. Last night I spent the night there. We flew border patrol around the LZ. Ever since the monsoon season started, the V.C. have been raising hell.

    The right side of my neck is all burnt. The empty shell flying out of my machine gun hit me there and they were hot.

    Only 17 more days and my platoon goes down by the shore for 90 days. It is going to be just like a vacation from what I have heard. I have enough hours in for my first air medal. I should be getting it soon. I should also be getting my aviator wings (or crew chief wings, same thing) soon.

    I am still doing fine. I don't get much sleep or eat regular but otherwise I am fine. I am going to go for now. I have a chance to get some sleep and I had better take it. So, tell everyone I said hi. Write when you can.

Love always, Larry

    P.S. Tell Dad I need a Door Gunner and for him to come on over. All you do is lean out the door and fire, plus there are rockets going off around 5 inches from you.

    Two Bits is what my camp is called.

* * *

By nature, I was more curious than Mama was comfortable with, and asked questions on every topic, relentlessly in search of the truth. There were so many hidden conversations that dried up when I came into a room, that I knew I didn't know everything. I remained curious about Larry's living arrangements and location, but they changed often, and it was hard to keep up with him. He spent much of his time at the LZs, which Daddy explained was short for landing zones, where helicopters landed and took off, and where Larry cared for his ship. And plugged the holes.

LZ English was Miss America's station, not far from Larry's earlier stations in An Khe, Bong Son, Kontum, Quang Tri, and Da Nang. They were all places located in the Central Highlands, south of the DMZ, surrounded by mountains and valleys to the west and coastal towns along the South China Sea to the east.

An Khe base camp was an immense complex with multiple landing strips and a steel-plated runway they called the "golf course." The top of the mountain marked the unit's territory with a large First Cav symbol, a horse head painted in bright yellow and black. The giant colorful symbol set the tone for Cavalry power and made the area easy to locate, becoming notorious for many reasons. Teenage soldiers spent rare sunny days there, where they could find nurses tanning on the hilltop.

At the base of the mountain, there were bunkers for sleeping, rifle ranges, and small landing zones for practicing, and plenty of artillery storage, all surrounded by perimeter wiring and fences. Nearby was a downtown area named "Sin City" that Larry visited, a place that Mama grumbled he should avoid like the plague. Because that's where "the plague" had indeed plagued him.

Bong Son had tents instead of buildings and no showers. Dirty, cold water was available for cleaning the combat mud, dirt, and rocket dust off at the end of the day. Soldiers slept on thin air mattresses, placed on top of ammo boxes that were nailed together as a makeshift bed frame, so they didn't have to sleep on the ground with the crawling creatures. Those bunkers were sprayed with rodent-killing aerosols to keep the rats and scorpions away, so if the critters didn't kill you, the toxic chemicals would do a number on your lungs.

Two Bits sounded like a nice camp until we saw the news reports. There were two living quarters, one placed beside the perimeter barbed wire that separated the camp from the village. We saw the faces of the Vietnamese children from some of the villages we read about in Larry's letters. Mama told me that Larry was there to

4. "Things I Don't Want to Talk About"

protect the children and they needed him like we did, only worse. One image scarred us all, when the television showed a young Asian girl not much older than me, holding a shotgun in one hand and a crying baby in the other.

* * *

3-Sept-67

Dear Mom and Dad,

 Sorry I haven't wrote in the last few days, but I have been real busy. I am in base camp now. I will be here for two or three days. My ship is having some work done on it.
 Was real happy to get your letter. I'm also glad to hear the doctor said you're fine. No, I don't get to see any TV over here. I would like to, but I doubt if I ever will. The food here at base camp is real good and it is also real good out in the field. We have three hot meals a day in the field. I told Jo all about the C rations.
 If the VC shoot us from the other side of the fence, we have to call up and tell the OD about it, and he tells us if we could shoot back or not. If somebody is shooting at me, I don't care where they are, you can bet I'm going to shoot back.
 Oh—I think my polits [pilots] turned me in for a purple heart. We went on a mission, and I was firing my machine gun while the rockets were going off. I got hit in the face by a rocket cap and all I saw was blood. My polits thought I got shot at first because the wind was blowing the blood all over and made it look like worse. I grabbed a dirty old rag and wiped the blood off my face and went back to firing my M-60. It hurt a little, but if that's the only kind of wound I get over here I will be happy.
 Things have really been bad lately. We were on a red alert for the last four days in the field. And 11 guys have been killed here at base camp. It is because of the elections going on. Have you been hearing anything about them?
 Well, I am going to close for now. I am going to see if they have done anything with my ship and go look up a friend of mine. Tell everyone I said hi and tell Tracy I said be good for me. I am doing fine and hope everyone at home is. Write soon.

Love always, Larry

 Did you get that 50c I sent home? I might get a '68 Chevelle.

* * *

 On my end of the world, there was color in all corners and rainbows were easy to come by. Crayola opened my senses to appreciate

Part Two

the vibrant hues beyond primary colors. Other than a whole lot of green, and the colors of the ocean he longed to visit on day trips, Larry's world filled with black and white images and ideas, and all his things were a dull Army gray. Or covered in brown mud. Nothing was ever mentioned about anything colorful in Vietnam until they started bragging about Larry's purple heart. I wanted to know exactly how it turned colors and if I could get one. I imagined a pink heart for me and a red one for Mama. My sisters needed to pick their own colors. I didn't give up asking about the purple heart and since I got scattered answers, I fabricated my own.

"How did Larry get a purple heart, Mama? Does he like it? Is it shiny? Can he see it? Can he send one home for me?" They wouldn't tell me he got injured, only that he would explain later and bring the purple heart home so I could see it. Since Mama repeated that Larry was starting to "drink the Kool-Aid over there" I figured it was grape flavored, and it must have traveled straight to his chest. It sounded like a logical solution to me.

That grape drink left a crimson dye on my brother's heart, that was the answer, that's how he got a purple heart. I figured it out. And once again, I wasn't entirely off base.

* * *

7-Sept-67

Dear Mom and Dad,

Hi, hope everything is fine. I am still laying around here at base camp getting bored to death.

I really should be thankful I am here at base camp. My camp out in the field got mortared two nights ago. From what I have heard, five guys were killed. They wasn't from my unit, they were from the 1/9th division.

I got a letter from you this morning. I sure was glad to hear from you. I had just about given up looking for mail. It had been about five days since I got any.

I really haven't got much to say because I haven't done anything since I have been here. I have just about finished painting the inside of my ship. It is starting to look real good now. They patched up all the holes in my tail boom from rocket caps and other things which I don't want to talk about. Now I have to spot paint my tail boom.

I saw what was left of a helicopter today. It went down yesterday. It wasn't shot down, the tail rotor came off. All that was left was the tail boom and there wasn't much of it left. When it hit the ground it blew up and killed the two

4. "Things I Don't Want to Talk About"

polits. They haven't been able to find the crew chief. After seeing and hearing things like that, it kind of wants to make me quit being a crew chief.

I found out a lot of the guys I went to school in Alabama with are right down the road from me. So far, I have seen three of them. I hope before I go back out to the field, I will get to see the rest of them.

Did I tell you we ain't going to that place by the shore? We are staying at the same place until Oct 15. Then we come back to base camp until Dec. or Jan. I heard we are going up by the DMZ next. I don't know if it is true or not.

Well, I am going to go for now. Tell everyone I said hi. Don't forget to tell Jane. Write when you can.

Love always, Larry

P.S. Ask Dad if he knows what a 50-cal. round looks like? It's about as long as this paper this way. That's what most of the V.C. use up north. Big ain't it?

* * *

Larry told the truth, but not the whole truth. There were things he never talked about, and he filtered his daily trauma to protect us.

The guys from the 1/9th division that got mortared in the field were ambushed by guerrilla forces on a back road of a rubber tree plantation. Their bodies were found stripped nude, full of bullets from execution style shots, some were tied together and weighted down with rocks and others pinned down with stakes in water-filled ditches. Even after they died, the enemy continued to torture their bodies.

The gunship that crashed was on a standard rocket run when the aircraft's tail rotor and driveshaft came off, reportedly due to "incorrect assembly." Pilot Captain Winston Robinson and his crew of four were from the same 2/20th unit as Larry, in C battery. The pilot tried to control the diving ship as it crashed into the trees. Larry didn't realize that three of his First Cavalry troopers ran to help the crew escape when the heat of the fire detonated the rockets. Eight heroes died that day. Their names joined countless others in KIA counts. Jessie Barlow, Walter Mack Phillips, and Loren Lee Morford tried in vain to save their fellow warriors, Winston Robinson, Paul Clark, J.D. Singleton, James Hembree, and Pryor Wheat.

Larry spent the day painting his ship after they patched the holes from things that he "didn't want to talk about." He distrusted his own ship's mechanics, yet he was proud of the new paint job on

Part Two

it. Daddy had plenty of reasons to distrust the Army and its aging aircraft, as well. He started studying helicopters and weapons from books he got from the public library. He didn't trust those flimsy helicopters to protect his son after hearing about all the crashes. Back in Advanced Training School, Larry had painted details validating Daddy's concerns in this letter to Mama:

> *From all the stuff I have learned about a helicopter and the way it is put together, I am a little afraid to ride in one. The rotor head without the blades weighs around 400 pounds and with the blades, it weighs close to 1000 pounds. The only thing that keeps it from slipping down the mast is two little split cones. Dad should know what they are. Just little things like that kind of make you afraid to ride in one. When the blades are spinning around 3300 RPM, it creates around 40 tons of centrifugal force and there ain't too much holding the blades or the blade grips on. It really surprises me how they hold together.*

He may not have been the smartest student back in Alabama, but he was spot on to question the safety of his future in the skies.

* * *

10-Sept-67
Sunday
Dear Mom and Dad,

    Received your letter yesterday. Sure was glad to hear from you again. Hope everyone is fine. I am still doing ok.
    I am still here at base camp waiting on my ship to get fixed. They told me yesterday that they changed their mind about putting in a new engine. Now all they have to do is put in a fuel boost pump and track my blades. So I will be going back to the field soon.
    Tell Peggy I said happy birthday even though I am late. I didn't even know when it was. It is hard to believe she is 14. I think she will change and become more grown-up.
    I wish we would have a cool spell. Even when it rains it is hot. The monsoon season hasn't got into full swing yet, but it will soon. It rains every day here but some days it only rains for a few minutes.
    Today at lunch we had all the chicken we could eat at supper and all the steak we could eat. The steak was cooked on the grill outside and it was cooked just right. The chicken was Southern fried, and boy was it good. It tasted almost as good as your cooking.
    I went to church this morning and had that little piece of bread they give you. After I came back from church TOP (our first sergeant) had me watering trees. As soon as he turned his back I was gone. When he found me he didn't even say anything. I thought maybe he had tripped and hurt his head

4. "Things I Don't Want to Talk About"

or something. Later I found out the major was back. He is nice to all us crew chiefs all day, but when the major goes back to the field he will turn back into the same old hard head.

Last night I was feeling good for some reason. I wasn't drinking or anything. He had a tree he was going to plant, so me and this other crew chief came up with a stupid idea to plant it. We knew if we did, he wouldn't notice it and go crazy looking for it.

While we were digging the hole, he came walking by. We put the shovels behind our backs, and he said, 'what are you up to troops'? We said, 'nothing at all TOP.' Then he went on his way, but it blew our deal about planting the tree.

We stayed up till 11 o'clock playing around and doing rotten things. At 12 o'clock we got up because we couldn't sleep. So, we had a beer and went outside in our shorts and played football.

I didn't tell you on my last letter about when we stole his Jeep and went riding around. It was fun until we ran out of gas. We were lucky there was a can of gas in the back. He didn't even know we took it.

I'm going to buy and get Tracy that jacket this month. I hope I can get back to town before 15 October. That's when I come back into base camp.

Well, I'm going to say bye for now. It is late and I have to make that 6 o'clock formation. If I don't, it will cost me $21.

Tell everyone I said hello. Write when you can. I need all the mail I can get to keep my spirits up.

Love always, Larry

* * *

Our family didn't practice religion, at least not like the McGuigan family next door with their Catholic rituals and ceramic figurines of Mother Mary. We prayed over meals on holidays and started nightly prayers at bedtime when Larry went away. All of us girls were sent to Sunday school at Sandhills Presbyterian Church and Mama joined us on special occasions, but Daddy never did. From our weekly bible stories, we knew that a mustard seed of faith was all you needed, and Mama took comfort in Larry's church attendance in Vietnam. He had a pocket bible and a Saint Christopher that would keep him safe until she got him back.

Larry didn't like to follow rules unless they mattered to him. And a whole lot of rules didn't make sense in his war. Not to my brother. He knew the worst thing that could happen already happened when they sent him to Vietnam. He was determined to have a good time despite the danger they put him in. Or, maybe because of it.

Besides the letters he received from home, the bonds of

brotherhood lifted Larry's spirits. When he arrived in An Khe, he met a kid from New York who was also a crew chief in the same unit. Richard Passer called Larry "Sonny boy" since he was a year younger than Rich and they connected on every level from the moment they met. Rich and Larry worked together every chance they got and kept things interesting around camp with their pranks when they weren't flying their ships and winning the war.

The unit major never liked the pair of goofballs. He respected their skills, so he tolerated their spirited antics as they tried to keep the "brass" scratching their heads. That was kind of the point and exactly as they intended. It felt good to push back against a system that let them down daily. Out of an estimated 200 formations, they were late for 199 and made no apologies. The Army threatened fines, yet the two friends avoided them every time. They agreed that formations were a waste of time when there was precious work to be done or fun to be had and got good at hiding in a foxhole or ditching the base camp when the time came to report in.

As senior crew chiefs, they were the go-to guys and never missed a mission when given the choice. Due to long days in combat, they were offered more grace than other soldiers in terms of rules and dress standards. The unit contained about 120 people, yet only a couple dozen others with the crew chief title fought the war like the two of them. They stayed busy in the grind of combat and faced enemy fire almost every day. Unless their ships were down, they were in the air. Their hair grew long, and their Army boots were never cleaned, much less shined. Rich and Larry avoided the "buttoned-up boys" with their clean shirts and manicured nails and kept to their own dirty world of "crewing and gunning."

Inside the crew chief tent at base camp, the boys bonded in the oppressive summer conditions, using sarcasm and pranks to stay sane. They dubbed themselves the "Scrufty Dozen" after the popular war film "The Dirty Dozen" with Charles Bronson. Each flight mission ended with a welcome shower after thick layers of rocket dust coated every limb of their bodies, clothing, and hair into areas unknown, which became an ongoing competition of its own. The crew slept every chance they got in the comfort of the tent, where

4. "Things I Don't Want to Talk About"

their buddies' cots were placed three feet apart on either side, close enough to reach out and slap each other when they felt the need. Which was often, by all accounts.

When Rich and Larry stole the major's jeep, Larry failed to mention he drove an hour away from base camp all the way to Camp Evans on a dark, sandy road long after lights out. The pair had to pass through enemy territory and had no way to contact anyone because a radio signal could be intercepted by the enemy. On the way back from Camp Evans, well after midnight and deep into the time when Viet Cong forces are most active, the jeep began to sputter. Larry looked at Rich, Rich looked back at his friend. No joke would be appropriate, as the engine failed, and the stolen vehicle stopped in the middle of the dirt road. The jeep had run out of gas. For a few minutes, they sat still, thinking they were doomed. They had long ago memorized the saying that "We own the day, but Charlie owns the night" and knew that the Ho Chi Minh Trail foot soldiers were probably not far away. Larry got out of the jeep and looked in the back, where he pulled back a tarp.

He smiled at Rich, and said, "Oh hell, there's a full can of gasoline back here." They filled the tank, released their pent-up fear through quiet laughs, and counted more of those lucky stars they were racking up. The major never found out.

I thought of Larry's nighttime adventure, dreamt of bouncing up and down on a leather seat next to him from the bumpy dirt road, and wished I had been there with him. Mama defended his actions by saying that without visible damage to anything or anyone, nobody was hurt by their impulsive jungle joy ride, and the Jeep was returned in one healthy piece, which was more than the Army could ever say about all the boys they stole from America.

* * *

15-Sept-67
Friday
Dear Mom and Dad,

   Hi, hope everyone is fine. I am still doing okay. Sorry I haven't wrote lately. Between eating and sleeping I haven't done anything else.

   I found out last night that on the 17th my platoon is leaving for that place by the shore. I just hope my ship is ready by then. It should be.

Part Two

All the guys came back in from the field yesterday. Last night, most of us went over to the club. I don't know how many beers or double shots I had, but when I got up this morning I felt like I had been run over by a truck. Just about everyone in the Bty. looked like they were half dead.

I haven't been up in the air for about 14 days now. So tonight I think I will fly mortar patrol with one of the guys just to see what it feels like to fly again.

Today I took out a $6.25 bond. The major said he would like for everyone to have one so I got one. Well I just got talked into going over to the club again tonight. So if I can write when I get back, I will finish this.

Well—here I am again. I just came back from the club. I ain't sober, but I ain't drunk.

They had a floor show and it was real good. There were five girls from the Philippines. They sang and played the drums and guitars. There was a whole mess of MPs there. They said they were there for the boys in A Bty., because we just came in from the field. The girls wore miniskirts, and they were mini.

They ain't too much going on here at base camp. I guess you know it's been 14 days since I've seen any action. But I will be back in action again soon.

Well I'm going to go for now. I am going to write some girl from Long Branch New Jersey. I don't know her but I'm going to write anyway. Tell everyone I said hi. Write again soon.

Love always, Larry

P.S. If you can, when you start getting them saving bonds, put them in the bank under Tracy's name.

* * *

This was one of those letters Mama would've skipped parts of if she read it at all. She would've erased the page if she could have. She felt Larry growing up much too fast, a little more in each letter. She didn't like his place in the war. Her young son was not prepared to handle the temptations or dangers around him. Or unlimited access to alcohol.

The job of the Artillery Rocket Association was to offer support to all allies on the ground. Infantry soldiers ("grunts") relied on flying gunships for many things, mostly to save their skins from desperate situations. The 48 rockets positioned under Larry's feet in a single pod could be delivered in four seconds. As the first and only ARA battalion in the world, the rocket men were notorious for the volume of firepower offered to the combat table at a moment's notice. Rockets were fired from the air with accuracy to destroy armored vehicles, brick buildings, and even cave openings.

4. "Things I Don't Want to Talk About"

Relationships between helicopter crews and infantrymen were strong, much different from other wars. The boys on the ground respected the hard-working gunships that delivered supplies and got them out of situations. Anytime there was an injured soldier, or forces were surrounded by enemies, they needed powerful forces to help the medevac team evacuate the injured. Infantry leaders lavished praise on the ARA forces, knowing the war could not be won without them.

Larry had convinced Mama that he would be safer in the air than on the ground, but she was learning that this war was unlike all the rest, and Larry had a pivotal job in it. It wasn't a job as a mechanic or a crew member working on a helicopter in a war zone. He did everything the helicopter did and would never stop until it stopped. And if it did stop, you had better hope that happened on the ground.

He complained when his ship was down, and he grew bored waiting to get back in the air despite the dangers. He yearned to fly. So even on days off, he volunteered to be the door gunner for the other crew chiefs. He tucked his small frame against the open helicopter door and leaned out as far as possible to shoot the M-60 machine gun, trusting the loosened "monkey harness" around his waist—and the bungee cord that held the weapon to the roof—would stay buckled tight when the ship turned and dipped. With one foot on the rocket pod, he reached far enough out to avoid shooting his own ship and fired rounds between the skids beneath him to protect the vulnerable belly of the ship. The ideal door gunner would be smaller than average to fit in the back of the Huey and leave room for the ammo. He needed agility to balance on a moving aircraft without adding extra weight to the pilot's equations.

Larry made an ideal crew chief for the U.S. Army. He carried a heavy load of ammunition with an abundance of adrenaline pumping as he leaned out and emptied his machine gun with little precision but plenty of balance. Those hormones would fight lack of sleep, bad nutrition, 120–140 mph winds, and other forces, even beyond the ruthless enemy. He followed orders he didn't agree with. He shot innocent humans and destroyed entire villages without hesitation, as

Part Two

he was ordered to do. He worked at his job in the air, while dodging ground fire from below.

None of us understood the magnitude of his job in the back seat of that Huey. Then again, neither did he. Not yet.

* * *

17-Sept-67
Sunday
Dear Mom and Dad,
   Hi, I woke up this morning and there were three letters for me laying on my footlocker. One was from Jimmy.
   Da Nang is up by the DMZ. I am about an hours flight from Qui Nhon. Qui Nhon is right on the coast and it is a very nice place. I was there once.
   My ship still ain't ready so I might not get to go to that place. The place is right below Qui Nhon. I don't know what the name of it is.
   They had my ship out on the flight line again yesterday to test fly it, but they found more things wrong, so they're working on it again. I don't know when it will be ready now. If I do get to go down by the shore, I will be flying missions for the unit down there.
   I wrote you a letter the other night, but can't remember if I mailed it or not. I can't find it anyplace around here.
   I hope everyone is fine at home. I am still doing ok. Do you know what a mongoose is? It looks like something like a cat but the face looks like a rat. We have one for a pet. We call it Marvin. We had two monkeys we caught but we gave them away when we came in from the field.
   Well I had better go for now. I got some work to do and it's time to eat. Tell everyone I said hi. Write again soon.
Love always, Larry

* * *

They called them giant rats without tails. The only crawling creatures you couldn't shoot. They also called the mongoose the national pet, or Vietnamese steak, depending on who you asked. But Marvin the Mongoose held a special place in the 2/20 unit and served an important purpose to keep away snakes, cockroaches, and mosquitos. The ferret-like creature lived in the crew chief tent and the guys enjoyed his company. Some mongooses could be mean, vicious enough to kill a python or a fox, but Marvin was a favored pet. He jumped around with manic speed, at arbitrary times, from the floor to the wall, and onto bellies that weren't covered by a mosquito net.

4. "Things I Don't Want to Talk About"

He was an insanely curious pet and kept the boys entertained and offered much needed comic relief.

At night, Marvin slept on top of Rich's mosquito net. The little rascal left his daily droppings on top of Larry's mosquito net, and every other guy's bedding in the tent at some point except for Rich. Rich joked that it was a hygiene issue. The boys gave him hell. He didn't know why Marvin chose him as the lucky one, but he respected Marvin and liked having him curled above him at night.

One day, there was a new guard on station who found himself in Marvin's company with no warning. As he patrolled the perimeter ditch line around base, he saw a large rat-looking creature running towards him, so he pulled out his sidearm and killed him with one shot. He didn't know it was a pet mongoose. The entire unit got mad at the f'ing new guy (an "FNG" was what they called all new arrivals). The FNGs could be easily spotted, with fresh clean clothes, short hair and boots still shined. This rookie FNG killed the Scrufty Dozen's furry mascot, and they were all pissed about it. The private who shot Marvin received an Article 15 Punishment from the unit commander, for firing a weapon in base camp without authority. Firing a weapon in base camp was a big no-no. Which meant of course, that Larry needed to test it.

When Rich and Larry weren't flying, they were bored, and when they were bored, they looked for trouble. They were cleaning their pistols one day and decided to push their luck. They carried Smith and Wesson .38 Specials at all times, but never needed to use them. As they were sitting out on the landing zone near Larry's aircraft, one of them suggested, "Hell, we should shoot these things." After a brief debate, they agreed. They popped several rounds in nearby sandbags, emptying their pistols at the same time. They saw people scatter, as guys either ran for cover, or ran laughing at the guys running for cover. Within a few minutes, they were told to report to the Executive Officer (XO) and knew they would get an official reprimand. Hopefully a free ride home. They entered the office together, disheveled, and dusty, holding back strong urges to giggle.

Part Two

The XO asked the pair why they discharged their sidearms. Rich told him that they were fighting the enemy.

The officer looked them up and down and asked Rich, "What enemy?"

Larry interrupted with the truthful answer, "Boredom." Rich shook his head in agreement and grinned. He couldn't hold it back any longer.

"Boredom, huh? You are two of the best crew chiefs we have while you're flying, but on the ground, you can be a real pain in my ass," the officer scolded.

"Thank you, sir," Rich replied. He meant it. He and Larry were both happy with the officer's kind words, and happy to push the brass buttons.

The XO told them to stay out of trouble, pointed to the door, and ordered, "Get back to the flight line and find some other toys to play with."

They laughed all the way back to the ammo pile, where they sat down and finished cleaning their sidearms, plotting their next imaginary strategy for winning this war without the Army's help. They took their jobs seriously and when they were in the air, they were all business. On the ground, all bets were off.

There was another time their luck prevailed. Driving out to the flight line, the boys jumped in a cargo truck with Larry behind the wheel and Rich as his passenger. Larry drove the truck right into the tail end of a parked helicopter. Rich never let Larry live that one down. The boys weren't drinking that day and never did any drugs, although they had plenty of access to both. They were too busy to bother, and had a ton of work to do, unlike many of the guys laying around stoned in the camp. When they realized that nobody noticed the crash, Larry backed the truck away, parked it, and the pair got out and went to work. They never came clean, and nobody ever asked them about it. With all the damage done to equipment and vehicles during Larry's war, it may have been overlooked with ambivalence. Or maybe they just got away with it, as usual.

※ ※ ※

4. "Things I Don't Want to Talk About"

17-Sept-67
Sunday
Dear Mom and Dad,

    I received a letter from you today, and was very unhappy to hear about Peggy. I just wrote her a letter and hope it will do some good. I really hate to see her mess up her life like I did. Every thing I told her in the letter I meant, and it's true.

    I would like for you to send me Bill's address. I want to write him and tell him what I think of what he is doing. You just don't know how mad I got when you said he would go to a lawyer, that really burnt me up. Bill could never give Peggy as many things as you and dad have given her or even as much love. I, myself would never go live with him. I never realized until I left home just how much I did have when I was living home.

    (Rest of letter is missing)

* * *

30-Sept-67

Dear Mom and Dad,

    Hi, I received a letter from you yesterday. Sure was glad to get it.

    I hope Dad will be alright. I don't mind at all if you use my money. It is there, and if you need it, it is yours to take. I just wish I could be home to help out.

    Things over here haven't changed much. I am back at base camp again. I just came back today. My ship has a very bad vibration, plus a few other things which make it unsafe to fly in.

    I guess you heard about the DMZ. That's where all the action is. Well from what I have heard, we are going up there. Things will really be rough if we do. That's where all the Marines are.

    Two days ago, I was on a mission and my machine gun jammed up. I had two rounds jammed in the chamber. I started to remove them and one of them exploded. You can thank the Lord I still have eyes to see with. Most of the time when we are working on machine gun passes, I don't have my face shield down. I was lucky and had it down. I pulled some of the metal from the shell out of my hand. It scared the hell out of me when it went off.

    I would like very much if you would send me some books to read. Just think in 10 months I will be home again. I hate to go but I have to get all my stuff fixed up. Tell everyone I said hi and hope they're fine. Write when you can.

Love always, Larry

* * *

Daddy had pain in his knee that began to get worse, so Larry started to worry that he needed to be home as the man of the house. With Daddy home more, we all united around Larry's letters. All of us waited in anticipation and became friendly with the mailman. When

Part Two

a letter arrived, it was big news. Sometimes we didn't get any for a week or two, and sometimes more than one came on the same day. If a letter was thick, we found coins, pictures, or slides inside. Once, he sent a poem. We began to gather at the dining room table for Mama to read them to us.

She had a collection of thirty or more letters by now, and they moved from a shoe box on the table to a location out of sight. Mama stashed them in an old sewing box next to her recliner, under the table that always displayed her latest novel and an ashtray full of cigarette butts. She didn't need to say it, I knew that box was off limits to most anyone. She made room in the box for every letter and kept them neatly stacked.

When she wrote Larry back, she did so in silence at the same dining room table, with her glass of iced tea perched on a crocheted coaster to protect the wood. We knew she would fill Larry in on our latest school activities, grades, and pets. We never got to read her words. They were reserved for Larry. Sometimes we wrote him, too, but mostly Mama told him what we needed to say. I sure hope she signed them all with Love always, Mama.

Our parents debated the topic of war a lot, and both were concerned, you could see it anytime Vietnam was mentioned. My parents stole glances during the news and whispered late into the night sometimes. Mama focused on trying to follow Larry's whereabouts. We all looked for the DMZ and grew frustrated when we couldn't locate the newsworthy "demilitarized military zone" that Larry mentioned more than once. The DMZ was where evil weaved through mountains and plains and crawled below our troops in a series of tunnels and trails that led to entire underground compounds. Nobody truly knew the boundary of the enemy's territory or what lay beneath it.

Without knowing his opponent, or where they might be hiding, Larry was playing hide and seek with the game of red light, green light mixed in. He kept stopping and starting and moving back and forth but did much more seeking than hiding. Many places he visited but he couldn't spell, and we couldn't pronounce, anyway. Foreign lands remained a mystery to us, and besides that, the people of

4. "Things I Don't Want to Talk About"

North and South Vietnam looked the same. The war was an impossible game to play fair.

* * *

2-Oct-67

Dear Mom and Dad,

   I got another letter from you yesterday. Am glad dad is doing fine. Hope he will be up and around soon. I hope I have enough money for you to use. Glad to hear Tracy likes school. I just hope she doesn't change her mind in the years to come.

   I went downtown today (AN-KHE). It is a lot better than Bong Son. I also stopped in "Sin City" too. I'm going to try and go back Wednesday to see this girl I met. She is a clean-cut girl and very nice. She ain't like most of the girls in town. <u>Don't</u> worry we are only <u>friends</u>.

   I am still doing fine. I have gained a little weight. Here is a picture of me and one of my buddies. That is his ship. Mine is all torn apart. But that's what our ships look like. His is a B model, mine is a C model. That's one of our pets laying under the ship. The other guy goes home in 29 days.

   Don't think we always have a hair combed and clean clothes on all the time, the only reason we do in the picture is because, it was taken just before we left for town.

   Well I am going to go again. I have a few more letters to write. Tell everyone I said hi. Send me some pictures of everybody, O.K.? Write soon.

Love always, Larry

* * *

On the back of the envelope, Mama made a list. She often doodled and left notes for herself and others. She had to plan in order to afford the luxuries she grew up taking for granted, and yet her fashion sense and desire for the nicest clothing and latest fashions for her girls didn't wane when money got tight. In cursive handwriting, Mama planned the next Polaroid memories, complete with fishnet stockings for someone on her list.

$2.30 Pants
$7.88 Coat
$4.99 Dress
$1.70 Fish-nets
$3.68 Slacks
$20.55

* * *

Part Two

4-Oct-67
Wednesday

Dear Mom and Dad,

    Well, here I am again. I got a letter from you and Joanna today and I also got one from Jane. Am having a good time over here now. I have been to town three days in a row now. If I get caught, they will hang my ass but it's worth it.

    I got the picture of you and Dad out of the album when I was home. The reason I don't have a jacket is because I had to turn most of my stuff back in the states.

    I sure hope things will be alright at home soon. I feel kind of bad because I ain't there to help. But there's nothing I can do about it. Did Peggy change her mind about living with Bill? I sure hope so.

    I got a picture of the girl I am seeing in town, today. She wrote something on the back of it but I don't understand all of what it says. She's really cute. But as I said before, we are only <u>friends</u>.

    Today when I went to town, I spent about an hour at Sin City and the rest of my time at Kim-Mai's house (her name). Her Mom and Dad even got along with me.

    Well, I better go for now. I want to take a shower before the water runs out. Tell everyone I said hi and hope they are fine. Tell Tracy I said be real good. Write often.

Love always, Larry

* * *

    Larry still didn't take the war seriously, not like Mama and Daddy did. My brother made the most of his time and had lots of fun but sometimes he yearned to get kicked out of the Army and sent home. Mama defended her boy and his role in the war. However, when the letters introduced her to his newest affection for Sin City, she questioned the Army's motives and blamed them for everything Larry faced. I never heard tales of Sin City, as Mama must have skipped those sections. Sin City may have intrigued and amused both Larry and Daddy, but it haunted Mama.

* * *

8-Oct-67
Sun.
AN KHE V.N.

Mom and Dad,

    Just a few words to let you know I am still around. I got the flu or something. I have really been sick the last few days. I am starting to feel a little better now.

4. "Things I Don't Want to Talk About"

Well—I learned my lesson about messing around with the girls over here. The shots I got to take just ain't worth the $4 I wasted.

My ship should be ready in the morning. Most likely I will leave for Tuy HOA tomorrow. My platoon is still down there, and I don't know when they are coming back. I haven't heard any more about us going up to the DMZ, so I don't know what's happening.

I hope everyone is doing fine. How is Dad coming along? And how is your back?

How much money are they sending you in them checks? I think they are messing up on my pay records The next time you hear from me I should be a SP/4. I made it last month, but they revoked all the orders and only one guy made it. There was only one slot open for SP/4.

Well, I am going to go for now. I got to get up early and go see the Doc. in the morning. Tell everyone I said hi. Only 9 months and 21 days to go. Write often.

Love always, Larry

* * *

He's learning hard lessons. And all the girl stuff, well, that got swiftly swept under Mama's rug like anything the least bit improper. He was busy growing up, Mama said. He wouldn't hurt a flea, Mama said. And if he did hurt anyone, it would've been against his will and better judgment. He knew better, Mama said.

Larry had a soft spot for animals and children, always pulling for the underdogs. One day, his pilot made him shoot a herd of water buffalo, which required multiple passes to penetrate the gigantic animals and get them all down. The last one fell into a ditch and kept pedaling its legs, wedged between the dirt walls, flailing in desperation as it lay helpless. Larry asked the pilot to let at least one live. He laughed in his face and teased him for his naivete and ordered Larry to kill it. The innocent animals were pets to the local farmers, vital to the livelihood of innocent families, and did nothing to deserve death in this senseless way. Larry learned to hate taking orders from pilots and started to question his loyalty to the cause.

Mama didn't like being out of control of things, and this war had become a big mystery and a serious threat, possibly at the expense of her first-born golden child. Now he was sick, and there was nothing she could do to help him. Mama had a birthday, which Larry never even mentioned in all those letters he wrote that first week of October. She blamed the Army for filling his mind with poison and cursed the heads on television that kept delivering awful news. Mama stayed

Part Two

angry for her entire 37th birthday. My birthday would be much better, and I knew my brother would never forget it. In fact, during the month of November, Larry mentioned my birthday three times in his letters. I hope she didn't notice.

* * *

10-Oct-67

Dear Mom and Dad,

I just got another letter from you yesterday and was glad as always to hear from you.

I am still doing fine. I feel much better now. I got some pills from the doc, and I ain't too sick now. Them shots I got also helped me out too. Next time I go to town, I will know better to mess around.

My ship still ain't out yet. They test flew it and found more things wrong with it. I don't know how long it will be, before it will be ready. I am sort of glad in a way because I don't want to go back to Tuy HOA anyway. It is nice down there but all the sand just tears up an aircraft.

I sure hope everything is getting better at home. Dad should be out and home by now. He is better by now, ain't he? I sure hope so. Glad to hear your back is getting better.

Does Tracy still like her school? By the time I get home she should already be in the 1st grade.

My best friend Rich lives in Kinston, N.Y. He was just like me before he came in the army. He is also a crew chief. He has only been here a month longer than I have. But he has been in the army almost 2 years. He spent a year in Germany.

I just came in off a mission. I rode gunner with my buddy. Every time I go up with him, we have fun. We made some of the fanciest rocket runs you ever saw. One of the polits is as old as me, but he knows how to handle a helicopter. On the way back we flew right into some artillery. I thought for sure we were going to get hit.

If I take an R&R, me and my buddy are going to Hong Kong. I don't know if I want to take one or not. I want to get a big 4 track tape recorder. They are really nice. It would look good sitting in the dining room.

Well I am going to close again. Not much more to say except that I miss everyone and wish I was home. Tell everyone I said hi and hope they are fine. Take care of your self and take it easy. Write often.

Love Always, Larry

P.S. Tell Jo my Buddy (Rich) is going to write her.

* * *

I did love school. But I lost things there. Mama was still wondering about the second raincoat that I misplaced, or my latest missing

4. "Things I Don't Want to Talk About"

umbrella or mittens. I told her I thought that little mean girl stole them all. Mama comforted me by explaining that some little kid probably needed them more than I did and promising to buy me replacements. Truth be told, Mama promised me I would lose my head if it wasn't attached, but I knew she'd get me a new one if it came off.

On rainy days I preferred playing games over reading, much to the dismay of my maternal bookworm. When I wasn't creating household dynamics with Ken and Barbie, dressing and redressing my life-sized go-go doll, or playing the role of Buffy with my Mrs. Beasley doll, I longed for the sun to come out in order to play in the yard with the McGuigan kids. Larry used to play with us. Now he was busy out riding rockets over Vietnam with no time for little kids. I told my friends where he went and tried explaining his job. We equated his fancy rocket runs with a ride down a slide on Milton Bradley's Chutes and Ladders board game. My brother was playing the real game, but his chutes were super slippery on those fancy rocket runs. And his ladders were never-ending. He was so lucky.

* * *

18-Oct-67

Dear Mom and Dad,

   Hi, hope everything is fine at home. I am still doing OK. Sorry I haven't wrote in awhile but I have really been busy. I went back to Tuy HOA for a few days. The day I got there one of my buddies crashed and the other got a hole in his rotor blade. So that left mine the only one flyable, and that's all I did was fly.
   Everyone in my buddy's ship that crashed got out OK but I don't see how they did it. I am sending a picture of his ship. The other picture I am sending is our last night in Tuy HOA. We all went over to the club and had a little fun.
   I ain't on them new Cobra's you hear about. The Cobra is smaller than the UH-1 Hueys and only seats two people. We are supposed to get some but I hope we don't. I won't get to fly anymore if we do get them.
   I don't get to see any of the shows or people. I don't know for sure if we will get to see that Bob Hope show or not. The only thing we have is Red Cross girls that come around and play games every once in a while.
   I was out on a mission today and while I was firing my machine gun, a rocket cap hit me in the hand and then in the face. I got cut in seven diff. places on the face. The polit saw all the blood and rushed me back to see the doc. I got fixed up and also got put in for another purple heart.
   We have moved out of base camp here in AN-KHE and are setting up base

Part Two

camp in Bong Song (Two Bits). I am still here at AN-KHE, and will stay here for awhile.

I got a letter from Butch, and he says to say hi. He is doing fine. He is driving a truck now for the 1st sergeant. He still wants to come over here. I got a letter from Dad the other day too. I was so happy I had tears in my eyes. It sure made me feel good to hear from him. Me and Mary Anne are still getting along fine. I get letters from her all the time.

Well, I had better go for now. I have been flying all day and I have mortar patrol tonight. I am dead tired. Tell everyone I said hi. Will see you in Aug.

Love always, Larry

Thanks for the money. I haven't even had time to cash it yet.
Here is a picture of the girl I see in town. Send it back soon.

* * *

When it came to being girl crazy, Mama claimed Larry was "born a Casanova" and couldn't help himself. All I knew was that he had a fan club of pretty girls in Jersey waiting for him to come home. My sister's teenage friends swooned over his military picture framed and hanging square on the wall as you entered our house. He reminded them of a young Elvis Presley with his slicked-back dark hair and Southern twang. Mama said he talked like Elvis on a good day, yet with no rhythm and two left feet all that would buy him was a cup of coffee, or something like that.

The boys in the First Cav called him the Rebel Yankee. He may have been from New Jersey, but he spoke with a sweet Carolina-bred accent that the girls fancied. He would be hard pressed to find many American girls in South Asia, other than the Red Cross ladies who delivered coffee and donut treats in their light blue Donut Dolly dresses. He didn't stop looking, and he didn't discriminate. The hooch maids came around to make sure the boys had plenty of local options at their disposal and Larry paid attention. The Army provided what the young men wanted, to keep them sane and keep them there. Cold beer and hot women were in high demand. Mama thought Larry had more than enough of both. Daddy disagreed with Mama but stayed quiet on the subject.

The Army had messed up her son's handsome face and Mama started to cuss about things more, complaining that the war should be over by now. She didn't like the mention of a second purple heart

4. "Things I Don't Want to Talk About"

and winced as she read it. He had a few good days hanging out in Tuy HOA, which was referred to as "Hell's half acre" by the American soldiers. Larry never mentioned that little detail.

* * *

Saturday
21-Oct-67

Dear Mom and Dad,

    Hi, hope everyone is fine. I am doing OK. I got a letter from you and Peggy today and was glad as always to get them.

    Well—I ain't going to wait and surprise you at the end of this letter so I will do it now—I was down at the PX today and saw something I have been wanting for a long time. It was a big tape recorder, and it is really nice. So, you know me, I had to get it—So here's the plan—I borrowed the money from my best friend Rich to get it. Well, he is going on R&R and I told him I would have the money for him. He leaves on the 20th of November. So, if it won't put you into too much of a bind with the payments and all I would really appreciate it if you would send me $110 in a money order to Richard H. Passer. Make the money order out to him. But now if you can't swing $110, I still have the $45 & will get paid $40 the 15th of Nov. I hate to ask you and all but I really wanted that tape recorder.

    I hope you ain't too mad. I am going to send the tape recorder home later. But really if you can send it, I need it before the 20th of Nov.

    My friend Rich is going to come home with me in Aug. I showed him Joanna's picture and I haven't got it back yet. Every thing around here has Joanna's name on it. I think he fell in love with her or something. He is sitting here writing her again. This makes three letters, and I don't even think she has got the first one yet. When we go to eat, he takes the picture out of his pocket and sits it on the table and looks at it while he is eating. When he is flying, he has it in his pocket over his heart.

    I think you would really like him. I know dad would. He is a regular nut. Just like me. We are always talking about our families and how it will be when we get home. But he has really gone nuts over Joanna. You should see him kissing her picture every night before he goes to bed.

    We really have a lot of fun over here together. It is like being back home on the street corner with the guys.

    By the way—if Joanna's boy friend's sister is 17 or over, not over 20, get me her address. Maybe I can get in good with her.

    Well, I am going to close for now. Tell everyone I said hi and hope they are fine. Glad to hear your back is better. Tell Dad to take care of his knee. So, write when you can.

Love always, Larry

    Tell Tracy I said hi and be good.

* * *

Part Two

Larry talks into a reel-to-reel recorder in his teenage bedroom, circa 1965.

    Larry found his best friend all the way around the world. Mine was right next door. His met him on a helicopter pad each day, and mine met me at second base, under the maple tree between our front yards. Betty and I would talk about the latest secrets and scandals I discovered in my public school or her second-grade stories about the nuns at St. Augustine's Catholic School. We compared wacky family stories, mostly mine, and shared our favorite snacks. Betty knew everything I struggled with and helped me process the scattered pieces, long before my puzzle even had a name. Adopted. Both Larry and I had been adopted by our Daddy. Another bond we shared, and something I never quite comprehended until I grew up and it mattered.
    Larry kept telling me to be good in his letters. Maybe it was a

4. "Things I Don't Want to Talk About"

Seven Crew Chiefs: left to right, back row: Robert Ennis, Ronnie Dunn, Larry Smith, Barry Brady, John Stewart. Front Row: Dawson Crews, Dean Demain, circa 1967 (credit John Stewart).

reminder, maybe it was a warning. My brother knew the whole truth and knew things would be easier if I stayed on my best behavior. So, I did. Except for that one day when I left my bike on the sidewalk and it was stolen, and I blamed my sister Peggy. I had no bicycle for the whole winter and got a spanking from Daddy, the only one he ever gave me. It didn't hurt, but I promised to be good and not blame Peggy anymore. I didn't want to be returned.

* * *

25-Oct-67
Wednesday
Dear Mom and Dad,
    Just a few lines to let you know I am still O.K. and doing fine. Hope everything at home is back to normal.
    My ship is down again, it's been down for 3 or 4 days now. I still have a vertical vibration. I hope they fix it this time.

Part Two

Larry poses with a UH-1 Huey helicopter "ship," October 1967.

I had guard last night. I didn't know it until I came back from town and I was half drunk. I couldn't get anything in town yesterday because I wasn't supposed to be there and if I would of brought something back, they would of known I had been to town.

I am taping songs right now. This tape recorder works good. As soon as I get tired of it, I will send it home. Next time I write I will send some pictures. I just sent some to Mary Anne.

If you can find my old tape recorder and get it to work, tape a letter to me. I think it will play on this one. My buddy Rich is still in love with Jo. I hope she writes him. I told him she would.

Well—as for the war, I don't guess I have to tell you about it. It's still going strong. We got some kind of a report from Honia, that the 1st Cav. ain't nothing but a bunch of killing dogs and if the 1st Cav. wasn't here they would win the war. They also said that the 1st Cav. would kill anything that gets in their way. It is also known that our ARA ships and go-go are the worst feared helicopters over here.

Well I am going to go for now. Tell everyone I said hi. I am always thinking of everyone and I will return home in Aug. Write often.

Love always, Larry Here's 10c.

* * *

4. "Things I Don't Want to Talk About"

Killing Dog. A title you wouldn't wish for your teenage son. I'm sure Mama skipped reading us those words. The news reports had a way of saying things that upset Mama, and some of Larry's words didn't help, either. She stayed up late at night more often, took more pills than usual, and went in and out of the hospital for what I was told were "female issues." I knew better than to question.

Daddy got sick, too. His ulcers got worse, and his knees hurt all the time. He stayed around the house during the day, so the best part was he was home to make me fruit salad, and my favorite egg salad in angel-shaped sandwiches on Wonder Bread. I never heard him complain, not once, but I could see his pain in his crooked walk. The biggest wish he had was to ditch the doctor's orders, trash the wooden cane and go fishing.

Life had never been better for me. I had Daddy's undivided time and soaked up the attention I craved from him. After many months with no pennies inside Larry's letters, those ten cents would be cherished above all others. My bubble was firmly intact, and my brother was winning the war. Larry had promised pennies and promised to come home soon and promised to keep his promises. And so, I was satisfied that all would be well. I was wrong, of course, and I got no further coins from my brother. Everything changed for him in the fall of 1967.

5

"War Is Hell, but the Girls Are Nice"

28-Oct-67
Saturday
An-Khe V.N.

Dear Mom and Dad,

Hi, hope everything's fine at home. I am still doing OK have been working alot but that's normal. Haven't heard from you in a few days. Hope nothing has happened. My ship is still down and I have no idea when it will be up again. Right now I am waiting on a rotor head. At least I have a chance to get it cleaned up some.

The next time you are in a hardware store, I would like for you to get me a few cans of wax. The paste kind, not the liquid. You just can't find wax over here any place. I got Tracy a jacket but it might be a little big. I didn't get one with all that stuff wrote on the back of it. If it don't fit, maybe you can cut it down or something. I haven't much to say because I haven't done anything but work. And nothing has happened around here lately. Well, I am going to be going again. Tell all the kids and Dad I said hi. Write when you can.

Love always,
Larry

P.S. Will send some pictures next time I hope. Rich said hi and he still loves Joanna.

* * *

28-Oct-67
Saturday

Dear Dad,

Well, here I am getting around to answering your letter. Sort of late but better late than never. So how is the greatest old man in the world doing? Your knee should be better by now or at least I hope it is. I am still doing O.K. Could be better but you know how things are.

It sounds like you really got it made. You just lay around the house and get $80 for it. I wish I could do it. I get $55 extra a month for flying. But every time I go up I am risking my life.

5. "War Is Hell, but the Girls Are Nice"

I was looking at the new Dodge Charger R/T. It looks pretty good this year. I can get one over here for $3,800 with everything. But by the time I come home the '69's will be out. I will just wait and see what they look like.

Well Dad, I am going to be going for now. I was really happy to get your letter and I hope to hear from you again. So, take care and be careful with your knee.

Your Son,
Larry (Smitty, Jr.)

P.S. War is hell, but the girls over here sure are nice

* * *

Daddy was home on disability leave after being thrown off the top of his truck when the truck tank exploded and knocked him off. He looked older to me at the age of 32 and limped around the house bored, ready to get out and do some fishing. His blurred vision drove him mad. The pain in Daddy's knee started after the accident, and the pain in his hip and the rest of his leg followed. He never recovered from the accident and would never work again, except in my Uncle Garner's grape vineyard in the Sandhills of North Carolina. That's where, in a few years, he would teach me to drive a tractor, hook a catfish and shoot a .22 rifle, before that tumor in his brain grew too large for cobalt treatments to help.

* * *

(A partially typed letter)

30 oct 67
MONDAY NIGHT
AN * KHE V.N.

Dear Mom and Dad,

Hi, Hope every thing is fine at home. I am still doing O.K. Right now I am on guard duty. I am pulling a 12 hour shift. Every hour I have to walk around the place. It ain't bad but I don't get much sleep. My typing ain't to good eighter as you can tell.

So Joanna got her driving papers. Now all she has to do is learn to drive. Is she going to get a car of her own? I got a letter form you today and was glad as always to hear from you. Glad to hear every thing is OK and that dad is getting around better. By the way how is your back ?

Nothing has changed around here. I am still working like hell and my helicopter is down. I think I had better finish this in writting. My typing just ain't what it used to be. The type writter don't work too good anyway.

Part Two

So you got another cat. I bet they are really a pain. Have you still got Smitty? By the way did you ever find my pet again?

Just think only 272 more day and I will be on my way home again. Boy, I can't waite untill then. I have been thinking hard about extending for six more months, but I am going to wait until I get real short before I make up my mind.

Well, that's about all for now. I got to go walk around for a few minutes. Tell every one I said hi and hope they are fine. I haven't mailed Tracy's jacket yet, but I will as soon as I can. Write soon.

Love alway's Larry

6-Nov-67
Day (?)

Dear Mom and Dad,

Hi, hope everything is fine at home. I am still doing fine. I got your letter with the check in it yesterday. Sorry to hear your back is acting up again.

I tried to give Rich the money, but he told me to send it back and to tell you to buy Tracy the biggest cake you can find. I let him read your letter and he won't take the money.

Rich is coming home with me in Aug. I think you will find him to be a very nice kid, He has really gone nuts over Joanna. He wrote her four times in two days, and I have never seen him write more than 1½ pages, but he wrote a 9 page letter to Joanna.

I don't want you to feel bad because you have spent the money. As long as there is money there, you are welcome to use it. Besides it ain't doing me much good while I am over here.

Mom, I don't want you to think I am telling you what to do, but I would like for you to do something for me. I got a letter from Peggy a while back and she sounds like she really wants to get along with you and Dad. She begged me to help her and tell her how to do it. So would you try to meet her on a halfway basis and try to be calm with her. I know and I think you know, when you get mad at Dad, you take it out on the kids. I would hate to see Peggy leave home like I did and end up like me. I know a lot of it is Peggy herself but if she does what I asked her to, maybe things will work out.

Them pictures are really cute. Which cat is which? I still haven't got any pictures to send home yet. My ship is up again, and I have mortar patrol tonight from 1–3. I also had guard all night last night. Well, I am going to go for now. Tell everyone I said hi and tell Tracy I said happy birthday. Take care and write often.

Love always, Larry

P.S. I got a letter from Bob & Gail Koonce

* * *

Bob and Gail Koonce became pieces of my puzzle. They were good friends of our parents and were in on the secret from the

5. "War Is Hell, but the Girls Are Nice"

beginning. Larry knew everything, too, but never treated me like an adopted sister. One day while Larry was away at war, Mama and Daddy sat me down in the kitchen to have a talk.

"We want you to know that we love you very much. You are special. You were chosen. We picked you because you are special." I didn't understand the title of being "special," but I knew Mama loved the concept, so I accepted it with ease. Daddy added, "When you have questions or want to know more, just come to us. We will always love you more than you know." I didn't care to know anything more and didn't ask questions. They picked me. That's all I knew for sure, so I made up stories. I envisioned an orphanage, and a room full of babies to pick from, including me, presumably the cutest one, that caught their eye and stole their hearts.

I worried about keeping the status of being special and not messing it up. I knew if I was not good, they could send me back. I knew how refunds worked.

I learned to leave the room when Aunts and Uncles came to visit, and more whispers started. I had my happy place, and I was happy in it. I left the drama to the rest of the house and escaped to my playroom, where Ken and Barbie had their own bullets to dodge and babies to choose.

* * *

10-Nov-67
Friday
Dear Mom and Dad,

Hi, hope everything is fine at home. Everything is OK here.

Everything is back to normal around here. I am flying night and day again. I have had one night off in five days. All the other nights I got to bed around 4:00. It is sort of rough, but my job is flying, and I love it.

Sorry to hear Grandmother can't make it this month, but she will be there later on. Glad to hear the weather is nice there. It is pretty bad here. We are in the middle of a Typhoon. I flew last night, and boy was it rough. I haven't flown yet today and I hope I don't have to.

Charlie (The V.C.) has a bad habit of hitting us when the weather is bad. They haven't hit yet but I got a feeling they will soon.

I want some paste wax like you use on a car. I want it for my ship. Get a good brand of wax, ok.

Will be looking for the boxes in the mail. You really got me stumped, I can't

Part Two

figure out what it is, I hope it is some under clothes and socks. I really need them bad.

This sure will be a lonesome Xmas without being home. With my luck I will have to fly Xmas day. Tell Tracy I won't be able to make it to her party, but my heart and thoughts will be there. Tell her I said Happy Birthday.

How come you keep writing PFC on your letters? It should be SP/4....

Here are a few pictures of me and my ship. I am going to start taking slides when I get some film and send them home. So, pick up a projector so you will be able to look at them. Rich has got some nice ones. He got some of the rockets in mid-air.

You know I haven't had any beer in quite awhile. Today I think I will get good and drunk. If my polits can fly drunk, so can I. Rich and I have already decided, the first day back in the states we ain't coming home. We are going to hit every bar we can find.

I would like for you to do me a favor ok. I would like for you to go price a Dodge Charger R/T "68" for me. With a 426 (425 H.P.) Hemi, dual 4 BBL with a 4 speed trans also with everything else on it. Black leather inside.

I want to see how much it would cost in the states and also see how much down and if you would be able to work out some sort of easy payments for a guy in the army (ME). O.K. I am going to try and get one. I really like them this year. Here is a picture of one. What do you think of it?

Well, I will be closing for now. Tell everyone I said hi and hope they are fine. Write often.

Love always, Larry

P.S. Here is a poem Rich made up. He is real good at making them.

* * *

Mama went back to work driving the high school bus and spent afternoons out of the house. The onset of processed food that flooded grocery store shelves became our norm. We lived on canned and frozen foods for the sake of time and convenience. It still beat my brother's Army rations, I'm certain, but the mere thought of Hamburger Helper still makes me queasy.

Sometimes I heard my parents' heated discussions about the car Larry left partially disassembled in the garage. It needed repairs they could not afford. It was newer than their own vehicle, yet not as reliable, so they needed to sell it. They didn't want to use Larry's car or rely on any of the money he sent home for his future. Mama preferred driving her own car when she wasn't driving the school bus, so Joanna learned to drive it and used it on occasion, mostly to the Kendall Park Roller Rink where she worked and where Peggy and I spent

5. "War Is Hell, but the Girls Are Nice"

Friday nights skating circles in short dresses, with our personalized skates, colorful laces and matching cases full of stickers that told the story of the times. Groovy. Peace. Make love, not war.

My parents tried to make sense of the challenges Larry faced. They asked him questions in their letters to get a better understanding of his living conditions. We all knew the truth would be inside each word he wrote, and nobody could take that away from us or tell us anything different. Larry reported the war even better than the TV did. His words were as good as gospel.

We knew the weather played a big part in his problems but may have never realized how big. While Larry flew night missions during the Pacific typhoon season within 6 days in early November of 1967, 40 tropical depressions formed and 35 of them became tropical storms. What Larry didn't know was that the real storms were still ahead. His happiest memories of the war were behind him.

6

I HEAR YOU

Life support feels much more like death support after a while. With every visit, you feel the weight of the decision. In your search for answers, you receive more questions. The physicians stay hopeful but offer no choices or advice. Be patient, they tell you. Nothing new to report. The nurses seem to know more yet remain diligent in their duty and stay quiet on his actual chances.

You take his left hand in both of yours, wanting him to feel your plea. "Please come back to us, please keep fighting to get back," you repeat at every trip. If he would do it for anyone, he would do it for you. He is also a fighter by nature, which offers hope that he won't stop fighting for himself.

What you need is a reaction. Anything. The energy shifts between your palms like a breeze full of goosebumps, startling you, and you drop his hand. Did he just, did he just move his hand? The attending nurse says it's probably a physiological response. You haven't seen any of those in months. *God, give me a sign.*

"Larry, I need you to give me a sign. I know you're still here, and you can hear me." He stares at you without moving. And then, a more certain response buckles your knees.

A single tear falls, as a slow blink releases the long awaited sign. The perfectly tragic answer rolls down his cheek, a tear so well-formed it is strong enough to reach the pillow but for the ventilator tube blocking the path. Studying the wet streak, you watch it puddle at the corner of his lips. The salty drop absorbs into his frail skin and enters back into his traumatized body.

You know what this means. You gotta get him out of here.

Part Three

7

"Charlie Don't Play Games"

> We should declare war on North Vietnam....
> We could pave the whole country
> and put parking strips on it,
> and still be home by Christmas.
> —Ronald Reagan, 1965

Larry's war was just getting warmed up. After summer passed and he survived those first 90 days in Vietnam, the Army moved Larry's ARA gunship unit into action. They added forces and relocated north as the United States implemented the largest offensive move in the war. In October 1967, General Westmoreland ordered more uniformed personnel and 3,400 helicopters to join the troops in Vietnam, spearheading the buildup of troops to more than 500,000 Americans. An additional 3,400 helicopters were deployed, creating an even more powerful aviation fleet for fighting the airmobile war. A plan that presumably would put an end to the years of conflict in South Asia and declare victory over communism. On November 17, President Johnson told Americans that "We are inflicting greater losses that we're taking. We are making progress" and there was "light at the end of the tunnel."

Larry moved closer to the Ho Chi Minh trail, where highly designed, massive underground structures gave the enemy distinct advantages. The trails and tunnels served as enemy supply routes, hospitals, and living quarters for the expanded enemy forces. Larry fought intense pitched battles with the well-structured North Vietnamese Army but also faced Viet Cong guerrilla forces that didn't have an organized military organization or rules of engagement. Small units of Viet Cong scattered the countryside, setting booby

7. "Charlie Don't Play Games"

traps to ambush our troops with elaborate plans to capture them as prisoners of war.

These new enemies looked different. Viet Cong forces wore checkered scarves and multiple types of hats and berets, instead of military helmets, and baggy pajamas in place of uniforms. Many were rice farmers with no training, supplied with weapons and troops by the NVA, eager to play the game of war in a jungle they knew well. They hid from American soldiers, knowing that in a true battle, there would be no competition. Viet Cong Communists wanted to overthrow the South Vietnamese government, which started with capturing Americans and their allies and ended in intimidation, sabotage, torture, and murder.

Also, there were the fiercely loyal, successful NVA forces who had been fighting for Communism for decades (also referred to as PAVN, People's Army of Vietnam). They had spent the last three years adding to their number of highly trained troops and stockpiling massive arsenal and field supplies in anticipation of the epic battles they planned to win in the year ahead. Everybody underestimated the power of the North Vietnamese Army, as they had their own troubles in leadership and politics.

Our other enemy came from home. Washington, D.C., officials continued to claim that the war was being won by America. By November 1967, the number of American troops injured reached over 100,000 and casualties added up to 15,058. By sheer numbers of kill counts, our side prevailed, and the enemy lost many more human lives, but the war of attrition waged against America came at a higher price than anyone wanted to pay. Graphic, heart-wrenching images plastered on the news would invade even the coldest of hearts.

The U.S. military's plan to inflict more losses than the Communist forces could sustain would never result in victory because we failed to recognize the nationalist zeal of the North Vietnamese. Even with far less power, slower technology, and many less combat resources, our enemies could defeat us and were defeating us. The bad guys were winning Larry's war simply by their unity, their collective will, and their common goal: to fight brutally at any cost, and never stop.

* * *

Part Three

14-Nov-67

Dear Mom and Dad,

    I received your letter the other day and was glad as always to hear from you. Would have wrote before, but haven't even had time to think straight.
    I went out to "Two Bits" (Bong Son) on the night of the 12th. I slept there and at 4:00 in the morning we were told to pack up because we were moving out. So yesterday afternoon we came up to this place called Kontum. Only my ship and two others came up. We had no place to sleep and nothing to eat.
    We finally got some C rations to eat, and when it came time to go to sleep everyone was saying they were going to sleep in the back seat in the helicopter. Our CO was flying my ship with a WOI {lowest ranking Warrant Officers, also known as peter pilots}. And do you think I was going to let them sleep on the seat? They sleep <u>outside</u> and I slept on the seat. I got up this morning and they wouldn't even talk to me. It was real cold last night and the bugs here are real bad. I was warm all night and the bugs didn't bother me.
    An advanced party came late last night and today they set up a few tents. It is real dusty and dirty here and when a helicopter came in, you can't even see because of the dust.
    A few of us took off and went down to the river and took a bath. It really felt good sitting there in the water and swimming around. Me and a few guys have already took off and went to town. We were supposed to be getting some water.
    The only bad thing about this place is Charlie (V.C.) don't play games. They even mortar places in the daytime. Yesterday at Dak-To, 143 men got killed. That is where we will be staying most of the time. There was one ship going in for a landing and it got knocked down by a mortar round. It wasn't one of ours but one of my buddys have already got two 50 cal. round through the blades.
    I was never really too scared to fly on a mission before, but I am now. Remember when I said we would most likely be going north? Well, we are working our way slowly but surely up there. One thing I am glad I don't have to ride on any convoy. This is all NVA country up here.
    I saw a French graveyard on the way up here and it was real nice looking. It is on top of a mountain and also kept up very well. That was when the French were over here and lost a lot of men up there. There are also a lot of French people living around here in these towns.
    Glad to hear Dad is O.K. and working again. And about Siam, I hope you and Dad are very happy with him. It is alright with me that you got him, I wanted you to get anything that would make you happy. And as for Tracy getting a bike, get her the one she wants and all them little do-dads that go on it. Tell her she don't got to wish on chicken bones anymore, whatever she wants, tell me and it is as good as hers.
    <u>Chicken bones never worked for me.</u>
    SP/4 is one rank higher than P.F.C. I made it on Oct. 4th. By the time I leave here I will be a SP/5 which is the same as a buck sergeant, but I want to be an NCO.

7. "Charlie Don't Play Games"

Well, I am going to close for now. Tell everyone I said hi and hope they are fine. Write often.

Love always, Larry

* * *

The Kon Tum Province in the Central Highlands of Vietnam had a small village with paved roads, streetlights, and outside cafes that sold Miller beer. The local girls were pretty, yet the American boys knew they could easily turn into enemy soldiers at night, so in time, they learned to avoid them.

In the field, living was much worse, and Larry's trip to Kontum proved it to him; there was no infrastructure, simply a remote compound surrounded by chain-link fencing with barbed wire on top. As they cursed the Army and waited for supplies and further troops to arrive, they passed the time playing in the dirt and complaining about the authorities that got them into this mess.

Dirt was my specialty, and Mama's dislike of it didn't stop me from seeking it out. Daddy encouraged getting my hands and feet dirty, having grown up with a weekly bath and tobacco-stained bare feet. He taught me all about nature and the fire ants who ruled the earth far under the ground beneath my red Keds. Uncle Garner had plenty of sandy hills full of them on his grape farm, marking the entrances to complex underground worlds. I knew they worked together like a well-trained army and each ant played an important role and helped the others. We studied their patterns in and out of the hills and saw evidence that they worked day and night and never rested. Sounded like Larry's army, relentless and overworked, with non-stop action that contributed to the success of the entire colony, each ant devoted to the cause.

Fire ants also provided entertainment for bored soldiers. As the boys waited with little provisions, they invented a battle of their own to pass the time. They dug a large hole, filled it with fire ants extracted from their nest, and threw in two slinky scorpions to fight. Bets were placed, probably with beer and cigarettes at stake. The battle began and the boys gathered around to cheer for their winnings. The scorpions took the early rounds as expected. Then, little

Part Three

by little the fire ants consumed the scorpions by their sheer numbers and devoured all evidence that scorpions were ever there. The fight proved true to life. Larry and his aerial rocket buddies would continue to fight like an army of ants. However, in the end, they would suffer the longest like the scorpions.

As my fifth birthday approached, Larry faced his biggest battle yet in Dak To, and promised me anything I wanted. Besides the doo-dad basket and purple tassels for my bike, having him home was my only wish.

* * *

18-Nov-67
Saturday
Dear Mom and Dad,

Just a few words to say hi and let you know I am still fine.

Haven't any new news to tell you so far. Things up here are rough as hell and I really hate it. I am not getting any sleep hardly and I get to eat once and maybe twice a day if I am lucky. I carry a case of C rations in my ship, but I have been eating them so much I can't stand them any more.

Right now, I am sitting in my ship at an LZ called Polly. We always come up here and wait for a mission. I was never as scared before as I was last night. We were called out on a fire mission because Charlie (V.C.) was blowing up an LZ with rockets. We were flying along side of a mountain where we was and he cut loose with two rockets. They went right in front of my ship, and you can believe when I saw them coming, I was scared. They were also shooting automatic weapons, but I was lucky and didn't take any round in the ship.

Yesterday on a fire mission, while I was firing my M-60, the polits door came open and "I" put four rounds through it. The polit is a new guy, and he has already been in four mortar attacks. Boy—that is some way for a new guy to start out.

Don't feel bad if you don't hear from me too much now, because we are really kept busy up here and I don't ever have any time off.

Sunday 19th

Hi, well here I am again. I am at Kontum right now sitting in my ship. I am thinking about taking the day off and going into town. That is if I can find someone to sit in for me.

Monday 20th

Well maybe I will get to finish this today. I am in bed, sicker than a dog. Not only that my nerves are a little shot.

Yesterday I took three rounds through my ship. One was through the windshield, one through the rotor blade and one through the drive shaft cowling (sp?). No one got hurt but we were all scared. They even shot down a jet

7. "Charlie Don't Play Games"

that was dropping bombs on them. So you can see things are pretty rough up here. I also had that new polit flying with me when I took the rounds.

I won't be flying again until I get better. I told my section leader that I wasn't fit to fly, which I ain't right now. He told me to take it easy and when I felt better to let him know and if I felt worse to let him know and he would see to it that I got proper care. I ain't sure but I believe I have the flu or something like it.

I found a letter from you today, which came a few days ago. That shows how much I get to come around in the tent.

I will write Grandad just as soon as I can. I will most likely start flying again tomorrow.

Well I am going to go. I started a letter to Mary Anne a few days ago, so while I have the chance I had better finish it. Tell everyone I said hi and hope they are fine. Write soon.

Love always, Larry

* * *

He told us he was okay in every letter until he wasn't. Now, he thought he had the flu. Mama assumed he had a nervous condition. She knew because she had one before and still got headaches that put her in bed for days. Larry had more pressing matters at hand, and Mama reminded us that what he needed was some home-cooked food, a good night's sleep, and a ticket out of Vietnam for good.

We never got a letter like this before, with three parts written over three days. Larry hoped for "proper care" and we wondered what that might look like in the jungle. We all hoped it meant a ride home, but "proper" was another relative concept Daddy didn't trust, and he said they'd probably give Larry a couple of aspirin and a shot of whiskey. We were all still betting on my dwindling penny collection and hoping on that wing and a prayer that Daddy still mumbled about. None of us were good at gambling. Well, except Aunt Louise at Sunday afternoon bingo, if that counted.

* * *

21-Nov-67
Tuesday

Dear Mom and Dad,

Hi, I received a package with the shoe shine kit in it today. I really like it and think it is very nice. I haven't signed my boots in so long, they would fall apart if I put polish on them.

I think I will give my polit a shock tomorrow by having my boots shined and

Part Three

my hair combed. My hair is so long now it hangs down in my eyes. I was told to get it cut so I did. I had it trimmed around the edges.

You won't believe this, and I still don't. I got a letter from Bill Reaves today. He didn't have much to say but at the end of the letter he said, "we love you." What do you think about that? I hope I won't hurt you and most of all Dad, but I am going to write them.

I am feeling a little better today but I'm still sick. My ship is still down. They are patching up the bullet holes and trying to get a vibration out of it.

I am sending a newspaper clipping about the battle near Dak-To. That is the hill we helped take and also where I took the round through the windshield. Also, that is where a jet went down.

Will close for now. Hope everyone is fine and doing o.k. Write soon.

Love always, Larry

* * *

Bill Reaves raised Larry as his own son, until Daddy came around. Bill was Mama's first husband and the father of Peggy and Joanna. Daddy kind of took his place when he legally adopted Larry and agreed to raise all Mama's kids as his own. Like Larry's war, things were not always as they seemed. Like me, Larry had more than one Daddy. The whole truth would evade us all for decades.

Larry cut his sharpest combat teeth in the battle of Dak To. The battle began with initiatives by the enemy earlier in the year and became part of several ground fights known as "the border battles," a precursor of the offensive fighting being planned for the end of 1967 and early 1968.

Enemy units were determined to rid the Central Highlands of American forces and poured thousands of troops into the area to destroy Special Forces camps located at the end of the Ho Chi Minh Trail. The Army's 173rd Airborne Brigade ("Sky Soldiers") and 4th Infantry Division's 1st Brigade answered the NVA buildup and the presence of the PAVN 1st Division. The fighting on the hills near Dak To led to intense, close-quarters conflict and one of the hardest fought battles of the entire war to date.

Rough terrain, steep limestone ridges, thick bamboo, shrub brush, and tall trees offered limited visibility and extra challenges, both on the ground and in the air. Nonetheless, the sky was crowded with Marine, Air Force, and Army helicopters to assist the troops on the ground fighting heavy, face to face, for three weeks. Air Force

7. "Charlie Don't Play Games"

Skyraiders dropped napalm on the ground in support of the infantry, as gunships assaulted enemy forces in rocket runs back and forth.

Flamethrowers shot through the sky, visible to Larry and Rich from their ships. The military warfare known as liquid hellfire used by Marine forces lit up the entire mountain for a moment, designed to confront and destroy dug-out enemies posed to ambush Americans. Being above the war offered several benefits. From the balcony seats looking down on the theatrics the boys in the air were spared from hand-to-hand combat. It didn't change the intensity of what they witnessed or the importance of their participation. For a portion of the extensive 22-day battle, they watched mass brutality unfold beneath them and couldn't do much to help. They could not land their ships to provide much-needed rescue assistance because of the rugged conditions and extensive enemy fire. And, without GPS tracking or "smart bombs," the visibility challenge meant a higher chance that any given rocket could go wrong and find friendly forces.

On November 19, American troops executed an assault on Hill 875 that would mark the final days of the battle. This final push up the hill resulted in one of the worst incidents of "friendly fire" ever recorded. A Marine Corps A-4 Skyhawk fighter-bomber mistakenly dropped two 500-pound bombs near the American perimeter. One bomb killed 42 Americans and injured another 45 after it exploded in a fireball and hit a tree, under which officers and wounded soldiers hid for protection. Larry told us this kind of thing happened more than you realized.

Heavy fighting persisted the majority of November as the 173rd Airborne Brigade fought up and down the hill, and both sides of the conflict sustained heavy casualties. Bodies piled up among the debris of the land and piles of human carnage could be seen from the air. The 173rd fought violently in the ground battle, beside napalm fires, as NVA and Viet Cong forces shot at them from every direction. American forces suffered thousands of injuries and kept the Division doctors too busy to sleep.

The 173rd Airborne lost a fifth of their total strength in those vicious fights. Over 170 U.S. troops were killed in Dak To in November and 718 or more were estimated to be wounded in the fighting.

Part Three

Sadly, the number of body bags was the measurement of the success of the Search and Destroy mission. Americans could claim victory since 1,400 or more enemy forces were killed. Several thousand NVA forces fled and escaped the area, but returned as soon as our soldiers left the area. The commanding officer Major Woliver, often told his troops, "We just kill 'em, don't count 'em," so the true number of killed is unknown.

Rich and Larry stayed busy the entire month of November 1967. On one page inside Larry's letters, undated, in bright green ink Larry shared limited thoughts on the infamous conflict: *"The fight up at DAKTO was one hell of a fight and I pray to God I never see one like it again."*

* * *

28-Nov-67
Tuesday

Dear Mom and Dad,

Hi, just a few words to say hi and hope everyone is fine. I am doing O.K.

We are moving back to Bong Son today. Last night they woke us up at 1:00 because we were getting mortared. So, I went up in the air and we shot our rockets. One (mortar) round got a direct hit on a tank, and it caught on fire. Soon it started to explode. Some how the guys got out and we went down to pick up the wounded and took them to the hospital. There were four guys all together. One had a big hole in his leg, one had his arm tore up, one was burnt real bad and one had his face all messed up.

So today I found out all of us in the ship were going to get some kind of medal. And they think it will be the Silver Star. I will let you know as soon as I find out. Rich got a bronze or Silver Star for doing the same thing. There was a newspaper man here and he took our names and stuff. So, it might be in the paper.

So how was Thanksgiving? We had a real nice dinner. It was just like being home. I got drunk that night and stayed at some girl's house until 1:30 AM.

I get in real good with the cooks and I eat like a king. One of the cooks is from Jersey City, he goes home in 9 days. Hope Tracy had a nice birthday party, sure wish I was there.

I sent Granddad a Christmas card the other day. I got up also got a Xmas card from Maude and she sent me $10. The only thing wrong, it is American money, and I can't spend it.

Well, I better go for now so tell everyone I said hi and hope they're fine. Tell Dad when I get home to have plenty of beer on hand (Shafer). I have made up my mind and I <u>am</u> going to get that Dodge Charger R/T. The more I look at it, the better I like it. Well, write often.

Love Always, Larry (Tell Jo I will give Rich the card) (I am getting short)

* * *

7. "Charlie Don't Play Games"

A few days after the American flag flew on Hill 875, Larry earned his highest award, a Bronze Star Medal with a "V" for Valor. After a newspaper reporter interviewed him about the events of November 27, he told us some of the story but minimized his bravery and spared us his own wounds, or feelings, or fears. Those would have to wait. He had saved a few soldiers in the normal course of daily duty. The Army acknowledged the "exceptionally valorous action" he took to save several lives. The Army commendation reads:

> "For heroism, not involving participation in aerial flight, in connection with military operations against a hostile force in the Republic of Vietnam, specialist four Smith distinguished himself by exceptionally valorous action on 27 November 1967, while serving as a crew chief on an armed helicopter during a counter mortar attack near Kontum, Republic of Vietnam. After his aircraft had landed, specialist Smith exposed himself to the hostile fire as he crossed an area to administer first aid and evacuate the wounded soldiers. His actions contributed greatly to saving the lives of several injured comrades. His display of personal bravery and devotion to duty is in keeping with the highest traditions of the military service and reflects great credit upon himself, his unit, and the United States Army."—By direction of the President of the United States.

All the guys extracted from the explosion made it to the hospital and survived except for one. Sergeant Sam Tenorio of the Blue Max ARA unit B/2/20 perished. Sam had volunteered to take the crew chief's mission that day. Larry never mentioned him or spoke of any further details on that day.

Following three weeks in Dak To, Larry's entire ARA unit received recognition for five days of intense action. The 2/20 ARA Battalion was awarded the Valorous Unit Citation. The citation is non-specific in the description, stating, "the officers and men of the battalion displayed extraordinary valor in accomplishing all assigned tasks in the face of almost certain death." We did not get details on the actions leading to this award.

Despite the impact that the First Cavalry had on this war and the overall superior dominance of our technology and Armed Forces abilities, the enemy never slowed down. It remained a war of will and Americans didn't know the whole truth. A few weeks before the exchanges in Dak To, President Johnson assured the nation that "the enemy knows he has met his master in the field," and called the military efforts in Vietnam a "campaign of optimism." Mixed messages were the only messages anyone got.

The North Vietnamese Army, PAVN and Viet Cong moved endless troops into harm's way and stayed prepared to replace them like war supplies. Move them in, take them out, move more in. They didn't care how young they were, how trained they were, or how many lives they sacrificed, the enemy offered endless human lives as their ticket to keep fighting. North Vietnam prepared to lose everything and keep fresh blood on their hands.

The enemy acted ruthlessly to even their own people. They tried to get the civilian population in South Vietnam to turn against us, even though our soldiers were there to help them. They spared nobody. Mothers and children became martyrs, and they used extreme measures to groom them. We heard tales of grenades in diapers, bombs in women's breasts, and teen girls as young as 12 or 13 thrown into uniforms and handed weapons.

One month, Larry's team of crew chiefs went through six different barbers, and every time a new guy came in, the place got hit with incoming mortars. Planted Communist spies held straight razors to our men's necks while stalking for inside information. Ruthless enemies knew no boundaries.

As bad as the prior month of battles had been on him, the bloodiest "watershed year" of the Vietnam War faced my brother in the days ahead.

8

"Still Here Raising Hell"

30-Nov-67
Wednesday

Dear Mom and Dad,

Hi, hope this letter finds everyone fine. I am still doing O.K. so far. Well now I am at (Two Bits) Bong Song (same-same). I got out here yesterday. I guess I will be here for a while.

Yesterday I got just what Dad would like to have. I got a complete tool set with a tool box. I kept complaining because I didn't have any tools for my ship, so they got me a whole new set.

I haven't got any mail in quite a while, they sent all my mail to Kontum yesterday, right before I came out here.

Haven't really much to say right now. I have mortar patrol tonight from 9:15 to 12:30. I sleep anyway, so it don't make any difference if I fly it or not.

Well, I'm going to make this short this time. Tell everyone I said hi and hope you're fine. Write soon.

Love Always, Larry

P.S. If you would, take a few pictures of the Xmas tree, with everyone there.

* * *

2-Dec-67
Friday

Dear Mom and Dad,

Just a few words to say hi and let you know I am still fine. Hope everyone is doing fine.

I want to thank everyone for the Xmas presents I got. They were really nice. The only thing that I have seen that reminds me of Xmas is when I was flying out here, we were flying above and through some snow white clouds.

Glad to hear Tracy liked her party. I sure wish I had been there to see her. I got that box of books and everyone is reading them. You know, I never did mail Tracy's jacket yet. I will one of these days.

I want you to buy Maryanne something real nice for Xmas. Let Jo go with you and help pick something out. Get some kind of clothes or something. Then get it to Jo and let her give it to Shirley and she will give it to Maryanne. I got a big box of cookies and stuff from Maryanne yesterday.

Part Three

Well I'm going to close for now. Tell everyone I said hi and hope they are fine. Write soon.

Love Always, Larry

Did you get a check for $420 or something around there? That was all my back flight pay and stuff.

* * *

8-Dec-67
Friday

Dear Mom and Dad,

Hi, just a few words to say hi and let you know I am alright.

Things have been sort of bad around here lately. Four of our ships went up on a fire mission the other night and everyone took rounds. My ship took it through the blade. Rich's took it through the Chin bubble. It went through the polit's <u>foot</u> and through the instrument panel.

The polit that got shot is okay. He only had 32 days left over here. Now he is going home early. He was also a very good friend.

I have been having some trouble with my eyes lately. I get real bad headaches. I tried to get back to AN-KHE yesterday but I couldn't get on the plane. I will be going back to AN-KHE in a few days to have a PE inspection pulled on my ship, so I will go see the doctor then. I ain't got any glasses with me, so I will get some more made up.

I guess by the time you get this letter I will be 19. I sure feel like I am getting old.

I think this war is starting to get to me. Ever since Dak-to, I have been jumpy. Every time I hear 105 [105mm howitzer projectile guns] go off or something, I get jumpy. I think my nerves are starting to go.

Hope everyone is doing alright. Has your back been giving you anymore trouble? How about Dad's knee, is it okay?

Well hope everyone has a Merry Xmas. Mine won't be complete because I won't be home, but my heart will be there with everyone. Thank Jo for the wallet, and Peggy and Tracy for the Jade East and thank you for the lighter. That lighter was very nice.

Maryanne and I are still getting along fine. If things are still okay between us when I get home and I think they will be, we are going to get engaged. How do you and Dad feel about it? Don't forget when I get home, I will be almost 20 and I know what I am doing. I want to settle down and raise a nice family and Maryanne seems like the girl to settle down with. I have known her for at least three years now, we know each other pretty good. We have never done anything together that she or I will regret. If you know what I mean.

Sometimes I regret that I joined the Army, but sometimes I feel it was the best thing for me. If I want, the Army will send me to school for 6 months when I get out, to a helicopter school. I have been thinking about it, but I don't know yet. A job with Bell Helicopter means a very good future.

Well I'm going to close for now. Take care and write every chance you get.

Love Always, Larry

8. *"Still Here Raising Hell"*

* * *

While Mama welcomed the idea of Larry hanging up his rebel hat and settling down, she never approved of Maryanne. Any girl he brought home would be scrutinized, never good enough for marrying her son. Mama made sure to voice her opinion on the matter, so we all knew where she stood. Her aching back didn't help the somber mood in the house or her patience for her son's return home.

Things with Larry would never be settled; at the hands of a machine gun, my brother became a hardened man inside an active combat zone and grew calloused by the broken system he grew to hate, all before his 19th birthday. His nerves were shot. Larry Ray Smith, the man, would be harder to love after this war got through with him.

* * *

12-Dec-67
Tuesday

Dear Mom and Dad,

    Hi, hope everyone is fine. I am still doing alright.
    I am back in An Khe now. I have been here three days and just now getting a chance to write. Have been working on my helicopter. I guess I will be here for a while. The day before I came in, I took two more rounds in my ship. One through the floor, which scared the hell out of me and one through the tail boom. Now I am getting a new tail boom.
    I have just about decided to quit crewing. I have taken six rounds in my ship in less than a month. I also found out today that one of my buddies that I went to school with in Alabama and came over here with, was killed a few days ago. And another one was sent home because he got his back busted up when his ship got shot down.
    I don't want you to have a bad Xmas because I ain't there. Don't worry about the money you spent for Christmas. As long as everyone was happy, I don't care how much you spent.
    I want to answer your questions about my helicopter. We don't always pick up wounded, but if someone is wounded and they can't get any medivac ship, and we are there, we will pick them up. I have only did it once, and that was up at Kontum, when we got mortared. I am going to get a <u>Bronze Star with the V</u> for it. That is what Rich got for doing the same thing. The V is for Valor.
    Our ships are gun ships. You can see the rocket pods in some of the pictures I sent you.
    Don't worry about me while I am over here. I will be all right and I will return home safe. I should quit crewing, because I would be a lot safer on the ground, but I love flying too much.

Part Three

    Thank you very much for the check. I will drink a beer for everyone in the family and about six for myself. My first night back in An Khe, I drank quite a few beers. They cost $.80 downtown, so I will drink over at the club. I will get more that way.
    Well I guess I will be going for now. I have four letters from Maryanne and I have to answer while I have a chance. Tell everyone I said hi and hope they're fine. Write soon.
Love Always, Larry 231 days to go

* * *

We came together at Christmas like no other time of the year. Everyone stayed home, we all got along, and each of us girls bought or made gifts for one another. Cookies and milk were left for Santa, and he would always finish them and leave behind a trail of too many gifts. This year was no different. Except, Larry and his presents were missing.

They let me help decorate the lower branches. My sisters argued over the proper placement of the tinsel and Mama insisted it be spread evenly, even though it wouldn't be as fun as throwing the shiny strings on like we wanted to. Even on the tree, there had to be order.

Daddy got out the reel-to-reel camera with the three large spotlights on top and blinded us on Christmas morning as we opened our gifts in our pajamas and squinted at the camera with sleepy eyes. Daddy's purpose came to life behind those spotlights, like he missed his calling in Hollywood. We were his leading ladies. If he pointed the camera at Mama, she blocked her face and stuck her tongue out at him.

Santa didn't have a chimney to come down, so Daddy left a key hidden under the front doormat. When I noticed a Kent cigarette butt burned out on the edge of Barbie's bedroom floor, I knew that Santa was cool, and smoked the same brand as Daddy. So, I made Barbie do some cleaning up and apologized to Ken for Santa's mess. The brown stain served as a reminder that burns leave scars. They cannot be removed or swept under the rug like Mama liked.

* * *

8. "Still Here Raising Hell"

16-Dec-67
Saturday
Dear Mom and Dad,

Hi, hope everyone is fine. I am still doing fine. I got another cold. The weather here in An-Khe is cold as hell.

I started to call you last night, but I changed my mind. I would've only been able to talk for three minutes and the guys that did call home came out crying and all. Besides, it would've just made me that much more homesick.

I don't even feel like it is close to Xmas. We have Xmas trees up all over the place and they just don't seem to mean anything to me.

Mom, I don't want you to get upset or anything, but I think I am going to extend for six months. I need the money to buy that car, plus I will need some for when I get married. If I do extend, I'm not going to fly. I will be a TI or platoon sergeant. I wasn't going to tell you until I got home, but I'd rather tell you now and not wait up to the last minute.

If I didn't extend, I would have a year and a half left in the states and most likely I would get sent to Germany, and I don't want to go there.

My ship is still down. They got my tail boom, but haven't got it on yet. I am trying to get a new engine and transmission. Mine are falling apart and I am scared to fly and it like that. I know it is unsafe, but the maintenance sergeant said it is okay. He don't know a damn thing about a helicopter and all the crew chiefs know it. But there's nothing we can do about it, because sergeant has the major all snowed under.

If I don't have enough money saved to buy the car, which I know I won't, do you think you could trust me to get a loan from the bank to pay off what is left? I know I will be able to make the payments.

Also, I would appreciate it if you could send me some money. I got paid yesterday and I am already broke. I paid everyone the money I owed them. I need around $40 or $50 to keep me up tight until next payday. If you don't have it, don't worry about it, I will be able to get by somehow.

Boy, I really got a lot of people mad. I was just joking around and ordered a new '67 helicopter. I thought it was funny, but a Major and a Captain brought the order form back and boy were they mad. They still don't know I did it and I hope they don't find out. But what can they do to me—send me to Vietnam or draft me?

Did you ever hear anything about Billy?

Well, I had better be going for now. Tell everyone I said hi and hope they are fine. Write again soon.

Love Always, Larry

Did Dad find out about the car for me? Tell him to write me a few lines.

* * *

It was the night of his 19th birthday, and he wanted to give himself a gift. He thought about it for a minute, deciding exactly what he needed. "Hey Rich, what do you think about me ordering a new ship? I mean, it's the least the Army can do for me, right?"

"Well, yours is always down, so you do kinda need one. Why not?" Rich concurred.

That's all Larry needed to hear, a little justification for rebellion. He got his hands on the order form to trade in his '65 Huey for a newer model and filled out the paperwork to make it happen. He had no authority to sign it, but that wouldn't stop him from scribbling the Major's name. My brother was pushing back against his war. If they wouldn't give him replacement parts for his flying carcass of a helicopter, he would get himself a new ship. Had it not been for one digit missing from the model number, that Huey would have been delivered.

Larry in dress uniform, circa December 1966.

One stray digit, like a single bullet, made all the difference in this war of bandaged parts and people. So far, Larry was able to dodge the danger and manage to escape any form of punishment, much like he did back home before the war. Still, luck was on his side.

* * *

20-Dec-67
Wednesday
Dear Mom and Dad,
    Just a few words to say hi and let you know I am doing fine. This is going to

8. "Still Here Raising Hell"

Teenager Honored For Bravery In Battle

In a recently released Army photograph, Kendall Park resident Larry R. Smith receives an Air Medal in Quang Tri, Vietnam, in recognition of his "combat aerial support of ground operations in Vietnam." A helicopter crew chief, 19-year-old Larry is due to end his vacation home Monday to return to airborne duty for six months additional service in the war zone. During his original year in Vietnam, he volunteered to return after taking a vacation in South Brunswick. The son of Mr. and Mrs. Kenneth V. Smith, ███ ██████████, he attended South Brunswick High School prior to his enlisting in the Army.

Larry receives Air Medal in newspaper article.

be a very short letter because I got a lot more to write. You wouldn't believe how far behind I am on my letter writing.

I am still here at An Khe raising hell. They still haven't fixed my ship yet and every day I am raising hell about it, but it don't do any good. I just plain hate it here.

It is only four more days till Xmas and I still can't believe it is almost Xmas. But I guess it is better this way, I won't be so homesick and feel so bad. But I wish everyone at home a very Merry Xmas and happy new year. You can bet I will be drunk on my ass Xmas and New Year's. Don't forget to send me some pictures of the kids and you and dad around the tree.

Part Three

Hope everyone is fine getting along ok.

We had a show at the club last night and it was pretty good. Little Joe Cartwright's father and his girl were there. His girl is 19 and really cute. Little Joe wasn't there, but his father is really something. He came out with some good jokes.

Did Dad ever go find out about the car I want? I will have a new car waiting for me when I get home one way or the other.

Do you know what I would like? Well, I will tell you. I would like a picture of "<u>everyone</u>" in a group. I had a picture of you, dad and Tracy, but I lost it somewhere. I still have the big one of Tracy.

Have you heard anything about Bong Song or Two Bits? Or about A.R.A.? That polit that I told you that got shot, well he is doing fine. I sure was glad to hear that. He was a good friend.

Well, I am going to close for now. Tell everyone I said hi. Tell dad to grab a chair, pen, and paper and drop me a few lines. I would like to hear from him. Well, take care and write soon.

Love Always, Your Son, Larry 218 Days to Go

* * *

His first Christmas away from home weighed heavy on Mama, and we all missed Larry more than ever. Pies and cakes lined the kitchen counter and the turkey barely fit in the pan it was so huge. It was the one season where Mama encouraged music, and Bing Crosby serenaded the house early and often. Mama got her shopping done by the first week of the month yet continued to add to the presents under the tree. By Christmas, piles of wrapped presents dwarfed the little tree. She bought more than she needed to, but Daddy didn't complain. We worked hard on the gifts we each sent Larry, to make sure they were things he needed and would enjoy, and we sent them early so he would have them in time.

Larry made very few requests. Write him back, write often and write soon. Send pictures of the whole family. And most of all, get that car in the driveway before he got home. A new Dodge Charger would give him something to look forward to, one dream he fully intended to achieve, and one that would offer immediate freedom when he got home. He wanted a Hemi engine to own the fastest car on the market in his budget. Some demons had to be outrun.

* * *

8. "Still Here Raising Hell"

24-Dec-67
Xmas Eve

Dear Mom and Dad,

Well here I am the night before Xmas and I don't even feel like it is Xmas.

I came out to Two Bits today to be with the guys for Xmas. I am sitting here with Rich now. He is writing to Joanna.

I got Tracy's picture yesterday and it was very nice. I gave Rich the little one like you said. She sure looks like she has changed a little, but maybe it is because I haven't seen her in so long. Only seven more months to go and I will be home to see everyone.

These first five months have really gone by fast. I just hope the next seven go by fast.

Maryanne has already got my whole leave planned for me. If I do everything she wants, I won't be home very much.

My ship is still down. I am waiting for a part that we can't get. So I don't know how long it will be before it will get fixed. I am going back to An Khe Tuesday morning. I come out here every chance I get, I just can't stand An Khe.

I won't get to see the Bob Hope show. He said he wouldn't put on a show for the 1st Cav. unless we brought all our guys in from the field. We won't get to see the show.

Just about everyone around here is drunk, even the B.C. (Major). I would be, but I just don't feel like drinking tonight. I had about two beers and that is all.

This is the longest I have ever been away from home at one time. I can't really say I miss being away from home too much, because I am busy all the time and don't think about home. When I am just sitting around alone, I get really homesick.

I went over to the Red Cross center one night and one of the girls wanted me to help make Xmas things. I did for a while but I started thinking about how it used to be at home at Xmas, when I helped fix up the tree and all. I had to get up and leave, just so I could get my mind off of it.

I can say one thing, even though I am in a war, I have had a lot of fun over here. I don't ever think about the war, unless I am getting shot at. I have also become very heartless for most of the people over here. Some of them are good, but most of them will do anything to get your money or kill you. When I first got here and saw how the people live, I felt sorry for them and now I know how they really are.

I have got where I can kill a kid 14 or so and it won't even bother me. I can remember on one mission I saw a woman working in a rice paddy and we were shooting up the place all around her. I cut her down with my machine gun and I am not sorry to this day that I did it. I would do it again and I know before I leave I will. So, you can see just how heartless I have got.

I just hope and pray that my kids will never have to go through something like this. You know if they would let us fight this war the way we wanted to, it would be over in no time at all. We can't shoot anybody or any place unless we ask. Like when we were out at Dak-to, we found some V.C. hiding in bunkers and we couldn't shoot because we couldn't contact the A.O. (the guy we have to ask). We found out later they put a bomb strike in there.

At least I have one thing to remind me of one of the worst battles I have ever been in and that is the Bronze Star with the V. That is one battle I will never forget.

I really hope everyone enjoys Xmas and has a good time. I won't enjoy it, but I will have a good time. Well, I had better be going for now. Tell everyone I said hi and be good. Write when you can.

Love Always, Larry

* * *

Other than one mention of feeling old, there would be no further acknowledgment of his 19th birthdate; there was nothing to celebrate except for the prospect of making it home, with 231 days left and counting. In numerology, 19 represents new beginnings and fresh starts. In spiritual circles, Angel number 19 is symbolic of the Alpha and Omega, the beginning, and the end. For Larry, the number 19 combined all the elements that turned a young boy into a man and the number showed up in his letters often. The trip across the world took him exactly 19 hours and marked his first steps on foreign soil; he wrote home to tell us. Little Joe Cartwright's 19-year-old "really cute" daughter drew his attention from the stage; he wrote home to tell us. He loaded exactly 19 rockets in his minigun after it jammed up one day; he wrote home to tell us. The newspaper reported him missing for 19 hours; he wrote to correct the reporter's mistake and let us know it was much longer.

My brother didn't care about his 19th birthday. He had no idea that 19 would mark his rite of passage and that it would be the age he never stopped living over, and over.

9

I FEEL YOU

"Squeeze my hand, can you do that for me? Here's mine." You get nothing in return. You try again, the other hand. Try again, blink, squeeze, look this way or that. Not a single returned command. His look continues to tell a different story, he is in there and speaking to you with every stare. He doesn't turn away, there is nothing coy left about him. There is no doubt inside his confident stare; he is speaking volumes. He is deliberating, you feel him trying. Nothing is delivered, nothing is received.

All your life, he has spoken slightly above a whisper, and you hung on every word he allowed in your presence. Now, even a whisper would be welcome. Just a grunt, or a movement, anything. Doctors assure you the recovery will continue to be slow, and not to expect too much too soon. Too soon? It's already been a lifetime.

"Can you blink for me? Just blink, so I know you hear me." Nothing. You take his hand, his calloused and rough skin replaced by bloated, smooth skin. It's much too warm. The fever has spread to every limb. You recognize portions of the man, lying still on the table with little fight left in him.

The Intensive Care Unit Desk phone number at the hospital in North Brunswick, New Jersey, is etched in your mind, and you wish you could erase it. Today, Nurse Sharon confirms that he is still critical, there have been no changes and his vitals remain steady. When you press her for any forecasting, she repeats her advice to not give up hope.

You realize that Dr. Stewart is telling you partial truths these days, like the rest of the hospital people coming and going. Their answers are too brief. Internal Medicine doctors, infectious disease

Part Three

doctors, surgeons, pulmonologists, and social workers tell you so many things that you start to document them with sketchy shorthand. None of it makes sense, still. The notes pile up, right beside your mounting questions.

He's on a ventilator, but awake. His eyes are open, but he is unconscious. He appears to be in no pain. He no longer needs the Tenormin or Plavix for his heart, or the other medicines that had stopped cold turkey: Restoril for sleep, Diazepam for nerves, Prozac, Ativan, Lipitor and Amdur. His daily dosage of coping meds, to help him breathe, sleep and deal with life, were replaced in full by a comatose state. They can't explain to you a logical reason for never closing his chest from the operation. Once he stabilizes, they will close him up, they tell you. Infection filters poison through his veins, keeping his heart working overtime and slowing any possible healing process. It's a vicious cycle, and his body continues to fight like it did those Viet Cong guerrillas. Ruthless. Endless.

There's one place in the hospital to sneak a cigarette, in the parking deck. One night you run into the night shift nurse who has been there since he was admitted. You open the conversation about the weather being so different than your home in North Carolina, and you remember her sharing a story about her own brother on a prior visit. Something about losing touch with her entire toxic family, with no further explanation. She takes a long drag of her cigarette and looks apologetic. You think back to the first time you met by his bedside, where she encouraged you to keep trying.

"You two are close, huh? I can tell by the way you talk to him. My brother and I were once like that. It's nice to see how much you care. I know it's a long drive for you, and it's been a long wait. He can hear you, so keep talking." She moves to extinguish her half-finished Marlboro light and turns away, signaling her exit. You want to stop her. "I'm sorry, what was your name again?" You see her badge yet want to pronounce it properly and open the conversation further.

"Marylee. Mom and Dad couldn't agree on my name, so they combined their favorite parents and went with the combo. Mary and Lee." You smiled at the canned response she no doubt had long ago memorized. Which opens the door for your real question.

9. I FEEL YOU

"Marylee, I need to ask you something. Is it possible for me to look at his chart? I need to see what happened on that operating table." She hears your sincerity and meets your eyes. It takes her a minute to answer.

"I can't do that, but I can tell you something, off the record. It should explain a lot." She pauses again and comes closer. She lights another cigarette after tapping the package against her palm to pack the tobacco, looking to you for further trust. You nod your head in agreement, making a silent pact of secrecy. Waiting for her to speak, nervous sweat beads on your forehead and chills run down your spine. You wonder if you are ready for the truth. Or any portion of it.

With a heavy sigh, she continues in a lower voice, "I was working the day your brother came in for surgery, I remember it well. Early arrivals always get our best selves; we usually aren't showered with skepticism until the afternoon. Not many days include a warm hug and a happy face balloon around here like Pediatric," she smirks, and goes on.

"Your brother flirted with me, and even got a rise out of the head nurse, who is known to be all business." That sounded like Larry.

"We sensed his sarcasm, and he joked around with us, even in his weak state. He told us he was 'just plain tired of being tired and hoped like hell that this surgery would help.'" She mimicked his raspy, low volume voice and smiled as she did so.

She continued. "He had been too tired to even drink, he admitted, and asked if I could be beside him with a cold beer when he came out of surgery. We both laughed, and the head nurse rolled her eyes and stayed busy with prep work. I promised to do my best and then winked at him before he started his countdown from 100. The surgery went well, for a few hours. A triple by-pass can take several hours, and we had five replacements on your brother. We knew it would be a long operation, and every completed artery brought a sigh of relief and a little break for the whole surgical team. So, when the surgeons got to the fifth and final artery, we started to relax just when things took a turn. We heard alarms, watched his heartrate escalate and blood pressure skyrocket. We never saw it coming."

The look on her face scares you. "What happened?" you ask,

Part Three

prompting her to finish, but also afraid of her answer. She nods to herself, convinced you deserve the truth. She looks around and finishes with a gentle touch of your shoulder. "Your brother woke up in the middle of surgery. *His eyes opened.*"

Part Four

10

"I Get Pills"

> To know war is to know there's still
> madness in this world
> —Lyndon B. Johnson

Larry admitted to tearing up when he received his second letter from Daddy. I wonder if those were common tears or rare tears. I wonder if they started early in the days of Larry's war and dried up as his deployment progressed or if the opposite was true.

He got our presents in plenty of time for Christmas. Mama sent him the most practical gift—a windproof Zippo lighter, handy in monsoons and typhoons. Larry and his Zippo were in good company; more than half of all American men smoked, so the refillable lighters were common. The lighters were instrumental in "Zippo raids" in Vietnam, where the practice of setting fire to straw huts ("hootches") often resulted in entire villages going up in smoke. Larry's war became known as the "Zippo War" and his Christmas present became his latest weapon.

Soldiers engraved their names, years served, and rank on the fronts and backs. Some included warnings to their captors if they became prisoners of war. Popular examples included:

> WE THE UNWILLING,
> TRAINED BY THE UNSKILLED,
> TO DO THE IMPOSSIBLE
> FOR THE UNGRATEFUL
> 10 MIN TOO LATE
>
> THE ONLY THING I GET OUT OF KILLING A PERSON
> IS THE RECOIL OF MY RIFLE
>
> I DIDN'T COME TO VIET NAM TO DIE FOR MY COUNTRY
> I CAME TO MAKE THE OTHER S.O.B. DIE FOR HIS

10. "I Get Pills"

ALWAYS RIPPED OR ALWAYS STONED
I MADE IT A YEAR, I'M GOING HOME

Larry's Zippo would soon be lost in combat, along with his camera, slide film, and favorite helmet. We sent him a wallet to hold money he wasn't allowed to have, and a bottle of Jade East cologne designed to spark his "inner confidence" if the ads were right. The tiger on the label fit in nicely with his jungle friends, I must have rationalized. We meant well. Larry needed so much this holiday, but nothing that could be wrapped in a bow.

* * *

27-Dec-67
Wednesday
Dear Mom and Dad,

Well here I am once again. I received a letter from you today and was glad as always to hear from you. Hope everyone is fine. I am still doing ok. I have got to get a tooth pulled as soon as I get up enough guts to go have it done. I have been taking pills and everything for the pain and it won't go away. It is one of the big teeth in the back on the bottom.

I am still An Khe and I hope to get back to Bong Song in about two days.

Well Xmas is over this year and it don't even seem like it has come yet. Had a very nice Xmas dinner (turkey & ham). I went out to Bong Song to spend Xmas with the guys. This is one Xmas I will never forget.

I flew for three hours Xmas morning for one of the guys, then I slept most of the day. In the afternoon, we loaded up a truck with candy, toys and all sorts of stuff and took them to some village. It really made the kids real happy. Then when we came back someone cut loose with a CS gas bomb and of course you know I didn't have my gas mask. I just grabbed a towel and put it over my face. It helped some. Half the guys were drunk and it didn't bother them anyway.

I got a card and letter with $5 in it from Bill (in NC) the other day. I just thought I would tell you. Bell Helicopter is in Texas in San Antonio.

Well, I guess I will end for now. Tell everyone I said hi and hope they are fine. Write again as soon as you can. Well, take care and write soon.

Love Always, Larry

I am going to have that tooth pulled in the morning, I can't take the pain anymore.

* * *

The boys in A/2/20 had a memorable Christmas together in An Khe. Red and green lights draped inside their barracks and an ample supply of liquid spirits kept them in a more festive mood than normal. They sang holiday tunes late into the night under the stars, getting more off-key and louder as the clock approached midnight. A cease-fire was in place and offered a moment of relief from the sounds of war. Larry volunteered for another guy's Christmas morning mission, so we figured out that with the 12-hour time difference, he flew in the skies at the exact same time Santa and his reindeer headed out of the North Pole toward New Jersey.

Duffle bags full of cards arrived wishing Merry Christmas, or Happy Hannukah, and offering prayers for safe travels home. Soldiers were inundated with deliveries, goodies like chocolate chip cookies, peppermint sticks, and penny candy. The Army fed them well with hot homemade meals, not unlike the spreads they were missing back home.

Hanoi Hanna became the female protagonist of the airwaves, filling the radio with propaganda to remind the boys that some civilian boy back home was busy loving on their girlfriend and that this was probably their last Christmas, so they should enjoy it. They regarded her words, cursed her daily, yet still respected her. She spoke harsh truths and gave them an annoying female figure to complain about when they needed to vent. Troops may have craved her candid words, after being lied to by so many. The truth hurt, yet it may have prepared the homesick boys for a bleak future after the war.

Rip the band-aid off, Hanna. We can take it.

* * *

29-Dec-67
Friday
Dear Mom and Dad,

Hope everyone is fine. I am still doing ok. Just a few lines to say hi and let you know I got the wax today. Thank you very much for the wax and books.

I had that tooth pulled yesterday and my mouth sure is sore. One side is all swollen up and looks funny. I hated to have it pulled out but they couldn't fix it and it hurt too much to let it go.

Well I am back in Bong Song now. I got my ship back this morning and it flies like a dream. I am going to start waxing it tomorrow if it is nice.

Do you know what a flight jacket looks like or is? If you do and can find one at a sports shop or any other kind of store, I would like for you to get me one and send it to me. I can't get one over here anyplace.

10. "I Get Pills"

It sure feels funny without that tooth there. It was the next to the last one on the left bottom. It didn't hurt when he pulled it, but after the stuff wore off I almost cried, because it hurt so bad. I have been taking pill after pill.

Well I had better go for now. I got to unpack all my junk. Tell everyone I said hi and hope they are fine. Write often.

Love Always, Larry

* * *

The excitement of a new year started with the 1968 calendar with fluffy kittens on top, that Mama hung up beside the refrigerator. She taped newspaper clippings all around the stained wallpaper beneath it, where orange and brown tea kettles repeated themselves, and where little hands were not allowed to touch.

She marked off each day with a happy checkmark covering the date, a countdown, and one step closer to Larry's arrival. When I offered to check it one day, she snapped, "No. I need to."

For three weeks, we got no letters. We had grown accustomed to receiving a couple each week, so the absence of them spoke volumes in the quiet rooms of our house. I never heard so little noise from my sisters, and they pretended to be friends for Mama's sake, who was climbing the walls and "worrying her whole head grey," Daddy claimed. We avoided the topic of the mail yet waited for the metal clang of the mailbox to know Larry made good on his promise.

All us girls, and Mama too, worked on homemade cards and mailed them early so he would get them in time for Valentine's Day. Mine had an accordion fold to it, and on each flap, I drew a crooked heart that I colored with my Crayolas. With 64 new colors and a built-in sharpener, my world was full of convenience, and vibrant options. Far from my brother's life. His days were consumed with little convenience and uncomfortable black and white choices. Stay busy or get homesick. Eat crap or go hungry. Shoot or be shot. Follow orders or do the right thing. Live or die trying. For me, the biggest dilemma involved picking Violet Red or Carnation Pink for the middle of the hearts. And there was Indian Red. Jo and Peggy both said, "NO!" on the Indian Red option. Larry worked in the Cavalry, who worked for the Cowboys, who fought the Indians. Indians were the bad guys.

* * *

Part Four

23-Jan-68
30 miles South DMZ

Dear Mom and Dad,

    Hope everyone is fine. I am still doing ok. Sorry it's been so long since I last wrote, but we have moved again and between flying and getting settled down I haven't had the time.

    We are up by a place called Hue. The place we are at there ain't nothing but hundreds of graves all over. We call it LZ tombstone. At night the ships go to a place called LZ Jane. That is 10 miles from the DMZ. We have got our tents up and when we get a mission, we have to run a ¼ mile to our ships. They have been talking today about moving up north more tomorrow. I sure hope not.

    The towns around here are more built up then they are down south. Also, more French people too. Up here it is a lot different kind of war that it is in the south. We are fighting only NVA and they have 105s, rockets, and just about all the stuff we have.

    We are working with the marines. I have talked with a lot of them, and they were telling me what it is like up here. The only good thing about this place is, we got good fresh state side milk. As much as I hated An-Khe, I wish I was back there. But I doubt if I will ever see that place again.

    They have some Navy people in Hue, and you should see the place they live in. It is like a real big state side modern apt. house. Some people just have it made and it sure ain't me. I am living and sleeping in my ship.

    I didn't even know Rich sent Jo some perfume. I will find out what kind it was, and when and if I ever get to go to Da Nang, I will try and get you and Jane some. Rich must of got it in Hong Kong.

    Glad you liked the tape. It will be awhile now before I can send any more. Just send me the same kind of tape I sent you. My tape recorder has the big 7" reels, but I can get my buddy's little tape recorder.

    I am going to think it over about the car. So I will let you know later on.

    Butch is O.K. I got a letter from him a few days ago and he is still in N.C. He told me he will be coming over here soon.

    Try a sporting (big) store. It is a <u>blue</u> flight jacket. They have the summer and winter kind, get the summer kind. No, there ain't any way I can get out of staying here that extra 6 months.

    Well I had better go for now. Tell everyone I said hi.

Love Always, Larry

* * *

At night the ships went to LZ Jane, Larry told us. None of us knew that the landing zone was part of the "Miss America Ridge" named after Jane Jayroe, the same Miss America he wrote about in his first month in Vietnam. The commanding colonel of the infantry, Fred E. Karmons, signed a true copy on a hand-drawn map of the area, with

10. "I Get Pills"

magnetic north key reference and geographic coordinates, showing the location of the ridge and the named landing zones. The area is just south of the Demilitarized Zone.

By the end of January, we got a letter, and Larry apologized for the delay in writing. The whole house sighed in relief. Mama's checkmarks lightened up. The same week, his audio recording arrived by mail. It was like having Christmas all over again, a gift for all of us. We listened to it twice together and stopped it a few times to hear all his words. He recorded it straight from the war, while he sat in the dark, and called us all by name. Mama was so proud of that little tape. We hardly recognized his voice; it had changed so much. He didn't say anything about my pennies, but I knew he would bring some home soon.

The recorder stayed on the Living Room hutch near Daddy's record collection, another area off limits to me. Mama could hear her son's sweet voice with a flick of a button and listened often. His deep monotone and relaxed sound reassured her that he was safe, for now. Helicopters circled over his head and interrupted his message more than once. Mama got close to hear in some parts, bending her ear to the speaker. Those Hueys never rested and beckoned him back to the unfriendly skies even as he took fourteen minutes to report home, unscripted, flex a few muscles, and spill his conscience.

* * *

AUDIO TAPE RECORDING, JANUARY 1968:

Mom, Dad, Tracy, Jo, Peggy, I don't know really how to start this thing off, so I'll start it off by just saying hi. I ain't too sure about this tape recorder, it ain't mine. Mine doesn't have these little wheels here, so if it don't turn out too good maybe the next one will.

That noise you heard at first was one of our helicopters just come in for landing, it just came off some kind of mission, I don't know what kind it was, I didn't go on it.

I hope everyone is fine and had a real nice Christmas and New Years. Mine was about as good as you expect it to be, but *uh* … that's the way things go over here.

I got your letter yesterday, Mom with pictures in it, and the check, and I'd like to thank you very much for the check, I really needed it. And the pictures were very nice … sure wish I could have been home for that Christmas.

I guess everybody at home is pretty mad at me now, because the day

Part Four

before I got your letter I went ahead and—*uh*—signed the extension papers. And I wish I had got your letter before that, I would have never signed them, knowing how bad you didn't want me to stay over here.

But *uh*—I mean—when I come back over here, I'm not gonna fly. I'm gonna stay on the ground, ya know, it's fairly safe anyway. At least I don't have to worry about getting shot up in the air and staying on the ground is pretty safe. Well, every once in awhile we get hit, but its not really—it's nothing bad.

I am back at ... right now. An Khe is the American name for it. My ship's down again, transmission was going, so they sent it in to get me a new one, so I told them about it last time I was in here to get a toe hole, and everything and they said it was safe to fly, so when I found out they were gonna put another one in it I come back here, I raised a little hell with the Maintenance, but still don't do any good. Maintenance we got back here is not too good, they don't care if they kill you or not ... all they worry about is just making sure they have enough ships flyable to fly the missions we get. They don't care what kind of shape they're in, just as long as they can fly.

Hey, I found out today where we're going, we're heading up north about 40 miles below the DMZ, and boy I sure don't want to go up there. I don't know what the name of the place is, its somewhere close to Chu Lai.

I guess you can tell by my voice I got quite a cold, I've been sick since— well, right before Christmas and I keep putting it off, going to the doctor, I get pills but that's about all. I got that tooth pulled and it didn't help too much. I got another tooth that's bothering me now, I gotta see what I can do about getting that one fixed. I hate to get it pulled because I don't want too many of them pulled. And I was going to go see the doctor this morning, but I got two machine guns, bunch of other stuff missing outta my ship and I gotta dig that up, cause I'll never be able to pay for all that. I think I found out where it is, I just gotta go pick it up now. I'm gonna go pick it up tomorrow morning and come back and go see the doc and maybe he can put me to bed for a few days, get rid of this cold because I keep walking around, running around in the rain and flying and everything, and it will never get better.

I didn't actually extend just for the money for the car. I know that you'd give me the loan if I really needed it. But I–I—really don't know why I extended, *uh* you know me I'm crazy and I do stupid things once in a while, and I just did another stupid thing. The first thing I did was join the Army. Quit school, leave home, few other stupid things I did. But, *uh*, at least this next six months I'll have some money saved up anyway, when I do get married, I'll have some money to fall back on and least I'll have money for the car, anyway. But I do want to get the car, I'd like to have it sitting there waiting on me when I get home. I should be home in early August, depending on when I take my leave.

I'll be home for 30 days and have to come back over here for six more months. *Hmmmph*, I guess you know I'm gonna miss Christmas, I'll be over here next Christmas too. And I can get out of it by extending six more months and I can take my leave in December and be home for Christmas, but that depends on how things are, if I decided to extend again and I know you don't want me to, so I probably won't. But I would like to be home for Christmas, so I'm sorry right now that I did extend after reading your letter.

10. "I Get Pills"

Don't feel too bad, all my other buddies they extended too. There's about 12 of them, we all extended so, you know, don't feel too bad about it. I know MaryAnne's not gonna be too happy about the idea but *um*, maybe I'll talk to her or something, I don't know.

I'm afraid when we move north this time, it's gonna be just like it was up in Dak To. I wasn't actually at Dak To, I was about 20 minute flight from Dak To, but we did all our fightin' up around there and I hope I never got to be in another fight like that again.

I've been thinking about that getting that car and come to the conclusion that I'm just gonna go ahead and get it through the states, I'm not gonna try to get it over here. It'll cost me about, well the cheapest, 38 and probably run me 39 with all the stuff I want. Yeah, there's too much red tape, papers and all this stuff you gotta sign and it's gotta be paid in cash before I get the car so, *uh*, I'd like, you know, for you to kinda do a little research for me, if you would please, and *uh*, see about the car, I mean the car itself, see how much it would cost and everything and *uh*, you know when June comes around, how much money I can save up with the bank and maybe put a down payment on it, work something out through the bank where I could pay some each month cause I know I'll be able to make the payments and *uh*, I would really like to have that car waiting on me when I come home, so I'd have a car and at least—Kenneth, I know, I know Dad would drive it around. He gets a kick out of driving fast cars anyway, he's still got a little bit of teenager left in him, I believe. You know, we're like father like son, and you know me I like to race and everything else, and *uh*, I know he would drive it around a little bit, maybe teach Jo how to drive it or something. Cause, it wouldn't cost too much more to get it in the states, and *uh*, well there wouldn't be that much paperwork, I don't think, well I don't know too much about it but at least I know there wouldn't be as much paperwork as there would be going through getting it here. So if you would please, I'd like for you or Dad one to check into it for me and kinda let me know what's—what it would be like so I'd have some idea of what's gonna happen.

That wax you sent me was really some good wax. I was waxing my ship a little bit today, and it really shines it up nice. That paint job wasn't too good, but it still puts a pretty good shine on it, so when I finished the whole ship, it looked pretty good.

Well, this side of the tape is just about ready to run out. I think, I don't know.

I'm sitting out in one of our Conex's, out here in the dark, 'cause I sat in the hooch, well everybody you know they come running through, and you know how guys in the Army are, they say things and stuff.... I didn't want to get on the tape, so I come out here by myself, out here in the dark.

So, *uh*, I want to see, put my lighter on here to see how much tape I got left. I'm gonna turn it over right now.

* * *

Well, here I am again, had trouble trying to get these reels switched around here in the dark, but I finally managed to get it done.

Part Four

That picture of Tracy on her bicycle is really cute, how come you didn't send me no picture of you and Dad and the whole family together. I'd really like to have one, you know, standing together. You know, I haven't had one, I got one of you and Dad and Tracy, but I lost it so you know I'd like to have one of the whole family together if you can send me one.

Yeah, I thought the people over in the states, the poor people really had it bad, but when I come over here and saw how these people lived ... the kids and everything at first, I felt sorry for them, because they live in houses made of mud, sticks, kids don't wear no clothes, til they get to a certain age, things like that. But after you've been here for awhile, you keep learning how these people work and everything, and after a while you don't even have no pity on them, people will rob you blind, they'd do anything to get your money. They don't care how bad it hurts you. After you stay here for a few months, you'd just a soon cut 'em as look at 'em 'cause thats the way people are over here—they're rotten, be sweet to you and nice, turn your back and they'll take what they can get off of you.

All I can say is I'll be glad when this war is over, and they can send all the guys back to the states where they belong. And not have to go back over here again.

Like I said before, the way they fight this war over here, and they keep going and going ... and going, a lot more years to come.

I still have that coat I bought for Tracy. I never sent it home yet, I just, I think I left it out in the field in Two Bits, I packed up my bags, jus—it should be in here tomorrow and I think I have time, I'm gonna go ahead and mail it home while I'm back here in An Khe, get it out of here. I just hope it fits her. I'm not too sure of the size, but I do hope it fits her and I will—I'm gonna get everybody something, I don't actually know what to get, a jacket or something but you know the clothes people wear over here, you wouldn't wear back in the world. So, I'll get some kind of doohickey or something. As for Dad, there ain't nothing over here that I know I could get him. I'll dig around, and find him something, but I know he wouldn't wear any of these clothes that these people wear. He wouldn't even be caught with them in the house. I'll try to find something.

Seems kind of funny to be taping a letter home. I don't know, seems kind of funny to me, you know sending something like this home, you can sit and hear yourself talking. It will be nice, you know, send me a tape back I can hear everybody talking and everything. Yeah, God, I don't know how I'd feel though to hear a tape like that, hear you talk and hear the kids and Dad talk on it, and it just, you know, seems kind of funny in a way. But I will look forward to getting a tape from you so I can hear everybody. I won't be able to see em, but at least I'll be able to hear what everybody says and everything.

Tracy—I don't know, she looks like she's grown a little bit to me. I know Peggy has, in that picture you sent me of her and Jo standing next to each other in that dress, Peggy looks like she's just a little bit taller than Joanne now.

Me, I'm still short. I don't know if I'm gaining or losing weight. Go out to the field, like get real good meals, we get real potatoes. They cook real good

10. "I Get Pills"

meals out there. Come back here to base camp and the food back here is not even worth eating, I'd rather eat C-rations.

Those strange noises you hear in the background is helicopters flying all around, they come and go all night long out here.

Dad might be able to outshoot me with a rifle, but I can outshoot him with a machine gun. I've had plenty of practice since I've been here. I'd like to bring the machine gun home for hunting, that would be pretty good, couldn't miss then.

I don't know if you've been reading anything in the paper about these M16's they got over here, but people say they jam and everything. In my opinion, if you get a good one, which I ain't got, they're pretty good rifles. They hit something; they tear it up pretty good. Mine, I'd shoot one round and it'll jam. I have to take something and knock it out of the barrel, send it in to get it fixed, they said it was alright and they give it back to me, so I don't even fire that thing anyway, I got the 38 pistol—I fired it about once. So once in a while, I'll fire it out the door of the helicopter, but usually I fire the machine gun. It's a lot more fun.

You read about these—our own guys killing their own guys. Well, I was up, well on a mission one day out in Bong Son, up by the ocean, South China Sea, and got these Chinooks CH-47 called 'Guns a Go Go' with 14 rockets, they got 250 Caliper machine guns on 'em, a bunch of 60's, and *uh*, I watched 'em roll in hot. Well they rolled in and they shot up, I think there was 15 wounded and 3 dead the last time I heard, and that was about two weeks ago, so it's been so long I don't remember. But that really happens over here. I've seen it more than once. To me it's a shame that they do something like that.

Like on Christmas night, a pilot who's a pretty good friend of mine, he's not in my platoon, he's 2/8 platoon I'm in 2/7. They were out flying mortar patrol, and they fired these H&I's, well it was to harass Charlie if he's out there any place, and *uh*, somebody has given them the wrong place to shoot, he fires and he—well, it wounded 3 and killed one, and that was on Christmas night. And I betcha, you can imagine how he felt, and a lot of other people felt. All it takes is one mistake, and a lot of people can get hurt like that.

That pilot that got shot that night when all four of our ships got shot up well, he's doing ok now, he's over in Japan and his foot's healing up pretty good, and they say he'll be able to walk again and they're gonna send him back to the states. He was supposed to go home in January, anyway. I was glad to hear he's doing pretty good. Only officer I know if you screwed him he'd throw rocks at you. That's how good a guy he was, he didn't care for the Army, he didn't even care about being an officer.

There's not too much tape left, at least I don't think so, last time I looked. And, I'd just like to tell everybody I said hi and I really miss everybody and I miss being away from home, but that's the way things are.

In a way I'm sorry I'm over here. But in a way I'm glad, somebody gotta come over, and it just as well be me. I'm in the Army. That's the way things go.

I'm gonna go ahead and say goodbye now before the tape runs out. So, tell everybody I said hi and take care. Tell Tracy I said, be good. Tell Jo and

Part Four

Peggy to do good in school, so goodbye and I'll send you another tape soon, and send me one back, okay?

Bye.

* * *

While I colored paper hearts for my brother, he poured his heart out in a tape recording and faced the largest military campaign of the war, the Tet Offensive. He left the comfort of the base in An Khe and relocated closer to enemy territory in Quang Tri once they were alerted to the advance of a major buildup by enemy forces. The Tet Offensive may have targeted the cities of Hue and Saigon, but within 24 hours the enemy descended upon our military forces all over South Vietnam. A coordinated series of attacks hit all major military outposts and over 100 cities. The elaborate surprise attack against our forces represented a turning point in the war.

Cavalry never retreats. They keep fighting, and while they may be weary warriors, they stay aggressive and go where the war needs them. My brother embraced this mantra. He relocated again, knocking on the enemy's front door where the North Vietnamese Army had stockpiled ammunition for a year and set up hundreds of ambush sites and traps in preparation for the Tet Offensive. Larry faced the most aggressive fighting in his deployment, at the height of the 13-year conflict, at the front lines of enemy territory.

Enter the Chinese year of the monkey. A circus, for sure.

11

"Have I Really Gone Crazy All the Way?"

Battles inside the city of Hue raged for weeks, yet Larry divulged few details about his participation. He didn't tell us that the North Vietnamese took over the city and arrested civil servants, religious leaders, teachers, and anyone connected with American forces or the South Vietnamese regime. He didn't mention that his enemies arrested and executed thousands of innocent lives and dumped their bodies in massive grave sites, or that piles of human carnage scattered the grounds beneath the very flag he planned to replace. The battle left 80 percent of the structures in the capital city destroyed or damaged, over 3,000 Vietnamese civilians massacred and 100,000 innocent people left homeless.

The First Cavalry Division, under the leadership of Lieutenant General John J. Tolson, marched in the skies to the enemy-controlled city of Hue, and joined the U.S. Marine efforts to recapture the imperial capital. The details of these military strategies took up little space in Larry's letters but would fill the history books and volumes of military documentation.

General "Jack" Tolson had taken command of the First Cavalry in April that year and would stay in position until July 14, 1969. He was a widely admired leader who helped develop the concept of Army aviation, and then implemented it in the Fort Rucker training facility where Larry tried his best to join the ranks of Warrant Officers / Pilots. Lt. Gen. Tolson, after serving as a World War II Paratrooper in the 503rd Airborne, recognized the need for air mobility to improve speed, efficiency, and safety. He helped carve out a piece of the skies used exclusively by the Air Force in the past, both

Part Four

tactically and strategically, which created the first Airmobile War in Army history.

The North Vietnamese and Viet Cong dominated for three days in early February. Enemy troops followed orders to "crack the sky, and shake the earth," and unleashed firepower for mass destruction. They peppered streets with bullets, from inside every hiding place they could find. They didn't care about the agreement that had prevailed over the history of the country, or the 7-day ceasefire that both North and South Vietnam agreed to observe three months earlier in observation of the New Year Tet holiday. They coordinated their planned launch of 84,000 troops and timed the attacks purposely on 36 capitals, 64 district towns, and most of the American military bases in South Vietnam.

Ten days prior to the Tet Offensive attacks, the Seige of Khe Sanh kicked off the most violent season of the Vietnam War. In a remote outpost near the Ho Chi Minh Trail in the province of Quang Tri, Communist forces (PAVN) outnumbered a unit of U.S. Marines by a factor of three to one, with an estimated 20,000 to 40,000 Communist troops moved into the area to threaten the air base at Khe Sanh. Larry wrote about working with the Marines, unleashing volumes of ammunition into enemy territory. He killed masses of human beings and wrote home to tell us just how many, and how. The Tet Offensive kicked off on January 31, 1968, and marked the worst battles of the war. It took Larry a week to mail the February 1 letter, where his heavy words filled the pages with his fears, masked by bravado and statistics.

Hidden in the creases of one short sentence, his heart breaks to go home.

* * *

1-Feb-68 (MAILED FEB 7)
Thursday
11 miles Below DMZ

Dear Mom and Dad,

    Hi, just a few words to say hi and let you know I am still doing O.K.
    We have already moved again and now halfway settled down. All I got to say for this place is I want to come home. This place just ain't for me.

11. *"Have I Really Gone Crazy All the Way?"*

We have killed over 100 NVA in two days, most of them with our machine guns. We got all kinds of weapons from the NVA. I landed and got a mortar tube and two packs and one mortar round. I couldn't pull the other mortar tube out of the hole. It was in cement. We also got 4 AK-47's, a sub machine gun and a 50-cal. machine gun. That 50 cal. was aiming at my head, with two dead NVA behind it. We really kicked some ass in the last two days, but it also cost us too. We had one ship shot down and the crew chief got hit in the side. We only have two ships flyable now and every ship but mine has taken hits. One of our ships today took about 10 hits on one mission. My ship is down now because of the tail rotor servo.

Last night my polit hit another ship while we were parking. It only tore the tip off of my blade, but really messed up the tail rotor on the other ship. I flew today but my servo went this afternoon. Yesterday afternoon we really had some fun. There were NVA all over the place and it was just like a lucky shot. They were running across open fields, and we just walked our M60 rounds up behind them and up their back. We killed 30 in that one place. We even had to call an emergency re-supply because we shot so many rockets and M60 ammo.

Three days ago, my polit saw two people hiding in the grass and I shot both of them. I put over 1,000 rounds in them and we got a gun the guy was carrying. The other person was a girl about 15. She didn't have any gun, but she was in uniform.

The place I am at is right outside Quang Tri. It is up above Hue. The NVA have taken over Hue and got their flag flying. But they won't stay there long. You wouldn't believe how many villages we have leveled around here. The NVA are in every one of the villages and when we get through, there won't be a village left.

Hope everyone is doing fine. We don't get mail up here but once every 10 to 15 days. If you see MaryAnne, try to explain to her I can't write as much. I am busy all the time up here.

Well I had better go for now. Tell everyone I said hi and hope they are fine. Write often.

Love Always, Larry

* * *

Larry's M-60 machine gun could fire hundreds of rounds per minute, with a caliber of 7.62 mm and a range of 1200 yards. With a longer range than the M-16 rifle, they called the M-60 the "pig." With his "pig," Larry killed face to face, proud of his kill counts. This byproduct of combat would haunt him soon enough.

After the Tet offensive attacks, everything about the American military strategy shifted. Perception of the war back home remained volatile and became even more swayed, thanks to continuous, lopsided press coverage of shock attack type journalism, continuous bomb dropping coverage, and graphic carnage in the streets captured on film with no edits.

Walter Cronkite, the most trusted man on television, took off his objective journalism cap and polarized public opposition when he spoke these words on television: "To say that we are closer to victory today is to believe, in the face of the evidence, the optimists who have been wrong in the past … to say that we are mired in a bloody stalemate seems the only realistic, yet unsatisfactory conclusion." On February 27 he delivered the news that the war was "unwinnable."

Not that Cronkite didn't speak the truth. Yet, his defeating stance provided a false victory for the Communist Army and deflated our troops in the field. His words fueled the fire inside our enemies and made things even worse for our soldiers fighting the front lines. They convinced many Americans that there was no way we could win this war, and the public became further disgusted by our participation in Vietnam and trusted the U.S. government even less.

The enemy's sneak attack may have been large and violent; however, overall, it was a dismal failure and a crushing defeat for the Communists. America's superior military forces overpowered the NVA at almost every point they met. Both sides suffered great numbers of casualties, from a blood bath of battles up and down the countryside. We killed them at a ratio of nearly 10:1 when comparing Viet Cong deaths with U.S. troops, a clear victory on paper. However, both sides claimed victory. By the middle of the day on the first of February, enemy forces retreated from the Quang Tri area. That was just the beginning of the attacks that included a series of intense combat sessions lasting several months. The enemy maintained control over Hue for almost a full month.

The war made less sense than ever as Larry continued to stay mobile, in the air, fighting with all the energy he could manage. He had no clue what a Tet Offensive was, yet he believed he was kicking ass, taking names, and winning the war for his country. He fought for patriotic, political, or dutiful purposes that he would never understand. He just fought.

* * *

11. "Have I Really Gone Crazy All the Way?"

8-Feb-68
Wednesday
Dear Dad,

Got your letter today and it sure made me feel great to hear from you again. Right now I am sitting in mine and Rich's tent over the top of a hot plate trying to keep warm. Don't let anyone tell you it don't get cold over here. I have froze my ass off for the last four days. It's even colder flying and trying to fire a machine gun.

I used to hate An-Khe but I would give anything to be back there now. This place is nothing but one hellhole. For some reason "Charlie" don't like this place. Every other night he hits us with rockets and mortars. I never did like a foxhole, but I busted my ass quite a few times getting into one since I have been up here. Every time I hear somebody yell, "incoming," I hit the first one I find.

I am still doing O.K. and crazy as ever. I just wish I was home and all I had to worry about was getting hit by a car. Up here we can't even go to town, so that leaves us without any girls. We can't even get any beer up here. We are in a bad way.

Mom told me what you said about renting a car. I have really gave it a lot of thinking. It is a good idea, but I am stuck on the '68 Charger R/T. I would really like for you to check on one for me. I want all heavy-duty stuff underneath, 426, 4 speed, bucket seats in front, all the teenage stuff. I am still a kid at heart. I would like to have it waiting for me when I get home if it is possible. I am not even going to take an R&R so I can pay for the car.

Hope everything is still O.K. at home. I hope we do go to N.C. beach for vacation. I would really like that. I think of that a lot, just lying on the beach with the whole family drinking a cold beer and not even thinking about the _____up army. I think I would kill the first slant-eyed person I see back in the world. All I want to see is round eyes.

I found out one funny thing about me the other day. I never went to church much, but we blew up a church and for some odd reason I couldn't shoot one round from my machine in it. I can shoot a kid, which I have done, but I just can't for some funny reason, bring myself to shoot into a church. I saw a guy with his leg torn off and he was watching me, it was just like he was begging me not to shoot, but I tore his head half apart and I got a kick out of it, but I can't shoot into a church even when I know there are gooks in it.

What do you think is wrong with me? Have I really gone crazy all the way?

Well, the lights just went out and the batteries in my flashlight are weak, so I will close for now. Take care and write again soon. I really feel good when I get a letter from you.

Your Son, Larry

* * *

In the thick of the action, he was eating and sleeping combat, and questioning his sanity. Things had become volatile in his daily

Part Four

life. We changed, too. We still ate breakfast and most lunches at the kitchen table next to the sliding glass door that led to the backyard, and that is where we began to pray more. We prayed in my school, too. Mama started to pray for all the soldiers in the war, not just our own. She prayed for the end of the war, and for peace among all nations. She prayed for the children in my school who lost their daddies and the kids in Vietnam who lost their villages. She prayed for the politicians and the news people who went to war, too. Once, Mama prayed for Larry's enemies and their children. All we could do was pray, so Mama asked it all for us, in the name of Jesus. It was one of the few times I remember Daddy bowing his head, so I knew I needed to keep my eyes shut tight. And there could be no fidgeting.

I cherished Jesus from a young age; I didn't learn from my parents so much as from Presbyterian Sunday school stories that repeated themselves. Combined with Catholic rituals that I witnessed from the top of the bleachers when the McGuigan family took me to Mass, the hierarchy of it all got tangled in my mind. Jesus had parents who didn't pick him, and his story had a sad ending. He was the leader of the children and took care of all of us, even orphans. I knew I would eventually outgrow him. However, Mother Mary, God, and the Saints were reserved for adults. Heaven was reserved for Catholics unless you were baptized in a pool of water. Jesus did the right thing all the time and loved all the people, yet God did some bad things when he got mad. God didn't have to tell you about his reasons for punishment, and he always got the last word. And like Mama, God didn't scare me, but I sure knew better than to doubt his power.

* * *

9-Feb-68
Thursday
Dear Mom and Dad,

Hi, just a few words to let you know I am still doing okay. Haven't heard from you in a while. Got a letter from Dad and Joanna yesterday. Hope everyone is fine.

Haven't really much to say. Haven't done too much lately. I have the whole day off today. We lost another ship. They were sling loading it out and about

11. *"Have I Really Gone Crazy All the Way?"*

1000 feet up the sling broke and down it went. Also another one of the guys got shot. He got it in the gut. He is going to be okay, and he is on his way back to the world now. Things have cooled down a lot, but we still get mortared every other night. Tonight we should get a full nights sleep. They hit us at 12:30 last night. I hate getting out of a nice warm bed, and jumping into a cold, muddy foxhole.

I am going to try and send another tape this week if I get a chance. Dad also told me about renting a car, and I have thought about it on a lot since he told me, but I am stuck on the '68 charger R/T. One of these days, when I get up enough nerve, I will have a picture taken of me with all that war stuff on we are supposed to wear. I never wear it, I carry around my M-16 half of the time and that is all.

I started carrying grenades and a M79 in my ship now. They are great for bunker and gooks hiding in a trench or foxhole. The M79 shoots rounds that are the same as grenade. It works pretty good.

Well I am going to go for now. Tell everyone I said hi. Tell Tracy I will see her this summer and that I love her. Write soon.

Love Always, Larry

* * *

I quizzed Daddy about the foxes that might hurt Larry in those holes if he kept jumping in their holes. He told me I asked too many questions, and that sometimes answers caused more questions, so they would have to wait for Larry to tell us more. My brother had a lot of explaining to do when he got home. I hoped he wouldn't forget about the foxes by that time.

* * *

14-Feb-68
Thursday Night
Dear Mom and Dad,

Hi, just a few words to say hi and hope everyone is fine at home. Things are still fine with me.

I got a newspaper clipping with my pictures in it and they said something about the medals I got. <u>I was just wondering if you had anything to do with that</u>. Or if the army put it in there. I haven't heard from you in quite a while. I got the cards, they were very nice.

I hate to bother you again about money, but I would like to have around $40 or $50. I will be going to Da Nang next month some time. I want to get a camera and some film so I can start taking pictures. I am going to take a lot of slides too.

You won't believe this, but it is true. We were on a mission and the lead ship saw two gooks and shot them. They landed and one of the guys was

Part Four

an officer. They took his pistol and left. There was a green bag about 10 feet from him and my buddy was scared to get it, so they left it. Later on, we found out the guy was a pay officer and the bag had $3000 in it. If my buddy had of got it we would've had $3000 to split between 8 of us. A couple of infantry guys got it, and they got $88 a piece. One thing for sure, that officer won't ever pay anyone again. The whole side of his face was gone. I sure wish I had a color picture of him.

I was also talking to an infantry Sargent that went out to where we killed them 30 gooks and he said they were so badly tore up that their clothes were holding them together. So, you can see what kind of damage them M60s can do. And they were killed with the M-60.

Well, I had better go for now. So, tell everyone I said hi and hope they are okay. 168 day. Write soon.

Love Always, Larry

* * *

Mama would skip all parts about gooks and missing faces, like other details that she didn't want to know, much less speak out loud. Sometimes when she read Larry's letters, she shut her eyes. Sometimes, she swallowed hard, placed the letter on the table upside down, and left the room. Daddy would finish reading and more than once, Mama went to bed without dinner. Late at night, I heard Mama crying for the first time. Soft sobs reached my room down the hall from my parents' room, waking me up to wonder more about what she knew that I didn't know. I pretended to hear nothing and went back to sleep.

* * *

18-Feb-68

Dear Mom and Dad,

Well, here I am again. Hope everyone is fine. I am still o.k. It is still raining and cold over here. I spent the last four hours out in the rain working on my ship and I am soaked now.

I got the two tapes and the letter yesterday. I really enjoyed them. It made me feel so much better to hear everyone. I have got the songs playing right now. I'm going to try and start a tape today, if I don't get too drunk. I got me a fifth of silver fox 80 proof yesterday. Everyone sounds the same. I ain't going to write much in this letter because I won't be able to think of anything to say on the tape.

I just ate a big lunch of two hot dogs and a spoonful of beans and two pieces of bread. And I couldn't eat the beans, they tasted like dirt. And a cup of real stateside milk.

11. "Have I Really Gone Crazy All the Way?"

What size boots does dad wear? I can get him a pair of jungle boots for the summer and a pair of stateside boots for the winter if he wants them. All of us crew chief and polits can't wear jungle boots anymore. They say they burn fast and will hurt our feet in case we have to jump.

Well I will close for now. Tell everyone I said hi. Send me some more tapes since you can. Write soon.

Love alway's, Larry 162 days + 180

* * *

Larry mentioned his tape player, hot dogs, and jungle boots, and complained about working in the rain for four hours; all the mundane facts he could muster. He confessed to buying 80 proof liquor but never explained why he needed the hard stuff.

The Vietnam War peaked two weeks into the Tet offensive. In the entire war's death count, the highest number of U.S. soldiers perished between February 11, 1968, and February 17, 1968. A total of 543 Americans were killed in action in those seven days. During that deadly week, the war silenced my brother. His truth would be untold. He never spoke about the events of February 16, 1968, on that day or ever again.

I grew old and gray by the time I learned the truth about Larry's war. It explained a lot.

12

I GOT YOU

They never tell you the whole truth. The anesthesiologist fails to mention mid-surgery protocol issues or problems with medication tolerance. The surgeons reported a successful outcome and told you all to go home to get some rest. It was only once his heart stopped in recovery and they revived him, that they called his wife with the update on his condition.

You keep asking why. Larry's DNR clearly states his wishes, so you don't understand how it remains in question. Your frustration is clouded by the medical explanations and terminology they throw around. They test your patience, so you never stop asking questions. How long was he not breathing? How long was he not alive?

No clear answer follows the script they have fabricated, so no clear answer is what you get. Liability attorneys are abundant and wealthy for a reason, known to be thorough, and overprotective for a client as big as a hospital system. You don't want a lawsuit, though. Just some answers. How can he go so long without blinking? Can he cry? How does digestion still work when nothing else does? What does his brain activity show?

He wanted his broken heart fixed. He had grown tired of being tired and badly needed some energy. Without steady blood flow, the heart works overtime so everything else moves in slow motion, and he had suffered in that reduced speed for years. He hadn't had the energy to complain about it. Prescription meds had failed to do their job, and all they brought were side effects and a pile of unpaid medical bills. He reluctantly agreed to heart surgery with severe skepticism. Doctors were always his last resort. As with most people of authority, he trusted nothing they told him.

12. I GOT YOU

Lord, give him an open road and another ride on his Harley. Just one more ride, one more open road for him.

On the last day before the surgery, you had taken your pictures together beside the dining room table. The same table where you dyed Easter eggs and ate holiday meals for decades, memories long ago forgotten. The table served as a backdrop for all the special occasions over both of your lives and many family photographs.

You urged him to smile, to which he mumbled, "I'm too damned tired to smile."

You teased him for his short haircut—the first in a decade or more—and insisted on a picture with the whole family, and one with you alone. Without his defining ponytail, his ZZ Top–style beard, or any trace of facial hair this clean-cut persona looked ready for a new heart. Larry finally allowed himself to trust the surgeons to open him up and fix him. After the pictures, he followed you outside, fighting a bitter wind in the January air to complete his sad goodbye. With no coat, he didn't complain as usual ("damn Jersey winters") and appeared determined to say something before you left. He walked you to the end of the driveway, to the edge of your childhood memories, where tall cypress trees lined the property 20 feet high, casting shadows on the snow-covered sidewalk beneath, waiting to be shoveled.

Before you got in the car, you asked his thoughts on getting married, and after a joke about staying single and sane, he gave you his blessing by nodding toward your boyfriend and adding, "He seems like a nice guy. And I will walk you down the aisle when the time comes. Don't rush into anything." You promised you would set the wedding date once he got out of the hospital.

He apologized for being so tired, and you apologized for leaving so soon. He paused, as if he had more to say, yet he didn't continue. He looked down at his feet and swallowed hard. He knew. Somehow, he knew it would be his last goodbye.

Part Five

13

"Thought I was a Gonner"

> You will kill ten of us, we will kill one of you,
> but in the end, you will tire of it first
> —Ho Chi Minh

We waited for more audio tapes, but none came. Larry's mention of buying a bottle of liquor worried Mama more than ever. Beer was one thing, but liquor brought out the demons in everyone, Mama said. Daddy agreed. He had spent his childhood avoiding his own father on weekends, which is when his dear mother worshiped Jesus, but his giant father worshiped moonshine. My grandfather, the "gentle giant" they called him, turned into a Primitive Southern Baptist preacher on Saturday nights. When he returned from his date with the bottle, he woke up Grandma and all six kids to gather around his makeshift and familiar "hell, death and damnation" sermon.

Standing in the living room on top of a wooden stool, with nothing but his baggy underwear on his body and Grandma's leather bible in his shaking hands, he put the fear of God into all those kids. Sylvester Ham Smith stood tall over everyone, at 6'6" not including the stool. It was no wonder Daddy avoided church. Those liquor demons threatened him as a young boy, and nobody named Jesus came to unlock the door when Granddaddy passed out, after locking the whole family outside in the cold night. But since Jesus was all that I had knowledge of, I put my faith in Him to bring my brother home safe like we prayed, and that Daddy would come around by that time.

* * *

13. "Thought I was a Gonner"

Feb. 21–68

Dear Mom and Dad,

    Hi, hope everyone is fine. I am still doing O.K. Not really much to write about, just wanted to write a few lines and let you know that I'm still fine. Got a letter from you yesterday, with the newspaper clipping in it.

    Today I thought I was a gonner for sure. We were making our rocket run and I felt something hit me in the head, it knocked my head back against the wall behind me. I grabbed my head but didn't feel any blood and I was still living, so I took my helmet off and it was covered with mud. I still have a headache from it. We were sort of low when we made our run. My ship is covered with mud. I chewed my polit's ass to hell and back. In the morning he will be out there cleaning it, and I will be there watching. I really get a kick out of chewing out an officer and making <u>him</u> work.

    Two days ago I grabbed a hold of a red hot stove pipe. I thought it was a tent pole, I didn't look because I thought I was standing next to the tent pole. I took my hand out of the bandage last night, I couldn't stand to wear it. My hand is still a little sore. As for the weather it is still the same, cold, wet and rainy.

    We also had another guy shot. He was one of the best polits we had. He got it through the leg and it hit his chest protector and it splattered, and some of it went into his arm. He will be O.K.

    Well I will close for now. Tell everyone I said hi and tell Tracy to be good for me. Write soon and often.

Love Alway's, Larry

* * *

    His writing changed, with three weeks in between letters, then one day in between letters. He forgot dates and wrote them in a different format than the rest of the letters. Larry admitted to being scared, and he must have been mixed up good to grab a hot pipe.

    Mama and Daddy agreed that they were proud of Larry, but they fought about why. Daddy said this war was for rich Americans to get richer, and Larry had been caught in the crossfire. Mama said that all this killing was at the price of our peace, not for peace. Jo and Peggy got in the conversation and spoke up about peace, too, and told us what their older friends were doing in Washington, D.C., fighting for peace and love. All I knew was, Larry deserved all the peace he could find in that ugly war, and we needed him to bottle it up and bring it home with him.

* * *

Part Five

Left to right: Dawson Crews, Orlando Sanchez, Dean Demain, Larry Smith hanging out on a rocket pod, a landing zone in Central Highlands of Vietnam, circa March 1968 (credit John Stewart).

6-March-68
Wednesday morning

Dear Mom and Dad,

    Hi, hope everyone is well and doing. I am still doing fine. I got your letter and another one with the check in it. Thanks for sending the money. I will be going to Da Nang in about two days, maybe tomorrow. I hope the beach is open, I will be down there all of the time if it is. The town itself is off limits, but the beach is about ¼ mile or less from where I will be.

    Have been listening to your tapes over and over. Can't wait until you send more. While I am in Da Nang I am going to pick up a lot of tapes so I can send a lot more. The weather got bad again, but started clearing up yesterday. I hope it clears up and stays clear. Haven't really much to say, cause I haven't really done too much. Haven't got the cookies or wax yet, but should get it soon. They have a lot of backed up mail in Calif. so it might take awhile.

    I am still planning on getting married and most likely it will be next summer

Left to right: Larry Smith, Dean Demain, Barry Brady (in John Stewart's arms), Dawson Crews, posing with a machine gun on sandbags in front of the crew chief tent, circa March 1968 (credit John Stewart).

Left to right: Ronnie Dunn, Dawson Crews, John Stewart at the crew chief tent, circa March 1968 (credit John Stewart).

Part Five

some time. You never did tell me what you and Dad thought about it. I don't think I would be making a mistake by getting married now.

Well that is about all for now. Take care and tell everyone I said hi. Write again soon and send more tapes <u>soon</u>.

Love Always, Larry

* * *

We each had our spots, just like every holiday meal gathered around the dining room table. We sat down to record an audiotape for Larry. Mama at the end by the hutch, Daddy by the front door, and us kids in the middle. Larry sat beside me when he was home, and when he left Peggy was quick to try and claim his seat. She didn't ask before pouncing into it, so Mama made her move back and we left his seat at the table empty from that point on—accompanied by a place setting at every meal. Mama had a direct line of sight to the front door, perhaps to will him through it with her dark stare, or to celebrate his surprise arrival.

We spoke into the small handheld microphone that was attached to the recorder on a short cord. We took turns as Mama stopped and started the tape. She prompted each of us with something she wanted Larry to know. "Ken, tell him what you found out about that car. Peggy, tell him about your math grades. Jo, remind him to send home a picture of Rich. Tracy, what about that tooth that fell out? Tell Larry about the tooth fairy visit."

She finished up with her own words for him to stay safe and come home soon, adding a final request. "Please change your enlistment status. The money is not worth it. You hear me? We need you home. Especially at Christmas."

* * *

7-March-68
Thursday morning
Dear Dad,

Well I got your letter yesterday and was glad as always to get it. Three letters in seven months, you're getting better. Hope you are still doing O.K. I am doing great. Hope Mom is better by now.

Well, ain't much happening around here. I have about had it with the people around here. They are really screwing over us crew chiefs. The operation officer and the new major we got is coming up with all kinds of new corny things.

13. "Thought I was a Gonner"

They are trying to tell us crew chiefs how to crew our ship and how to take care of them, and it ain't going over too good with us. I told them today if they didn't stay off my back, they could shove the ship with a full load of rocket. I never payed any attention to them, but today they started with the time on my ship. Every 25 hours we have to pull an inspection and every 100 hours we pull a real big inspection, which takes a few days. And every 300 hours we go to a unit that pulls the whole ship apart for an inspection. Well, I am almost due for the 300 hour one and only have 2:45 minutes of flying time to go. It takes 1:15 to fly to Da Nang where I have to go, which only leaves me an hour of flying missions. They said this morning to fly the 2:45 here and then fly it to Da Nang. I know it don't sound bad to you, but they ain't supposed to fly it past the 2:45. They did it once before like that and the ship crashed. You probably don't fully understand but it is really very dangerous. I could explain it better talking to you but since I can't, I will just have to write it.

Ever since the new major came in, this whole Battalion has gone to hell. There have been days where people got so bad and I couldn't put up with them, I just came in the tent and hit the old bottle. When I got feeling right, I went back outside and dared anyone to say anything to me. What they are trying to do is make this place just like state side, they can't get it into their thick heads that this is a combat zone.

I guess it is wrong to kill people, but you got to remember it's him or you, I had much rather it be him. That day my two friends were killed, it made me want to even kill more. It's not like having a friend killed in a car wreck or just up and die, I don't know why but it is a lot different. You look at the bullet hole and where your friend was sitting, all you see is blood and parts of him. You would have had to been in my place to feel and understand it.

The weather has sure cleared up. It is so hot now I can't stand it, before it was so cold, I couldn't stand it. I would go out and clean my ship, but if they know so much about crewing a helicopter let them do it. Being a crew chief and having a helicopter of your own is something to proud of over here, but there ain't a crew chief in this Bty. that cares about his ship now. All we care about now, is if the ship goes up and we are in it, that it makes it back down. Well, any way ---

When I get to Da Nang I ain't going to do nothing but lay on the beach all day and spend the night at the club. The town is off limits so I guess I can forget about the girls. Besides I am getting married anyway.

Well, I guess I better be going for now. I have a lot more letters to write and since I am just sitting around, I might as well write letters. Take care and write again real soon.

Your Son, Smitty Jr.

* * *

We all claimed the nickname. "Smitty" was embroidered on Daddy's work shirt, and the same name we picked for the puppy we got from the pound. And Daddy called me that sometimes. We all

Part Five

had a unique attachment to the sentiment that represented Daddy's heritage, and now "Smitty, Junior" named himself after the man who raised him as his own. It may have been the only part of the letter that made Daddy happy to get it.

Daddy didn't read his letter to us. When he handed Mama the paper to add to the collection, he looked mad, something I had never seen. He spent the rest of the weekend in the garage and Mama said to leave him alone.

Larry looked forward to a beach trip on the coast. His plans sounded inviting, with no clue as to the action ahead of him. He was headed to the second-largest city in Vietnam next to Saigon, referred to as "Rocket City." Da Nang Air Base was a constant target by local Viet Cong "sappers" that raced through the compound throwing gas grenades and bomb satchels while the NVA mortared the area with long-range rockets. Nobody liked Rocket City or the muddy bunkers they had to jump into there.

Da Nang held large amounts of herbicides called Agent Orange for practical and tactical use in eliminating thick jungle coverage and crops. Dioxin and other harmful chemical ingredients in Agent Orange sprayed from above to decimate all living things it landed on. A single aircraft could hold enough to render 300 acres of forest useless, leaving behind nothing. Some targets died instantly, like animals and plants, and others suffered in silence for years with invisible wounds. A vacation in Da Nang could end with damaged body organs and tethered nerve endings. Agent Orange, a brand logo of the Vietnam jungle, became the silent killer of friendly fire.

* * *

25-March-68
Monday
Dear Mom and Dad,

   Hey, just a few words to let you know I am still doing fine. Hope everyone at home is the same. I am still here at Da Nang and having a great time. They say I might be leaving in 3 or 4 days, I hope not. I got the cookies, books, and wax. Thank you very much for them. I sent some of the cookies back up north for the rest of the guys. There's not really much to say because I ain't doing

13. "Thought I was a Gonner"

nothing but eating, sleeping and drinking. I only got 4½ months to go before I get home. I can't wait. I have only been home 28 or 29 days in 18½ months.

Did Dad ever find out anything about the car? If you can I would like for you to make a down payment on some insurance, and then when I leave to come back over here I will cancel it. That way I will be covered while I am home. If you can, try to save a few hundred dollars, so I will have something to have some fun on. If we go to N.C. we will need two cars and I will have to have money to get down there and back on.

Well, that's about it for now. Tell everyone I said hi and hope they are still fine. Write often.

Love always, Larry

* * *

Americans had grown further disenchanted with the war and their president. President Johnson and his disillusionment of optimistic reports of victory fell on hardened ears weary of our place in this war. On March 31, he announced that he would not be seeking reelection to the presidency. Many hoped that a new president like Robert Kennedy could end this war. In some views, the old Commander in Chief abandoned his duties. President Johnson left his post in the middle of the fire that he helped stoke, while the embers still burned, and the flames danced around my brother and his buddies.

* * *

31-Mar-68

Dear Mom and Dad,

Just a few words to say hi and hope everyone is fine.

As for me, I am still in Da Nang and doing fine. You will have to excuse my writing this morning because my hand ain't too steady. It is only 8:30 in the morning and I did some drinking yesterday. I went swimming yesterday for about an hour and the water was real nice. Right now I got a cup of homemade ice cream, which was made last night. I got to let it warm up because it is hard as a rock.

I don't know if I told you this or not, but I was thinking about something you said on your tape, about me being in the middle of all the fighting. I guess you were talking about the fight at Hue, well I wasn't there. I meant to tell you this before. I am way up north from Hue, so don't worry about me being there. I was there but moved out before the fighting started. The place I am at now is about 2 miles S.W. of Quang Tri.

A good friend of mine named Barry Brady came down two days ago to get his ship fixed. He lives in Hightstown, N.J. He has a brother over here in Da Nang. We went over to see him, and I can't believe the camp he is in. It is just

Part Five

like back in the states. They have a swimming pool, an indoor movie just like one in any town, street signs on all the streets and their bathroom is just like one in the states.

I got that check cashed at last and got a camera and a lot of film. I got mostly slides. So now when I come home, I will at least have some pictures to show you. Since I have been down here, I have put on some weight, mostly from all the beer I drink every night. I got a pair of ox blood boots from this guy in the Navy. I am the only guy in the Army with red boots. I wear them too, I got them on right now. People down here don't know if I am in the Navy or Army.

I saw a ring I am going to get before I come home. It costs around $200 but if I'm going to get married, they say you are supposed to be engaged first. I am going to borrow the money from the guys and pay them back each month out of the $40 I get. Don't say anything to MaryAnne about it. How is Doug and his wife making out, and what is Robert up to? Did Robert ever get everything straightened out about the money?

Well, I will close for now, hoping everyone is fine and doing O.K. Everyone take care and be good. Write soon and send more tapes. I got some tape down here and when I get back up north I will send one.

Love always, Larry

* * *

When the boys from the First Cavalry came into a town, all the locals knew it. The field units were not hard to recognize and were happy to get a slice of civilization. First Cav boys were the rowdy bunch, the unkempt crew that marveled at the sight of a street sign, or indoor bathrooms. Sometimes they flushed over and over to watch the water swirl and listen to the sound of simple comforts they didn't realize they missed so much.

My brother wore oxblood red boots to be funny. Keep people guessing. And maybe because his flight boots were deemed worthless, with thin layers of leather that he had worn out with help from monsoon-level waters on the ground and rocket cap burns in the air. He would soon wish he had his jungle boots back.

* * *

8-April-68
Monday
Dear Mom and Dad,

Hi, just a few words to let you know I am still fine and still down here in Da Nang, but by the time you get this letter I should be back up north.

13. "Thought I was a Gonner"

You will never guess who I got to see the other day. Billy Robbins, he is here in Da Nang, and he is an MP, how about that. I spent one day with him but haven't been able to get over to see him again. I got his address from a girl I know, and I started asking around and sure enough he is here. He's doing real good and looking about the same. He has lost a lot of weight, but I still wouldn't fight him. I am going to try and get a three day in-country R&R here and stay with him. I don't know if you remember Johnny Gallagher, Jo does, but he was killed September 14th over here.

That Steve guy sounds like a nice guy, but don't you think it is a little early for Jo to get married? They haven't known each other that long, and things just might not work out after they are married. If she wants to it is up to her. But you tell her I said when I come home in Aug. and we go on vacation, I want the "whole" family together, not just part of us. A year over here fighting a war is a hell of a long time and I want to at least have the whole family together for a while.

You didn't have to go and order all them under clothes for me. All them old ones lying around the house would've been good enough for me, but I thank you anyway. I haven't got them yet, but I will let you know as soon as I get them, and size 11 is just right.

I have gained a little weight since I've been here from all the beer I put away every night. I had to go get another tooth fixed, it was one of my front ones. He drilled a hole in it and said to let something or other drain out. It has been 2½ days now and the tooth is better. I am going back in the morning to get the hole filled.

Not much more to say except that I miss everyone and wish I was home. Tell everyone I said hi and hope they are fine. Write often and send more tapes.

Love always, Larry

* * *

Billy Robbins was the first black person I ever met, one of Larry's best friends. Billy came over at Christmas time in 1966 to visit Larry, and he wore his fancy uniform. Between his bright personality, formal dress clothes, and ability to easily touch our ceilings, he filled the room with his officialness, and as Larry's best friend, was the most important person in the world to me. I was honored when he ate dinner at my kitchenette table where he had to squeeze his large frame into a toddler-sized plastic chair and endure several pictures at Mama's insistence. His starched image softened the minute he and Larry started wrestling and let me join in. Mama got more pictures.

After looking for Billy for months in Vietnam, Larry finally found his friend and they spent a few days together. At that same

Part Five

time, the shocking assassination of the famous civil rights activist, Martin Luther King, Jr., took place in Memphis, Tennessee. On April 4, Mr. King died from a single bullet at the age of 39. His death came after the killings of John F. Kennedy and Malcolm X, and just months before Robert Kennedy was slain. All these deaths tied to conspiracy theories that involved local, state, and federal governments, the FBI, CIA, and the mafia. Violent riots erupted in major cities across America, racial conflict prevailed, and people flooded the streets in protest for multiple reasons. Nobody trusted anybody.

Like the war, the spring of 1968 was eventful in our home in Kendall Park. Joanna did not marry Steve; she broke up with him. She wouldn't tell me why, which made me question romance and marriage, asking questions that got ignored by my sisters. Easter came, complete with all my favorite traditions, coloring eggs with Daddy, chocolates delivered by the Easter Bunny, and a giant basket left overnight full of toys. Along with the basket I got a large box from Mama. When the box moved it scared us all, so Daddy helped me open it. I looked inside to find the real Easter bunny. My fuzzy friend, who I creatively named Peter Rabbit, was the first pet that was all mine to care for. I fed Peter and played with him day and night, made him a home inside the box with old blankets, and gave him a good life hopping around our yard munching on blades of grass. One morning after just a few weeks, Peter Rabbit wouldn't wake up. His eyes were open, but he couldn't move, and his body was hard and cold when I touched it. Mama didn't understand why I cried all day long and bought me a wind-up stuffed animal version to take Peter's place. She flipped that emotional suppression switch like a pro.

We gave Peter Rabbit a proper burial in the backyard. Mama decided we should not tell Larry about Peter, so we never spoke about my rabbit ever again, just like Joanna never spoke about Steve. There are things we don't need to speak out loud, even though they are a part of our heartache for valid reasons. That's what I learned in the spring of 1968. Lift rug, sweep feelings.

Then, my brother became famous. He escaped the bad guys with the help of some Jolly Green Giants who took him for a ride in a flying net. Details from my brother's search and rescue mission filtered

13. "Thought I was a Gonner"

Billy Robbins "wrestles" with 4-year-old Tracy, 12-26-66.

Billy Robbins with Tracy in her "Rite Hite" kitchenette, Christmas 1966 (12-26-66).

Part Five

through the house and consumed conversations in the neighborhood. Reporters called to talk to Mama and came out to the house with the biggest camera we had ever seen. With the help of my all-too-familiar diet of canned sweet peas, I invented my own version of Larry's rescue. A bright green man as large as the block, wearing a dress made of green leaves and a hat to match, saved my brother with a swinging net that swooped him up after he was stranded on a deserted island for days, all alone and surrounded by snakes and alligators. *The Jungle Book* once again served as my reference guide, and except for the green man and swirling alligators, I wasn't too far off.

My brother was brave, that I knew. And I knew he devoted his life to that flying ship, until it broke. What I didn't know is that a broken ship would hand deliver his biggest fear—being captured in the trap of a Viet Cong guerrilla. Happy Valley was the enemy's playground, and my brother landed with his Huey in the middle of their dirty sandbox.

14.

"Got Shot Down"

In the month of April 1968 several military operations kept the First Cavalry and others busy fighting the war near the border of North Vietnam. Operation Delaware committed the 1st Cavalry Division and the 101st Airborne Division, along with South Vietnamese forces, to several preplanned strikes in the A Shau Valley. The A Shau Valley held significant value to the U.S. Army as a strategic location that straddled the Ho Chi Minh trail. The massive raid near the Laotian border began on April 19 amid bad weather, and Communist forces shot down ten helicopters on the first day. On April 21, fighting in the area increased and American troops moved deeper into the A Shau Valley. Larry's ship would be among the statistics of at least 60 helicopters and one C-130 airplane that were shot down or damaged before the campaign ended in mid–May.

Close to A Shau Valley was Happy Valley, as the U.S. Marines named it, an area known to be Charlie's TAOR (Tactical Area of Responsibility). It served as a staging area for Viet Cong and North Vietnamese Army forces, where they launched large rocket attacks against Marine installations, especially aimed at Da Nang Air Base to the northeast. The valley was 20 miles south-southwest of Da Nang, not far from the DMZ. With a shallow basin, rugged terrain, and triple canopy trees, the Happy Valley promised extra challenges for a helicopter. Add monsoon weather, heavy fog, and hefty winds, along with a depleting source of fuel, and the stakes were higher than ever to survive in a helicopter inside Larry's war.

* * *

Part Five

Monday
22-Apr-68
Quang Tri

Dear Mom and Dad,

    Hi, how are you? I guess you must of thought I got lost or something.
    Want to hear a joke—well I better tell you now, because it might be in the paper and I don't want you to see it in the paper and get all shook up. Well here's the joke -----I got shot down Saturday afternoon, how about that? As a matter of fact, two of us went down together. Ain't that a big joke. Well that ain't the half of it.

* * *

With fuel, ammo, crew, and engine checks all in order, Larry took his position in the back left cargo area and buckled into the seat of the UH-1 helicopter. A belt of heavy ammunition draped across his chest to feed the machine gun. Leaving his seat belt loose allowed him to hang halfway out of the aircraft to shoot with more precision. It also helped to avoid shooting your own ship, as he had learned the hard way.

Larry called out, "Clear and untied," and the pilot responded, "Coming through," as he hit the starter. Larry could do these steps in his sleep, they have been performed hundreds of times before this day—slide the armor plating forward and close the ship's doors, put on a helmet and plug it in, and grab the M-60. Larry found comfort in the whine of the turbine engine. The heavy pattern of the main rotor's thud behind him, the heartbeat of the helicopter, "whop-whop-whop"—assured him that the gunship, his gunship, was ready and able to take flight. Like his ship, my brother aged with every flight but remained prepared to perform his best despite his exhaustion.

The day started like most, with uncertainty for the events ahead and plenty of prayers for survival. Ammo was loaded, and 48 rockets filled the space beneath the soldier's boots. The Blue Max Huey team included my brother and seven others from his Alpha Company, 2nd Battery, 20th Artillery. Larry thought the worst of his time in Vietnam was behind him and bragged about being "short," convinced he would avoid heavy pockets of attacks and be assigned light-duty missions going forward.

14. "Got Shot Down"

Larry's mission on this day included two gunship Huey helicopters, each with four soldiers. Pilot and co-pilot in front, crew chiefs and door gunners in back, the eight men from the A/2/20th with the call sign "Blue Max" took to the skies. Larry's ship was the lead ship, with Captain Mills as Aircraft commander and Lt. Hawks as pilot, and SP/4 Howell as door gunner. The wing ship was piloted by AC Chuck Germeck and Warrant Officer Raymond, and the back seat held Larry's friends Barry Brady and Rick Leroue.

Rick usually served as the door gunner for Rich Passer, but he volunteered to help Barry Brady on this day. His job as an ammo humper paled in comparison to the action of helping friends shoot the bad guys. He could thank Rich Passer for his new position. One day while Rich worked on his helicopter on the flight line, he noticed a small fellow working down in a hole, where ammunition was stored. The guy worked by himself, head down, in the ditch. His job involved opening ammunition boxes and putting rockets together.

Rich yelled down to him, "Hey you! Come on up here." Rick looked up, and without a word, climbed out of the hole and joined Rich at his aircraft. Rich could tell he was a timid guy. He asked his comrade, "You like what you're doing?"

Rick replied, "Yeah, it's all right," as he shuffled his feet and kicked up some dirt. Rich surprised the ammo humper with his next question, "You wanna be a door gunner?"

Nobody ever volunteered for the position of shooting out the door of a moving helicopter, so any willing men were welcome to join the ranks of the "Shotgun Riders." Some action outside of the mud hole could be good for the young soldier, and they always needed gunners, so Rich figured it would be a good match, especially since he didn't top 120 pounds soaking wet.

Rick looked surprised and mumbled, "Well I need to think about it." He took a breath, and answered the invitation with enthusiasm. "Yeah, I think I would." Rick was excited to move beyond his days in the ditch. If he was going to be stuck in Vietnam, he should see some action. Rich put the young man to work on his ship right away. Rick Leroue learned to fire and fly, with about five minutes of on-the-job instruction.

Part Five

The cast of eight set out early on Saturday morning, April 20, 1968, to complete the mission they had received one day earlier. An Air Assault mission could mean several things—to move troops in or out, to provide reconnaissance, explore and gather information, perform a raid, or search and destroy. Today they were called upon to support a troop insertion into the A Shau Valley by the 227th Assault Helicopter Battalion (AHB).

Referred to as the "Hog Gun Team" by their unit major, the two crews left LZ Sharon near the city of Quang Tri, climbed 5,000 to 6,000 feet to clear the clouds, and flew west. Some predicted that the A Shau Valley area would be the last stronghold of the enemy, and the North Vietnamese Army would surrender by the end of the summer. They highly underestimated their enemy. There would never be a surrender.

When the team of ships reached the valley, they descended through a small opening in the clouds to get a visual of the valley floor. These "sucker holes" were subject to close up as soon as aircraft descended through them, in claim to the name. Once they landed in the A Shau Valley, the boys paired up with the assault team and the Command and Communications (C&C) ship. The C&C ship controlled the mission and coordinated all radio contact. With multiple transmissions cluttering the airways, a C&C ship needed to pass on vital communications to each party, while navigating possible radio frequency interception by the enemy.

Insertions of troops were time-consuming and chaotic. Depending on conditions, one aircraft at a time could drop off troops. Harsh landing conditions tested the pilots' skills. The top of the mountain was pock-marked with craters from airstrikes and the remnants of some trees scattered about the landing zone, limiting spots large enough for the helicopter to safely maneuver to the ground. The descent angle was steep, and the fallen trees and tree stumps made it impossible to touch down safely. As Larry's team arrived, they watched a helicopter lose control and crash into the LZ, rolling down the slope before some trees stopped it from plummeting down the mountain.

The control ship left to refuel, and Larry's ship and another ARA

14. "Got Shot Down"

team stayed on station. But soon after the C&C departure, clouds grew thicker, cutting off the last remaining spots of entry into the valley. Waiting for the command ship to return became a dangerous promise to keep. As the skies grew darker, the hog gun team took to the radio with the news. "This is Blue Max Two Seven. Sorry but the weather is not an ally today. We are low on fuel, and we are going to have to leave. The clouds are closing in on us, and the C&C bird may not be able to get back with you either, if this weather don't improve."

"This is Cougar One Seven, Roger. Understood. Thank you for all your support."

The team's exit from the valley brought incredible challenges. Like flying through a maze, the crew found each canyon or header a dead end. The conditions forced the team to turn back into the valley to try another route. They attempted to fly out at a low level through the side valleys. They searched the eastern side of the valley for a passageway, taking fire as they looked for a way out.

Nothing disabled the pair of aircraft to affect their continued operation. However, both ships suffered severe damage from the shots. Getting out of the A Shau Valley became their newest mission.

Extreme weather conditions and the chaos of repeated hits to the ships disoriented both pilots.

The Hueys tried to head south toward base camp, hoping they had enough fuel. They managed to stay together but struggled to get oriented inside the violent storms. The ships needed to find a friendly landing zone to refuel if they couldn't make it to their base camp in An Khe, but they drifted off their map. As they made their final mayday calls, the radio went dead, and they landed deep in the Happy Valley. Which was anything but happy.

* * *

We went down in a valley with mountains all around. We didn't crash, we landed nice and soft. We grabbed all the ammo and guns we could carry. We left one M60 in my ship because it didn't work and we threw away two M-16's.

* * *

Part Five

The final radio signal received from the Hog Gun Team in the Blue Max ships came in at 1530 hours.

Captain Mills reported, "Mayday, Mayday, Blue Max 2–7 and Blue Max 2–8, low on fuel with shots to tanks and rotors, fighting with the weather and Charlie. Forced landing, both slicks with unknown coordinates. Send help. Out." Their coordinates were in the satellite vicinity of ZC 009663, yet they had no way to determine or report that information.

Hueys always flew in formation. Cavalry pilots were trained to synchronize landings. The two ships entered Happy Valley together, surprising a company of guerrilla forces. The gunship team faced a determined and strong enemy force who laid out the welcome mats for a couple of lost American crews and their flying rocket machines.

They drifted down gently as Captain Germeck found a clearing near a small stream to land beside with Captain Mills' crew following. Captain Germeck landed just as door gunner Rick Leroue opened fire. The ship lowered into the makeshift landing zone, and had to clear the enemy out, or risk an ambush. Within a few minutes, Larry's whirlybird joined Rick's on the ground, landing softly beside him, directly in the path of his friend's bullets.

Rick had to cease fire and gave Larry a hard time about it. "Hey man, I was shooting right there. You had to get in my way? Those were the closest gooks I've ever seen."

They landed on the sacred home turf of a communist enemy with a distinct disadvantage. They were outnumbered by a significant factor that nobody cared to know. Navigating unusual conditions, they had to think fast. Their infantry skills were rusty. Their boots were not made for running. They were not prepared for hiking through mountainous terrain or navigating thick jungle by foot. The clock worked against the Blue Max squad.

Neither ship had fired any rockets, so they were fully loaded with 24 rockets on each side, now rendered useless. They were forced to abandon the rockets with the ships. The soldiers loaded themselves down with all the ordnance on board. Larry left his new camera behind, with the photos he had taken on the slide film he planned to send home. It was not deemed essential.

14. *"Got Shot Down"*

Captains Mills served in a prior capacity as an infantry officer, so the team felt lucky to have his insight but didn't really know him. He and Germeck grabbed the emergency kits, which included survival tools, an emergency radio device, water, MRE (Meals Ready to Eat) food rations, and several smoke grenades.

Radio signals required a direct line of sight, so communicating with the missing crew would be impossible on the valley floor. After finding no radio signal, one of the Captains ordered the troops to move. "There's no reception, and we're sitting-fucking ducks right here. Leave your helmets and anything that won't kill a gook. Head for the mountain."

The men left helmets and cameras but loaded up their bodies with an M-60, an M-16 with four clips, two bandoleros of ammunition, an M79 grenade launcher with 13 grenades, and a 38 sidearm pistol.Packed like mules, weapons lodged in every feasible place, they left the safety of their ships and ran for cover. They headed toward the mountain, fueled by pure adrenaline running through rice paddies, and dodging man-sized sharp blades of elephant grass like a race through a jungle maze. Running fast and hiding well would be their plan of defense. Well, that and the bungee cord-rigged grenade that Barry Brady attached to the inside of his helicopter door.

* * *

We went part way up the mountain and stayed there for the night. About 4:00 Sunday morning Charlie came. He blew up my buddy's ship and sprayed the woods we was in with bullets. They really had a good time with the ships. They put on our flight helmets and played polits. Meanwhile here we were in the trees shaking like hell. They sprayed the woods a few more times and had a real good time throwing grenades.

* * *

The airmobile gun team needed to get out of Charlie's sight and find cover until daybreak. The hill next to where the ships landed had a bluff facing the aircraft, a broad, steep face of the mountain. They trekked their weapons to the base of the mountain, hoping to climb to the top and set up a perimeter. The eight men spread out, keeping their eyes open for any signs of enemy presence. After climbing for a couple of hours, they positioned themselves in a heavily thicketed area and set up a firing position. The crew could not make it to the top because of the terrain and their heavy loads.

Not much moves at night in Vietnam, except for sneaky Viet Cong troops and slinky critters, so any movement or human sound could breach the security of their tiny force. Rick, Larry and the others spent the night hiding in the trees, frozen in silence near their fellow crew members, perched between tree limbs. They kept a finger on a trigger and an eye on the darkness and drifted in and out of shallow sleep.

Right before dawn at 0400 the early rising enemy troops showed up in tribal fashion, full of fresh energy and an army of raging guerrillas, loaded with ammunition. They attacked the two Huey helicopters, and sprayed the woods with bullets, trying to entice return fire from the Americans, knowing they had not gotten too far in the valley's rough terrain. The "Indians" tossed grenades around in different directions trying to hit the "cowboys." The boys had to dodge fire while staying still and silent. It took all their will not to fight back.

Larry had a bird's-eye view of his ship being destroyed. The shots engaged the rocket pods and some of the 48 rockets launched from the ships, shot straight forward, and exploded into the side of the cliff directly below where they hid. The team felt the impact and sat helpless as the ground under them shook from multiple explosions. There would be no shooting back, no revenge, and no war cries. They focused on shallow breathing and communicated with simple hand motions. Rick later described his intense urge to smoke, saying "I just wanted to light up, my nerves were so shot. It killed me not to smoke a cigarette."

Viet Cong didn't have any types of aircraft, so the Huey gunship and rocket pods intrigued them. Larry watched as one guy put on his Army helmet, climbed into his seat, and pretended to be a U.S. Army soldier. Larry would have been highly pissed off, but slightly amused.

* * *

> When daylight came, we started moving up to the top of the mountain to try and get radio contact with someone. We didn't have radio contact when

14. "Got Shot Down"

we went down. They came up through the woods, or I should say jungle, because that is what it was—and I mean <u>thick</u> jungle. They kept spraying the trees to try and get us to shoot back.

We got to the top and got radio contact with the C130 and he got us some E-1A's for air support plus all <u>three</u> battalions of 2/20 and all kinds of gun ships. When them E-1A's got there, we were surrounded by Charlie's. They (E-1A's) got a fix on us and then started blowing up the mountain all around us. We were so happy we almost cried. The E-1A's are sky raiders from the Air Force. They got <u>60</u> rockets, <u>4</u> 20mm guns, and 1 mini gun. We had four of them and two of them had napalm bombs on them. They blew up my ship, plus our own gun ships helped.

* * *

Larry and his team searched for a radio signal as they ascended the mountain, knowing it offered them a lifeline. Captain Mills and Captain Germeck alternated mayday calls on their emergency radios. As the men climbed the rough terrain, Charlie found the chase engaging and moved in closer. As they topped the ridge of the mountain, Captain Germeck heard a response to one of his radio broadcasts. They expected a Blue Max squadron buddy, but instead, it was a C-130 Air Force aircraft. The four-engine command ship had been flying figure-eight patterns from Da Nang to the DMZ and heard the distress calls from the Army radio signal.

As long as the rescue nets could reach them, the boys knew they would be back at base camp for dinner. The hopeful eight crested the mountain with renewed faith. They were certain their First Cavalry squads would be on the way to save their asses. They celebrated with small hugs and silent fist pumps, not too jubilant, knowing that the worst was yet to come.

As they waited for rescue ships to come on station, Larry's team saw groups of Viet Cong encircling the hill below him, searching for the downed crew with a vengeance. The cloud ceiling remained too low to get a visual on the C-130, but knowing it circled above helped them relish the fact that a rescue crew would soon be on the way.

The military branches rarely commingled in Vietnam, except in extreme situations. The C-130 commander scrambled two Skyraider pilots stationed at Pleiku, a nearby Air Force base camp, to assist in the rescue. The Skyraider pilots, affectionately called "Spads,"

Part Five

scrambled some Jolly Greens from Da Nang to bring in the hoist nets to assist in rescuing the men. The Skyraider pilots were from the 6th Air Commando Squadron in Pleiku. With motto in hand ("Anything, Anywhere, Anytime"), the Spad pilots stayed prepared and flexible in action. The Sandy squadron from Thailand usually covered search and rescue, but the 6th Air Unit got called in to help when Sandy couldn't cover ongoing rescues fast enough. Since the new assignment covered South Vietnam, that meant the squadron would always have a contingent in Da Nang. The Skyraiders offered the closest and fastest assistance to search efforts. Skyraiders were the most heavily armed attack planes in the region and the largest combat aircraft in the world.

Each A1-H Skyraider "ship" was loaded with six pods of rockets, multiple machine guns, a mini-gun, and tons of napalm. The complex cockpit illustrated the vast capabilities of this fighter jet. A Skyraider ship could lift more than twice its weight, making it one of the strongest and most capable machines in the war. When empty, it weighed 11,000 pounds, yet it could lift 25,000 pounds. In addition to absurd strength, Skyraider "spad" fighter planes could hold 8,000 pounds of ordnance and fly 350 miles per hour. That equates to a massive amount of power for one plane, with one man aboard to manage it all.

Spad pilots Captain Tom Stroud (Spad 11) and Captain Lyn Oberdier (Spad 12) were on "sunrise to sunset" alert. Each week, one of the four squadron's flights rotated from Pleiku to Da Nang to serve a one-week search and rescue alert duty. Captain Stroud flew the lead ship as flight leader, with Captain Oberdier as his wingman. Stroud, a 26-year-old pilot, had served five months in Vietnam and Oberdier had arrived one month earlier. When the alert bell rang early that morning, the pilots scrambled and followed orders to head to Happy Valley. They jumped into their respective aircraft, single-engine, single-seat A-1H–model planes. The order began with the first task of finding the ground troops. Fighter pilots Stroud and Oberdier would then secure the area with strafing fire to keep the enemy pushed back while the rescue helicopters did their part to get the men out.

In addition to the Skyraider fighter ship, the Air Force flew several types of aircraft, but the Jolly Green Giants ranked among the most notorious. These military machines were originally used to transport troops and supplies, increasing America's advantage of speed and deployment capabilities, and the later model HH-3E earned the title of the Jolly Green Giant. It distinguished itself in rescue operations of downed airmen and was three times the size of Larry's Huey helicopter. This dedicated air rescue version boasted in-flight refueling capability and shatterproof canopies over the windshield covering the cockpit. The Jolly Greens were stout helicopters, plated with steel armor sides and powerful hoists for rescuing from a hover. They worked hand in hand with Skyraiders on most rescue missions.

The C&C C-130 aircraft commander issued directions to the pair of Skyraider fighter pilots to fly toward the general location where the distress radio call was detected. Lead ship Captain Tom Stroud tracked an electronic signal transmitted from Captain Mills' radio on the ground, enabling him to pinpoint their approximate position in the valley.

Skyraider pilots Stroud and Oberdier had been recently assigned to the business of search and rescue, and this would be their first mission in that capacity. It would also be their most memorable.

* * *

They were shooting so close to us that rounds were hitting 10 feet in front of me.

* * *

The Blue Max teammates watched enemy forces closing in on them up the hill. Chaos ensued as gunfire shot around them from all sides, from both enemy and friendly fire. Thick clouds dulled their sense of sight and sound. Adrenaline provided fuel for their last push to freedom, and it was all they had left in the tank.

The commander radioed to Captain Mills, "Blue Max Two Seven, en route to your location, request you pop smoke, over."

The smoke served as a beacon, to locate downed men in the thick jungle. If Charlie intercepted the radio signal and overheard the command, he would pop his own smoke to confuse and trick our men. If

Part Five

the enemy failed to use the correct color, it backfired on them. Once the canister's ring got pulled, the grenade spewed thick smoke that rose high above the canopy of trees. The Army used yellow, blue, red, and white to change things up, and today the smoke was white. A cloud of desperation filled the sky and proved promising.

The Spads located the downed men, assessed the situation, and went into full action. While the lead pilot, Stroud, spoke to the C-130 C&C aircraft above, he also relayed directions to his Spad partner, Captain Lyn Oberdier, and stayed in constant contact with the troops on the ground. Stroud knew he could count on Lyn; he was top in his graduating class and a well-respected Air Force officer he had worked with for a few weeks since Lyn's arrival in Vietnam.

While shooting his own weapons and maintaining control of the aircraft, Stroud orchestrated the actions of the entire team and kept everyone informed minute by minute on the rescue plan. The soldiers on the ground stayed close together while the Spads aimed fire to continually push back enemy forces and buy time. While the V.C. tried to invade the Americans' perimeter, Stroud had to work hard to keep the men calm, reassuring them that a rescue ship was on the way. If the V.C. didn't kill them, the sustained waiting and growing chances for captivity just might.

The familiar sound of whop-whop-whop never sounded so sweet. When the hum of the first Jolly Green echoed above, the clouds and grenade smoke dispersed, and so did the fear that had piled up in the men over the past two days. Larry and his buddies finally used their voices, yelling praises through the flying dust and shouting expletives over the comforting sound of helicopter blades overhead. They cursed Charlie and praised the Air Force in the same breath.

Jolly Greens flew in teams of two, one known as the high ship and one as the low ship. The low ship would pick up the downed men while the high ship provided backup, hovering in sight of its partner. The Skyraiders kept up the strafing fire and commanded the team's efforts.

Jolly Greens 28 and 30 arrived on station and directed the men to a small clearing down from the top of the hill. As the first Jolly

14. "Got Shot Down"

Green pulled in, he hesitated and went into his hover directly above the men. Met with heavy fire, he had to lift up as soon as he arrived. Jolly Green 30 went in for a second attempt at the rescue but was soon driven off by intense enemy ground fire and suffered extensive damage. Running low on fuel, the second Jolly Green couldn't complete the mission and had to return to Da Nang. The grounded soldiers watched in defeat as their rescue ship flew out of the valley.

Jolly Green 28 remained in position but refused to go any lower without backup. Captain Stroud discussed the situation with the C-130 C&C aircraft and found that the nearest replacement of Jolly Greens would take 45 minutes to arrive. At the same time, his own aircraft was running low on ammunition and could not sustain strafing efforts that long. Oberdier's ship was handicapped in the same way with limited ammo and low fuel.

Captain Stroud, fully cognizant that the way to any successful mission was to get in and get out as fast as possible, persevered despite the ever-diminishing odds. The Jolly Green's departure demoralized the men on the ground and made Stroud's job of reassuring them more challenging. He called for backup Jolly Greens and hoped they would arrive in time.

The team had shown their cards to Charlie and was running out of resources. Charlie learned exactly where the boys were located and moved in tighter with even more fury and determination to find and capture the American boys who so far had managed to escape their wrath.

* * *

> They got two big Air Force helicopters to get us out. They had to use a hoist to get us out. They got us out about 2:00 Sunday. You wouldn't believe how happy we were. If we would have been there another 2 or 3 hours we could of hung it up, all 8 of us would have been done for.

* * *

Stroud saw dozens of Viet Cong forces surrounding the ground crew. He called C-130 C&C aircraft and scrambled two more A-1 alert planes from Pleiku, but they were an hour away. There was a radio signal from some F-4 planes above that volunteered to come in and

Part Five

help Stroud and Oberdier. The McDonnell Douglas F-4 Phantom was considered one of the most versatile fighters ever built, and the first Navy fighter adopted by the Air Force. The powerful ally would have been a welcome addition, except for the fact that F-4s boast a top speed twice the speed of sound. With a minimum attack speed of 600 miles per hour, they can't manage anything slower. Stroud thanked them and sent them on their way.

Communication continued between Oberdier, Stroud, and the remaining Jolly Green 28. Stroud provided mission updates at every turn. He radioed the C-130 and Jolly Green, kept Military Assistance Command informed in Saigon, and constantly assured Captain Mills and his men on the ground. Pandemonium ensued as enemy forces gathered momentum during the delay. The mission worsened, and the chances of success were dwindling to zero when Stroud heard a promising sound. He searched the skies.

He radioed Lyn Oberdier and said, "Lo and behold Spad 12, would you look there! The Army sent in the Cavalry gunships, coming to help rescue their men." They flew in formation, two by two. A string of eight Huey gunships approached the Happy Valley with retribution on their minds. Fellow crew chiefs, gunners, and pilots from all three battalions of the 2/20th ARA converged on the scene. In true form and fashion, the First Cavalry came to save the day. Sound the bugles.

John Stewart, a crew member of one of those gunships, remembers the moment they intercepted the radio signal and found their missing friends. The entire platoon had searched day and night and tried not to give up hope of finding their buddies. When they got the news, they looked forward to this moment of vengeance to help secure their friends' rescue.

Stroud put the Cavalry gunships to work. All eight Hueys emptied their machine guns and launched all their rockets into the enemy's valley. After beating the area up pretty good, seven of the eight ships went back to their home base to reload, including John Stewart's. The commander of the squad, Major Clarence H. Woliver, call sign Blue Max 3, stayed with the rescue mission. "Clancy" or "Woliby," as he was called around camp, took full responsibility for the men in his unit and would never leave any of them behind.

14. "Got Shot Down"

The team remaining—Two Skyraiders, Jolly Green 30, Major Clancy Woliver, and his gunship crew—worked together to put a bandage on the situation until rescue ships arrived once more. To keep the enemy guessing and preserve depleting levels of ammunition, the four remaining aircraft made passes at the ground with alternating dry and live fire runs.

Stroud remained determined and maintained continuous contact as his disjointed team continued their bombing and strafing passes for 45 more minutes. No men had been lost, and Stroud stayed the course. He informed the team that backup Jolly Greens were moments away and ready to wrap up the mission.

After sufficient neutralization of the enemy, Stroud initiated the final rescue attempt. Jolly Green 21 came in first and lowered a hoist from a high hover, about 50 feet above the treetops. The rescue hoist has a very long wire cable and an electric motor that lowers and retrieves it, along with an attached "jungle penetrator," a torpedo-shaped piece of metal about three feet in length that helps the rope get through a thick forest without getting tangled. The penetrator has two seats folded up on each side, about six inches wide and 18 inches long. Soldiers unfold and straddle the seats, wrapping their arms around one another on the swinging ride up through the jungle. The hoist pulled up the first two men to the Jolly Green platform and repeated the steps for the next two. Four of the crew members were safe, and the ship ascended, hovering to watch the others follow suit.

Jolly Green 28 lowered the final hoist. Just as Lt. Hawks and Larry were getting on the seat, Vietcong forces came within feet of the pair and Larry faced his opponents eye to eye. He swung the hoist around and emptied his machine gun. Hawks fed the ammunition for Larry as they were lifted into the air with hearts pounding. It may have been Larry's finest moment in combat. Nobody ever knew. "All survivors secured. Let's get the hell out of here," Stroud broadcast to everyone, adding, "Pleiku backup will finish up."

As the Jolly Greens circled the area with the eight shaken rescued crew members, the men watched their fellow ARA gunship, Commander Woliver and crew, make a final show of victory in the

Part Five

valley. The Commander ordered complete destruction of any remnants of the fallen Huey ships to make sure they were rendered useless, creating fireworks displays from dozens of undetonated rocket explosions.

As the mission ended, the 6th Air Commando's two Skyraiders from Pleiku arrived fully stocked with ammunition, ready to finish the destruction of Happy Valley. Stroud thanked them and watched as they happily pounded the hill with dozens more rockets and dropped 500-pound bombs of napalm. Napalm burns at 3600 degrees Fahrenheit, hot enough to melt steel, hot enough to render Larry's ship useless and destroy everything in its path. The rescue and retribution jobs were done, and done well.

The last remaining job for Stroud and Oberdier was to escort the Jolly Greens as they flew the rescued soldiers over to Da Nang. Their search and rescue job would be complete once all crew members were safely on the ground. As they flew away in the Jolly Green, Larry and Rick watched the air fill with smoke from the final explosions. Their pounding hearts began to relax and finally, they allowed smiles to emerge from their filthy faces. They were lucky to be alive, free, and heading to their home away from home, with a whole new appreciation for the luxuries of a tent, a cot, and a mosquito net. They were heading to home to Sharon, sweet landing zone Sharon.

*   *   *

> They took us to Da Nang to get a check up, they gave us big shot of VO or something to drink and then took us to the mess hall and we had two big steaks and ice cream.
>
> That camera and film I bought in Da Nang went with my ship when it burned so I guess you can forget about the pictures. I put it in for combat loss so I will get the money back.
>
> Today I slept till 10:00, got up and cleaned the tent and didn't do nothing all day. I think I will take the day off tomorrow too. I don't guess I will fly for awhile now. I am going to start learning about the Cobra's but I don't care, I am too short to fly.
>
> Here's what I want on the car—a "426" engine, all heavy duty stuff underneath, bucket seats, 4 speed trans, and I want it the same color as the picture I sent you of it and black inside. I am doing fine so don't worry about me, I will be home in Aug.
>
> Well the lights go out in a few minutes so I had better close for now. Tell everyone I said hi and hope they are fine. So if you see anything in the paper

14. "Got Shot Down"

about us going down, don't worry. You know how the papers are. So take care and write soon. Send some more tapes.

Love always, Larry

* * *

The Jolly Greens flew the Blue Max team to Da Nang, where they were treated to the finest delicacies available to a soldier in a war. The meal would be the best the Army could offer as a "welcome back" celebration and appreciation for a job well done. After what they had faced over the preceding 24 hours, steak may have been a little difficult to digest, but I am sure it was a welcome treat.

Blue Max crew of eight rescued from Happy Valley; back row, left to right: Capt. Mills, Lt. Hawks (Pilot), Warrant Officer Raymond (Pilot), SP/4 Howell (Door Gunner). Front row, left to right: Warrant Officer Chuck Germeck (Pilot), Richard Leroue (Door Gunner), Barry Brady (Crew Chief), Larry Smith (Crew Chief). South Vietnam, April 1968 (credit Richard Passer).

Part Five

Tom Stroud (left) being congratulated on completion of duty by Lt. Col. Corey (right), Pleiku, South Vietnam, September 1968 (credit Tom Stroud).

With the customary handshakes and formalities complete, aircraft from the 2/20th flew the team back to their home base where the rest of the Blue Max boys were waiting for them, and the moment their ships touched down and the team of eight emerged, the rest of the unit piled on top of each other in a heap of happy hugs and celebration. Rich gave Larry hell for eating the Air Force's fancy food offerings, but Larry wouldn't turn down a good steak. The crew of grateful boys arrived in time to crash their own memorial service and party the night away.

Stroud had orchestrated a brilliant combat rescue on a stage of complete chaos; he recruited actors from different military branches, coordinated actions of multiple aircraft and weaponry, and directed each participant to a lead role. The Skyraider captain didn't take credit for the rescue success and instead insisted that it was a team effort.

14. "Got Shot Down"

Tom Stroud on the wing of an A1-H Skyraider, Pleiku, South Vietnam, early 1968 (credit Tom Stroud).

"All of us got them out. What would I have done if the Army's Hueys hadn't shown up, I don't know, we didn't have enough ammunition, so they were a godsend. It was not common to experience cooperation like this with the Army and Air Force working together, and it was my honor to be a part of the team." Stroud remains humble to this day.

Major Clarence H. Woliver of Blue Max 3, the Army commander that assisted in the final trifecta of subduing the V.C., issued a letter to the commanding officer of the 6th Air Commando Squadron of the U.S. Air Force. In it, Major Woliver recognized the valor of the Air Force crew on this mission. He wrote, "The highly accurate fire support and professional direction of this mission by Spad 11 and 12 contributed immeasurably to the successful accomplishment of this mission and the saving of eight American lives that otherwise would undoubtedly be lost."

Part Five

6th Special Operations Squadron Headquarters at Pleiku, call sign "Spads," 1968 (credit Tom Stroud).

In addition, a letter of appreciation was sent from Lt. Colonel Kenneth D. Caughron, commander of the Da Nang Jolly Green Giant Squadron, expressing deep appreciation for the assistance rendered by the Spads with the words, "The task that the Spads accomplished was done in a professionally classic manner, in that it was the way that a mission should be prosecuted. One earnestly wishes that future missions could be accomplished the same way."

Lt. Col. Caughron went on to praise the collaboration, writing, "Through the ability, loyalty, and dedication of Captain Stroud and Captain Oberdier, our Jolly Green crews were able to bring home eight Americans alive, yet we received no battle damage. In view of such circumstances, mere thanks almost seem inadequate. I am very proud to have been associated with them."

Captain Stroud was awarded the Silver Star, the third-highest personal decoration for valor in combat. This would be the only Silver Star he received. His commendation read:

14. "Got Shot Down"

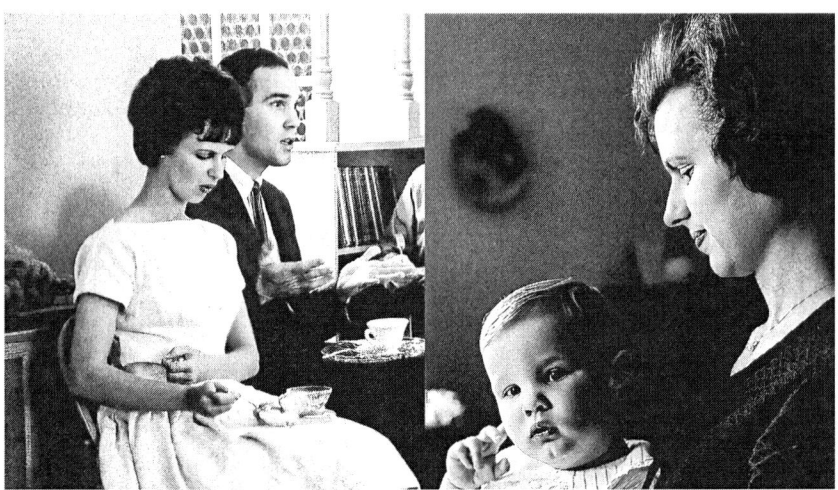

Left: Carla and Lyn Oberdier before the war; right: Carla and one young child, circa 1967/1968 (credit Carla Johnson).

> "Captain Tommy R. Stroud distinguished himself by gallantry in connection with military operations against an opposing armed force as an A-1H tactical fighter pilot near Da Nang, Republic of Vietnam, on 21 April 1968. On that date, Captain Stroud supported a rescue of eight army helicopter crewmen who were surrounded on the ground in hostile territory. In mountainous terrain under a low cloud cover, Captain Stroud made repeated rocket and strafing attacks to suppress hostile forces attempting to overrun the downed airmen. With complete disregard for his own personal safety, Captain Stroud delivered his ordnance at a very low level in an extremely hostile environment in order to permit Air Force helicopters to pick up the eight crewmen unharmed. By his gallantry and devotion to duty, Captain Stroud has reflected great credit upon himself and the United States Air Force."

Captain Stroud never met Larry, but he did meet Captain Mills. "I'd like to shake your hand, sir," Mills told Stroud after saluting the Skyraider. Following a firm handshake and a grateful look that spoke for itself, Mills thanked him for sticking it out for so long. "Glad to meet you, and happy that your men are safe and sound tonight. I wasn't sure I would ever meet the man on the other end of that weak radio signal. Good work, Captain. Let me know if you get fed up with the Army and want a place in the Air Force." Stroud saluted him back.

Part Five

Lyn Oberdier and fellow Skyraider Pilots, circa 1968. Lyn is second from the left on back row (credit Carla Johnson).

Stroud didn't get an offer to join the dinner, but he couldn't be more satisfied. Nothing could taste better than having his first rescue behind him with zero casualties. Not even steak and ice cream.

15

I BEG YOU

Your single subject black notebook fills up with nauseating terms and dead ends. The doctors try to explain your brother's body's reactions, the seizures he has been having, and the restlessness you see through his moving closed eyelids. He's fighting, even in his unconscious state. His file includes several concerning, deteriorating prognoses. Neurological Deterioration, MRSA, Serratia, Pseudomonas Yeast. Probable Anoxic Episode during Hemodynamic Instability. Endless issues tend to erupt from six months of putting a brain on hold.

You document the revolving diagnoses, hopeless updates, and conflicting information from the medical community with precise dates and names. The notes pile up, producing no answers and no remote plan of action. Calls to the realtor, his workplace and friends, the Boy Scout troop, attorneys, Veterans Administration facilities, social workers, and constant contact among them all keep the family busy up and down the East Coast. Bill collectors and collection agencies, followed by legal issues involving tenancy in common, guardianship, probate, and foreclosure all complicate the situation, and the family grows weary trying to survive the long days.

The dining room table becomes a war zone of its own. Documents gather dust, envelopes that nobody cares to open, knowing the one-million-dollar maximum lifetime healthcare coverage has been exhausted. Piles of evidence add up as funds decline and everything is in the red. It's the same wooden table where you heard his words all those years ago, wrapped in red, white, and blue envelopes, and where your penny collection awaited his return. The table where all things sweet in your childhood happened. And where the bitter war interrupted your peaceful home.

Part Five

He gives you nothing but perpetual blank stares. He shows a will to stare directly into your eyes, interrupted by too few random blinks. *Get me out of here.* His piercing optics still send you a clear message. Every time. *Get me out of here.*

You cover his dry, cracked lips with lip balm. Try to pry open his mouth, hoping the forced movement triggers a sound, knowing it will annoy the hell out of him. No response.

With each passing day and no improvement, it gets harder to hope. His open chest remains, inviting infections that still come and go, with fluctuating high fevers. There is enough neuro activity for the hospital to maintain the possibility of recovery. You are beginning to think otherwise, as much as you want to be wrong. He sleeps more.

Your sister-in-law starts clearing out the house. She has adored your brother since the day they met, despite their rocky marriage and years of challenges, and she stands by his side stroking his hair and straightening his pillows. On one of your visits, she hands you a large wooden box late one night.

"Do you wanna see these? They are your brothers' letters to your Mom and Dad during his time in the Army." She knew you would want them. Details from those days are foggy, your penny collection long ago forgotten and the war a distant memory. You stay up late, poring over his words. The stories entertain you, amaze you, and frighten you. Heavy drinking, wild women, hanging out of helicopters, simple, rebellious acts he hoped would get him court-martialed. Your brother shared personal tales of combat inside infamous, volatile battles he never spoke of ever again. He was a decorated hero, and you never knew.

A remarkable number, 99. Among them, over 30,000 words. Written in a voice you have never heard, by a sweet young boy you don't recognize. He needs to hear about what you now know. Sharing these truths could set him free from the bondage of his worst memories. Talking to him about his days at war may be the one thing that gets a reaction out of him. He's a captive audience, so it's worth a shot.

Your visit begins and ends with this declaration, and it takes all the bravery you can muster to let the words out.

15. I BEG YOU

"I have your letters. The ones you wrote us from your days in the Army." You wait for movement and continue when there is none. "I can't believe the stuff you did over there, or how bad the situation got for you. I've learned so much about the war, and about what they put you through to fight in it. I never knew."

You wait for movement, any suggestion he hears you. You squeeze his hand, hard. Nothing. You continue with more conviction.

"I wish, well I wish I had known this all before now. You lived through hell and wrote home to report it to us. Your words from the frontlines of that war speak for all those who didn't come home, those friends they took from you. They need you, Larry. We all need you. Please. Keep fighting."

Larry is trapped inside his own mind. He has not spoken or even moaned or grunted in all these months and the hell he is paying on the inside may trump all the hell he's already lived through on the outside. With Cavalry in his blood, you hold on to the hope that nothing is impossible for your failing hero. Your brother continues to fight, with a speck of resilience still in his eyes.

What you can't see, though, is that his physical body is starting to rot from the inside out.

Part Six

16

"We Go Where the War Is"

> We seem bent upon saving the Vietnamese from Ho Chi Minh, even if we have to kill them and demolish their country to do it. I do not intend to remain silent in the face of what I regard as a policy of madness which, sooner or later, will envelop my son and American youth by the millions for years to come.
> —Senator George McGovern

As Mama got everything ready for Larry's return in the summer of 1968, she cleaned the whole house and everything in it. She moved furniture around and made space on his bedroom walls for the awards and medals he would bring home with him. I relinquished my playroom to give him his room back, happy to relocate my mini kitchen to a corner in the living room to make space for his grown-up stuff coming soon. I helped Mama count down the warm days until the date of August 5 arrived, and she planned our annual family vacation trip to the Jersey shore for the very next week.

I overheard Mama and Daddy in more than one heated discussion about Larry's Charger, they were always debating both sides of money problems, and broken cars, and problems with engines and such. Mama liked to spend money, but Daddy liked to save it for rainy days. He didn't grow up anything like she did, and his days as a truck driver brought in just enough to pay the bills, so he kept having to remind Mama of those things. She couldn't have everything she wanted like she got as a child.

On the back of Larry's latest envelopes, Mama wrote this note: "Saw on TV. 1965 Pontiac. Only $550 in Pa." To which Daddy, exercising his own laws of relativity, answered in neat and respectful handwriting beneath, "I don't have 550.—Ken."

16. "We Go Where the War Is"

* * *

24-Apr-68
Wednesday
Quang Tri

Dear Mom and Dad,

Just a few words to say hi and let you know I am still fine. I forgot to tell you in my last letter that I got the under clothes so thank you very much. They all fit really good.

Right now I am in my tent drinking a beer, matter-of-fact it's my third one. While I was in Da Nang I got back on the beer kick, and I put on a lot of weight.

I am also mad as hell. I got a cobra, but today they put me on another Huey. I don't mind flying but I can't stand to crew a B model Huey. I used to have a C model. If they keep me on it for more than a week, I'm going to tell them to hang it in their ass, because I will quit.

I hated to tell you about what happened to me, but it is supposed to be in the paper and you know how they can build up a story. So don't worry, I'm just fine, still a little shook up but I will get over it. You won't believe how much it cost to get us out. <u>Two</u> million, $500,000. It's hard to believe, but it's true.

What is the deal on Joanna? Is she getting married or not? If she ain't, I ain't leaving here until around the 7th of August. I would like to know for sure. If the guy ain't bothered to write or call in seven weeks he must not care very much. Myself, I think she is too young. I am still planning on getting married, but it will be in Aug of 69.

Well I guess I will close for now. Tell everyone I said hi and hope they are fine. Take care. Write often.

Love always, Larry

I don't know who I would vote for, because I don't know who is running.
P.S. No I wasn't at Khe-Sanh. I was still in Da Nang.

* * *

Money and math intrigued me, as I continued to count and recount my dwindling pennies. Starting with one cent as my baseline made it hard to imagine two and a half million dollars, the price of my brother's rescue. I began to question the value of other things, even the price of my own adoption. Pennies took on more value as the coins failed to multiply as I had hoped. I never realized that as hard as Larry looked to find them, American pennies would not be found in Vietnam. In my mind, the war stole my brother, and my pennies, and one day they would let them come back. Daddy and Mama talked about money a lot and it never seemed to be a happy subject. Daddy

Part Six

grumbled that war was all about money. "War is a damn business," I heard more than once.

At some point I realized I needed more silver coins to go with my pennies if I was going to have something special, so my currency collection took on larger expectations just about the same time Mama bought me a cuss box for Daddy to fill up. The small wooden box with a slot on top proved more lucrative than I expected. On one side it read:

> Cussing ain't the nicest thing
> And friends fer you it shore don't bring
> But if you really got to sayem
> Here's the way you hafta payem

On the other side, it listed "The Payoff":

> One CUSS just a Nickel,
> Two CUSSES just a Dime,
> Three CUSSESS you really 'oughter,
> Put in the box at least a Quarter.

Daddy filled up that box for me in no time. Larry was cussing in his letters these days, too. There seemed to be a pattern, Mama even let a couple h-e-double-l words out.

His old Huey gunship was like a Model T compared to the jet fighter–like Cobra helicopter they had him training on now. When the two ships worked together in the skies, the Huey's job was to draw fire, while the Cobras came in to clean up behind them. Cobras would soon replace all the Hueys since they had more power, more maneuverability, and flew at almost twice the speed. Larry's Huey gunship would go 120 mph and the Cobras would top out around 220 mph.

* * *

30-Apr-68
Tuesday
Quang Tri

Dear Mom and Dad,

 Just a few lines to say hi and let you know I am still doing fine. Hope everyone at home is fine too.

 I got the pictures, and they are very nice. I sure wish you would of sent one

16. "We Go Where the War Is"

of yourself and Dad. But the kids look good. Jamie is really cute, can't wait until I get to see him. Sorry to hear about the kittens dying, but there will be more, and at least you still have one. Also hope Tracy makes it in the hospital this time.

I got a letter from Butch the other day he is doing fine. He is way down south. I knew Artie's marriage wasn't going to last. I know Artie like the back of my hand. He just ain't the marrying kind.

Not much hopping around here. I ain't flying anymore so don't worry about me anymore. Besides that I am too short to fly. Only three more months and then I will be home.

I taped another tape to you but never did mail it because it didn't come out so good. So I will try again some other time. So the vacation plans still on? I hope so. I am really looking forward to it. It's really going to feel good going on vacation and being with the whole family again.

Here is a newspaper clipping about us when we went down. They tried to make the polit sound good by saying they were the last ones out. Me and my polit was the last ones out and we were there longer than 19 hours. You will get to meet the crew chief of the other ship that went down when I come home. He lives in Heightstown.

I heard I made SP/5, but I haven't got the orders yet so I don't know. I should find out soon. It's about time I made it too. Four times before I got knocked off the list for telling them what I thought. Tomorrow I get one of my medals, but I don't know which one. So I might get all three. I never got any yet because they are real slow about getting them to us. I will let you know when I get it.

Not really much more to say so I will close for now. Tell everyone I said hi and hope they are fine. Write often.

Love always, Larry

Let me know for sure if Jo is getting married so I will know when to come home.

* * *

Romance confused me like math. Larry thought Jo was too young at the age of 17 to get married, the same age Larry was when he left home. Meanwhile, he was planning a marriage to a girl who stayed mad at him, he had not yet graduated high school, hadn't bought a ring and couldn't afford one, it seemed. All the talk of it seemed like a big sore subject. I had never seen my parents kiss like the neighbors' parents and didn't want them to, I was certain. I never saw them embrace like the couples on the Harlequin romance book covers that Mama devoured, and I knew it would be weird if they did.

I guessed that Joanna was like Artie, not the "marrying

Part Six

Left to right: Larry Smith, Tracy Smith, and neighbor Jane McGuigan visiting in our front yard, Kendall Park, New Jersey, circa 1967.

kind." I wondered if Mama and Daddy were the "marrying kind," or if I would grow up to be the "marrying kind." I think Jane McGuigan next door was the "marrying kind" since she managed to have it all and keep it well organized. She dressed up in heels each day to go to her important job at the *Princeton Packet*, raised five kids plus me most days, and had a newborn son ("cute" Jamie). Jane always cooked, wore an apron, and never fixed her plate until everyone left the table. She enjoyed her cocktails, floating in the pool, and loved when we gathered at the piano. In contrast, my own Mama didn't like most music, despised water in her face, and never drank alcohol. But she did like Jane McGuigan, we all did. Jane was a good listener, a devout Catholic, a great party host and the mother we all secretly wished we had. Including Mama.

* * *

16. "We Go Where the War Is"

5-May-68
Sunday
Quang Tri

Dear Mom and Dad,

    Just a few lines to say hi and hope everyone is fine. I am still doing real fine myself.

    I am flying again now, but not because I have to, because I want to. I stayed on the ground for a few days and did nothing all day. I got real bored and had to do something. I ain't flying steady like I used to, so don't worry. If you read anything about the A SHAU valley, that is where we do our flying. It ain't as bad as it used to be now, so don't worry if they build it up big in the paper. I will admit it ain't the best and safest place to fly, but we go where the war is.

    I haven't heard from you or anyone in a long time. I sure hope everyone is okay. Well I had better be going for now. I got to leave soon for the valley. Tell everyone I said hi and hope they are fine. Write soon.

Love always, Larry 92 days.

* * *

    My tonsils grew too big for my throat and had to be cut out while I slept. During recovery, I made friends with a little boy from the burn unit. We could see each other through a small window, that had a deep ledge big enough for my twirling wind-up bunny rabbit to entertain him. With a smile in his eyes, he explained what happened.

    "There was a big boom, something exploded in our house." He got quiet when he told me. I didn't ask questions. I could see long brown curly lashes that sweetened his gaze, and a small amount of his lips that moved very little when he spoke. I studied those lips and lashes, since they were all that I could see. The rest of his face was wrapped up.

    "I wish I could see all of your face. I can't tell when you are smiling or sad," I told him on the second day of our friendship through the glass.

    "My bandages are coming off in a few days. I will be okay then. You can meet my whole face!" He spoke louder with this promise. However, the next day my departing ice cream treat ended my hospital stay, and despite my protests to see my new friend, they took me home without seeing his unveiling. We never said goodbye. Maybe that was best.

Part Six

I wondered if his "okay" would be the same kind of "okay" that Larry assured us of in every letter. The same kind of "okay" that meant everything would be back to normal, even if you couldn't see it.

* * *

10-May-68
Friday morning
Dear Mom and Dad,

   Hope this letter finds everyone well and fine. I am still doing O.K. Not really much to say, for I haven't done much but fly every once in a while. I sure hope everyone is fine. I haven't heard from you in a month or so. Haven't heard from nobody in a month.

   I couldn't wait any longer for an answer on Jo getting married, and I had to tell them when I wanted my leave. I will be home somewhere between the first and seventh of Aug. I hope sure hope the car will be there waiting for me. Make sure it has a 426 and a 4 speed trans in it, with bucket seats and a console.

   Yesterday I went swimming all afternoon in a lake. I got a little bit too much sun. They got me pulling guard again, but it won't last too long.

   I am supposed to get a bolt action sniper rifle to bring home. All the flight crews are supposed to get one. It is part of the stuff they captured from the valley. I also heard that we may move way down south by the big city. If we do, I may get to see Butch. If he is where I think he is, he is right outside a R&R center.

   Well not really much more to say, so I will close for now. Tell everyone I said hi and hope they are fine.

Love always, Larry
Write soon.

* * *

They sold Larry's old car to save the insurance money and repair bills, and it helped pay a down payment on the Charger, complete with leather bucket seats and a console, like he asked. They scraped together enough money to cover the insurance and argued over how to surprise him. Mama wanted to pick him up at the airport, Daddy wanted him to see it in the driveway when all us kids could be there. We couldn't all fit in that car, and Larry would have lots of stuff to fill the trunk.

The *Princeton Packet* published the latest story about Larry, and Mama couldn't wait to show it to him, but still kept it secret. The Charger had been purchased and would be waiting on him. Mama

16. "We Go Where the War Is"

especially liked the part that predicted all would be well, which proved at least in her mind that he would no doubt come home to his fast car and loving family.

The paper reported, "Larry will be home, in a manner of speaking, for a month. His new automobile, equipped with a Hemi engine, is ready for him in the family driveway. His mother, who has put approximately 300 miles on it, has to admit that 'it really moves.' Larry is coming home to quite a lot."

* * *

14-May-68
Tuesday
Dear Mom and Dad,

Hope this letter finds everyone fine. I am still doing O.K. I got a letter from you yesterday and was very glad to hear from you. For awhile, I thought you had forgot about me. I also got a letter from the people next door with the pool. Hope Tracy is better by now. Does she still like school? Sorry to hear about the cat getting sick, hope she gets better.

Don't worry about me. I ain't doing any fighting any more and I ain't flying at all now. If things don't change soon I am going to start flying again. I pull guard 4 out of 5 nights, pull detail, plus they expect me to keep up a helicopter. If I start flying again I won't have to put up with that. You would think that there would be a lot of moral in the Bty, but there ain't any in this Bty. I am going to try and get into the same unit as Butch. If they don't let me, I am going to the inspecting General and find out why, and then I will tell him just how this Bty is. I know he will straighten this Bty. out. I could tell you things about this Bty. that you wouldn't believe.

Today I worked all day on my cobra. I put on rocket pods, cleaned the mini-jam, and washed the helicopter. It don't sound like much but it took all day and I didn't goof off either. Tomorrow I hope to go for a ride in it.

Not really much to say because I haven't been doing nothing but working. I still don't know for sure if I made E5 or not. I heard I did, but I haven't got the orders yet.

Well I will close for now. Tell everyone I said hi and see them in Aug. Write soon.

Love always, Larry

* * *

Daddy's lessons took me years to understand, but they applied in all parts of life. Everything is relative. Wealth, peace, the injustice of war, and life in general, all relative. And apparently much more complicated than necessary.

Part Six

People and pictures in the news puzzled me, and Daddy reminded me that there were at least two sides to every story. We saluted the flag, but some people burned it and called themselves patriots for doing so. We were proud of our men and women in uniform, but some people called them horrible names, and spat on them when they came home from fighting for our freedom. Songs on the radio, pictures in the newspaper, and heads on the television told us different stories about the same stories. I felt sorry for the Asian kids hiding out in the tunnels or running away as their entire world disappeared into the smoke of battle. The chaos of mad people everywhere on TV began to look all too familiar. None of it made any sense in my young bubble. Our family kept trying to figure it out and read between Larry's lines for the answers.

* * *

18-May-68
Saturday
Dear Mom and Dad,

   Received your letter yesterday and was glad to hear from you. You will have to excuse the writing tonight for I am dead tired and can hardly hold the pen. I had to pull the oil cooler out of my ship today, which took 4 ½ hours, and of course I got covered with oil. I have to put it back in tomorrow, and I sure ain't looking forward to it.

   I will be looking forward to the pictures of Jo, and I also want some of you and Dad, and don't forget.

   I hope Maryanne ain't too upset. I did write her a letter about other girls, but she took it wrong. I do care for her very much and love her, but I don't think I can get it across to her. I haven't heard from her for over a month, so I quit writing, but what you said about her liking me in your letter, it makes me feel bad because I hurt her. I am going to write her tonight and hope I can get things straightened out between us. I would like for you, if you will, to see her for me and try to explain to her how I feel about her. Not getting any letters from her is getting me down, and you wouldn't believe how many times I have tore the tent apart after mail call and I didn't get a letter from her.

   I will be coming home sometime between the 1st and 7th. I am coming home with 2 buddy's who live close by. I will be home by the 12th.

   Haven't been doing nothing but working on my helicopter lately. Everything seems to be going wrong with it and it only has 35 hours on it. We only have 3 people that went to cobra school, and I am just learning, so there are only four of us to do all the work on four cobras, plus we have to crew one. That adds up to a lot of work and hours. And to think I got to come back for 6 more months of this.

16. "We Go Where the War Is"

Well, I will close for now. Tell everyone I said hi and hope they are fine.

Love always, Larry

If you order the car now, will it be there by Aug.?

* * *

22-May-68

Dear Mom and Dad,

Just a few lines to say hi and let you know I am still doing fine. Hope everyone at home is the same. Well, it is <u>starting</u> to get hot around here again. Yesterday it was 110 and no wind at all. Today it is hot, but there is a little breeze blowing.

Here are a few newspaper clippings you might like. That 37mm is really something. You should see how big the round is. Also, some of them are radar operated. That is just one of the tricks they got. I thought the fight at Dak-To was bad, but the fight in the valley had it beat by a long shot.

I wrote Maryanne a letter the other night and tried to get things straight with her. I will let you know how things turn out if she writes back. I tried to explain to her that she took the letter wrong, but you know women are.

I have been thinking about when I get out of the Army what I am going to do. I would like to get my own truck and lease it out to some company and doing the driving myself for awhile. I don't think it's a bad idea, but I would have to have someone go in with me. I am going to write Dad and find out some things about it. I just don't think I could make it working on helicopters for the rest of my life. I am sick of them now.

I just now received a letter from you with the paper, is it about the car? I knew it would be high, but I will be able to make the payments. Don't worry about me driving fast when I get home. I am still a kid at heart, but I have learned my lesson from the past about cars, and I ain't about to mess this one up. Besides that, I ain't even sure I can drive it, it's been so long since I have drove a car.

I am really sorry to hear about Lotus dying. As I said in my last letter, I want you to get another one out of my money. I had rather see you have the cat then me get a new car.

That makes me mad about Jo and Peggy. I am going to write them a letter and hope they will listen to me. I would hate to see them start out like I did. I know how big of a mistake I made, and I would hate to see them make the same mistake. I ain't much older than Jo, but I guess since I have been in the Army, and being over here I have grown up some, and I can see how stupid I was.

Well, I will close for now, so I can get a letter out to grandmother. They have got me flying mortar patrol every third night, and I have it from 9:30 to 11:00 & 12:30 to 2:00 tonight. So tell everyone I said hi. Do you want that paper back about the car? If so I will mail it to you.

Love always, Larry 70 some days to go.

If you think you can drive the car, go ahead and try.

* * *

Part Six

Larry didn't know that Mama had tested the Charger. She was happy to put the first 300 miles on the car, especially after his last postscript which read like a dare. It was the least she could do for her son coming home from war with medals, to work out the kinks on the new car and make sure it was ready for him. Plus, she had her own demons to outrun, and maybe that Charger gave her the speed she needed, too.

My sisters fought about everything and nothing. Between the two of them, their monthly cycles, continuous hairdo maintenance and boy troubles, along with Larry's adventures, I got a good glimpse of harsh teenage lessons. They taught me about fighting and standing up for yourself and speaking up about your beliefs, and things that exploded—inside and out. I wasn't sure I ever wanted to grow up.

We buried Lotus Blossom, Mama's beloved Siamese cat, in the front yard under a lotus tree Mama bought and Daddy planted. It would get about six feet tall and serve as home base for wiffle ball games, shedding delicate pink reminders each spring, representing another loss we never discussed.

* * *

27-May-68
Dear Mom and Dad,
    Just a few lines to let you hear from me so you will know I am still doing O.K. Haven't really much to say, but I was just sitting around waiting to fly my last period mortar patrol. I flew from 2:00 to 3:30, now I have it from 5:00 to 6:00. I would go to sleep, but I hate getting up again. I got up late the first period.
    I should have a real good tan when I get home. It's been over 100 the last few days. And I never wear a shirt. Right now, I have a good case of sunburn.
    Well, I got to go for now, will finish tomorrow.

28-May-68
    I received a letter from you today. The one with the picture of Jo in it. She really does look good in that gown. I can understand how you felt about the guy not showing up and all. I feel twice as bad as you do about it. That was about as low as anyone could get and I swear when I get home, whoever he is, he will regret it. It was bad enough he hurt Jo, but hurting you is another thing. As long as I can still fight, there ain't nobody in the world going to hurt my family and get away with it. I guess she didn't go to the prom at all, did she?

16. "We Go Where the War Is"

Well haven't got much more to say, so I will close for now, hoping everyone is find and doing O.K. Write soon.

Love always, Larry

How did Dad feel about the guy not showing up?

* * *

In the days leading up to Joanna's senior prom night, we all shared in the anticipation of the occasion and the house felt lighter for the first time in a long time.

As she transformed her hair, makeup, and wardrobe for the day, my big sister turned into a princess. We all played a part in her preparation. My job was to hand over the bobby pins, and they needed a lot. Mama spent "a pretty penny" on the chiffon, sage green dress. I perked up at the penny reference even though I had resigned myself long ago to give up on receiving any more. Mama ignored my sudden interest and pulled Jo's hair tight into a bun to feature her high cheekbones. That bun looked painful, given fresh memories of the nightly ritual of Mama brushing out "rat's nests" from the back of my head.

When Joanna finished getting ready, she looked royal. She polished off the look when she slid

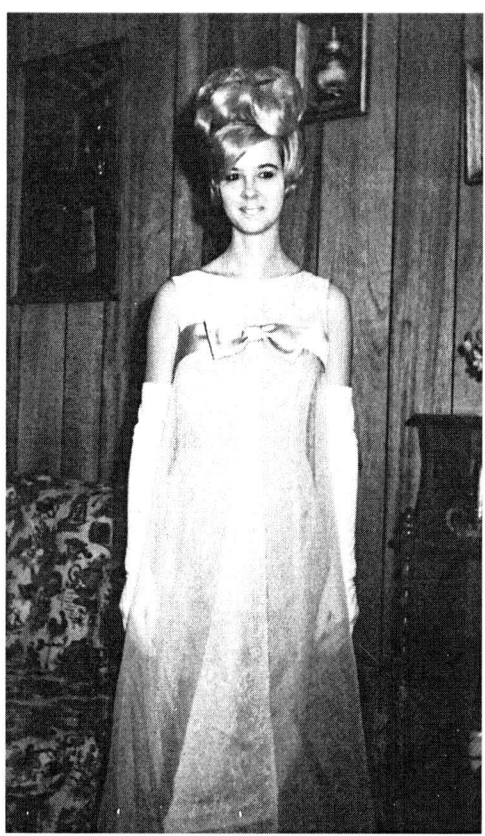

Joanna poses for the camera before her prom date arrives. May 1968, Kendall Park, New Jersey.

on silky white gloves that went all the way to her elbows. Daddy took pictures, Mama took pride, Jo smiled as big as ever, and the Polaroids turned out perfectly. Then, the jerk never came. Her face melted. Black mascara left dark trails down her rosy cheeks, and I saw her cry for the first time in memory, crushed by the realization that he wasn't late. He wasn't coming. She had been stood up. Daddy couldn't handle girl tears, so he promised her a daddy-daughter date that cheered her up. "I will take you to see the Radio City Rockettes in New York City, just you and me."

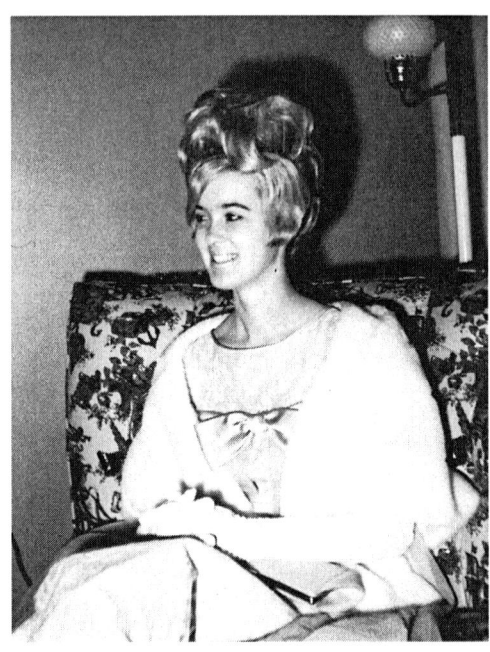

Joanna waits in a stunning fur shawl for a guy who stands her up for the prom. May 1968, Kendall Park, New Jersey.

Daddy's solution lightened everyone's mood, except for Peggy who got mad because she wasn't invited. Daddy reminded her that a prom would happen for her one day. Mama shook her head and bit her tongue; besides her "honesty is the best policy" mantra, she always said "if you can't say anything nice, say nothing at all." So, that's what she did when she stomped out of the room mumbling.

When Larry heard that guy stood up his sister, he wanted to handle things. He figured he would have plenty of fight left in him when he got home to take care of everything and everyone. Our brother was wrong but with the best intentions. That jerk was lucky Larry never found him.

17

"Shove the Mini-Gun"

30-May-68

Dear Mom and Dad,

    Just a few more lines to say hi and let you know everything is O.K. with me. Hope everyone at home is still fine.

    Not really much to say because nothing has happened around here. All I have been doing is working on my helicopter everyday. I flew mortar patrol last night from 8:00 to 9:30. I was lucky and only got one period of it.

    The letter may not be long, but at least it is something to let you hear from me and let you know I am O.K.

Hi Folks (Rico)

    That's my buddy Rico. He should be coming home with me. I got a letter from his mother yesterday, which really surprised me. His wife left him a few weeks ago and his mother wants me to write her and let her know how he is and everything. So I am going to write her today. Don't say anything in your letter about this, ok? He don't know his mother wrote to me.

    Well I am going to close for now so I can write a few more letters. Tell everyone I said hi and hope they are fine. Write soon.

Love always, Larry

    P.S. Your son is now a SP/5. I got my orders yesterday, but I made it May 7th.

* * *

They changed the rules in the middle of Larry's war. First, he was called a patriot and sent to war to serve his country with honor. Then, he was questioned on why he did it. While our young men in uniform clung to the memories back home and the dreams of returning, fighting through hard and long days with that vision in mind, many were answered with "Dear John" letters from their wives and girlfriends. Loneliness took on new meaning in combat.

    Soldiers had to fight in a faraway war and fight their own people back home, too. Their intentions were questioned, their methods

Part Six

were misconstrued, and their reasons for going to war didn't matter among the popular vote. Public opinion turned against the war and soldiers were victimized by a broken system of misinformation.

* * *

31-May-68

Dear Mom and Dad,

Well, here I am again writing a few friends to say hi and let you know I am still okay. I am sending a picture of all of us that were shot down. I will tell you who everyone is when I get home.

Haven't really much to say. I just want to send the picture home before it gets all messed up. Hope everyone is still doing fine. By the way, are you going to have plates on the car when I get home and have it ready for the road for me? If you have to, put it in your name if that's the only way you can get it on the road for me. I will have it changed over when I get home for good in Jan. Also did you save me a few hundred to blow while I am home? I will need it.

Well, I will close for now. Tell everyone I said hi. Write soon.

Love always, Larry

* * *

3-June-68

Dear Mom and Dad,

Received your letter today with the newspaper clipping in it. Was very glad to hear from you.

No, I ain't at Camp Evans, the one that got blowed away. I am about a 20 min. flight north of there. I remember when it happened, cause you could see the flames from up here. I am at a place called LZ Sharon, right outside of the city Quang Tri. We haven't had any trouble here with rockets or mortars in a long time.

I am still doing real good and getting shorter every day. Only two more months to go before I come home. I don't know what day I will be there, but it will be before the 12th. I will most likely call (send me the phone number) when I get to the airport and have you come pick me up.

Did I tell you I got to fly in my new helicopter? I flew in it twice and also tried flying it myself. It is a hole lot different than my old helicopter. It is hard to explain about it in a letter but maybe when I get home I will tell you about it.

I am enclosing two slides of my old helicopter. They were taken on the way back from Da Nang and two days before we got shot down. Also here is a slide of an artillery strike going on. When we left, that village was no longer there.

We have had two real bad rain storms in the past few days. It really cooled things off quite a bit.

17. "Shove the Mini-Gun"

Slide of Huey helicopter over the China Sea, June 1968.

Slide of Huey #58473 over the Central Highland plains, June 1968.

Well no real news, so I will close for now hoping everyone and everything is fine at home. So take care and write soon.

Love always, Larry

* * *

Part Six

While Larry moved around landing zones through artillery strikes in monsoon rains and learned to crew a Cobra, I spent the summer learning to swim without floats and master the game of Marco Polo with the big kids. With the long days of summer, fun in the backyard pool started early, continued well after the dinner hour and made our skin stay wrinkled until they made us go inside at dark. Cousins came to visit every weekend.

The family stayed busy and moved with a lighter step, knowing Larry would be home soon, but we traveled through the house in different ways. Peggy stomped to gain attention or ran to avoid chores. Joanna glided, or maybe it was the walking-on-egg-shells thing she did best, but you rarely heard her or felt her enter a room. Daddy limped and shuffled. Mama somehow moved from room to room in a blink. Me, I mostly skipped and twirled.

* * *

4-June-68
Tuesday
Dear Mom and Dad,

Hope everyone at home is still doing fine. Everything is just fine with me. Everything around here has been real nice and quiet. Not really much to say, I have two pictures I want to mail home so I thought I would write a few lines. I have mortar patrol tonight from 3:00 to 4:30. We might not fly because it is raining and cloudy out.

One of our ships went down today. The engine went and they had to make a forced landing. No one got hurt. The polits did a good job in landing it.
Last night us crew chiefs had a party for one of our polits that left today. You wouldn't believe how much beer we drank. I got to bed around two and got up around 7:00 and I still couldn't walk straight. When we have a party, we really have a party. I think Dad would like some of our parties.

I hope Jo and Peggy quit messing around in school. You know—you never did send me a picture of you and Dad. I am still waiting for it. Well, I best be going for now. I got to get up at 2:30 so I better try and get some sleep. Tell everyone I said hi and hope they are fine. Write soon.

Love alway's, Larry 60 day's

* * *

7-June-68
Friday
Dear Mom and Dad,

17. "Shove the Mini-Gun"

Hope everyone is fine and doing o.k. I am still doing real good and getting shorter every day. I got a letter from Billy Robbins yesterday. He is still doing fine and only has 20 some days left over here. He tried to extend but they wouldn't let him, because he has got too much time over here already. That nut loves it over here.

Haven't got a letter from you in the last few days, but I hope to get one soon. I keep worrying that something may happen at home, and I won't be there. Rich Passer left today to go home. He took his leave early. I gave him your phone number (I hope it was right) and told him to call you for me.

Still nice and quiet around here and that's just the way I like it. I heard on the radio yesterday that Kennedy was shot and killed. I also heard that they got the SOB that did it. Sometimes I think it is safer over here then back in the states. If the people want to kill, send them over here and let them have at it. There's enough NVA running around to last a life time. I think Kennedy would of won this year too.

Well, I will close for now so I can get this in the mail before goes out. Tell every one I said hi and hope they are fine. Write soon.

Love alway's, Larry

* * *

They were talking about something besides the war. Robert Kennedy, President John F. Kennedy's younger brother, was shot to his death, hours after winning the Democratic presidential primary in California and giving his victory speech. The country mourned his death, but also more than the man himself, as they faced the continuation of a war that promised to have no end in sight.

* * *

7-June-68

Hi Dad,

How are things with you? Everything is fine over here at least with me. Nothing much going on around here now. Every thing has been nice and quiet. I ain't usually doing nothing anymore but working on my helicopter and I do just as little work as I can.

I have been thinking alot about getting a truck when I get out of the Army and lease it out and maybe as the years go by, start my own little trucking business. What is your point of view on this? I have got to do something for a living when I get out and one thing for sure it ain't going to be helicopters. I want to talk to you more about it when I get home. I know you have always wanted to get a truck of your own, so maybe between you and me, we can come up with something. I am really serious about this, so give it some thought and let me know what you come up with. You know a lot more about leasing out trucks and all the business part about it than me. Who knows, we might end up with a big business. You never can tell. And as for a driver, you got me. I know it will take alot of money. As soon as I get the car paid off, I am going to save all I can, and I can get a loan from that G.I. bill thing. I don't know how mom will like it, but if you will go along with me, that's going to be my future.

   I am going to send a little story with this letter and what ever you do, don't let mom see it. It is sort of dirty and unfit for a woman to read. You might get a kick out of it. Pass it on to the guys at the shop when you're finished with it.

   Only 59 more days and I will be on the way home and I can't wait. I sure hope we are still going on vacation to N.C. I also am planning on going to Mich. for two days, too. You should see what I got waiting out there. If I showed you her picture you would want to come too.

   Don't forget when I get home we are going to do some beer drinking together.

   I had to go work on my helicopter for a few hours, but I am back now. I only have about two hours before I got to fly mortar patrol. I have it from 8:00–9:45, 11:30–1:15. So I will close for now and as soon as you can, write back and let me know what you think about my plans.

Your son, Larry

* * *

Larry didn't know about Daddy's double vision or headaches. Daddy still couldn't work, and stayed irritated more often, which was out of his character, so we all knew something was wrong. Daddy and Mama never told Larry about the diagnosis and didn't want him to know that his plans for a partnership could never happen. They wanted Larry to keep dreaming, and as long as he did, he would fight to make it home.

* * *

11-June-68
Thursday
Dear Mom and Dad,

   Received your letter and as always was glad to hear from you. I am still doing fine and counting the days. Hope everyone there is the same.

   Not much really to say, cause I haven't been doing nothing but working on my helicopter and flying mortar patrol every third night.

   You can look for me to be home around the 7th. I will be leaving here on the 6th. I will have 30 days leave, but no matter what my orders say it won't start until I step foot in the house, and I might even stay a few days extra. I know more about how the Army works now, and also me being an E5 I can get away with a few extra days. I am going to try and get a 10 or 15 day extension on my leave when I get home. I don't know if I can or not but it is worth a

17. "Shove the Mini-Gun"

try. They cheated me out of some of my leave time the last time I was home, but they ain't going to do it this time. I got a letter from Maryanne yesterday. I wrote her back and hope things work out o.k.

The other day I was helping one of the guys take all the guns and stuff out of his ship, and one of the nails on the ammo box went half way through my wrist. I was lucky it didn't hit the vein, but it came close. It is really sore now. It didn't hurt when it happened, but looking at it sticking in my wrist sort of gave me the chills. The way it was bleeding, I thought for sure it hit a vein.

Well I am going to close for now. Tell everyone I said hi and hope they are fine. 56 days and I will be on my way. Write soon.

Love alway's, Larry

* * *

Mama didn't like the sight of blood, and so I didn't either. A nail through his wrist, the thought of a broken vein, or blood pouring from his arm would bring Mama to her knees, and surely, she didn't read these details. If she had, I would have pictured Larry as a mystical figure, right up there with Jesus, like matching heroes on a pair of crosses. Their similarities would have made sense. They both suffered to help other people. Both tried to help the sickest, poorest people and the children. Both were in Vietnam, I was led to believe. Larry was coming home, I was told. I wasn't so sure about Jesus.

* * *

15-June-68
Saturday morning
Dear Mom and Dad,

I ain't doing nothing but sitting around so I thought I would write a few lines. Haven't done anything all morning except unjam my mini gun and load up 19 rockets.

Yesterday I took a ride to Camp Evans in a Jeep. It takes 20 min. by helicopter and we made it down there in 35 min and made it back in 30. We had a fast jeep, plus we had a trailer on the back. Only one big section of Evans got blown away that night. The main food, ammo, and fuel supply place. Charlie really did a good job on it. I got a few pictures of it, and some pictures of one of the 37mm guns.

Not really much to say 'cause I ain't doing nothing but laying around all day. Hope everyone is fine. I am still doing O.K. and only 51 more days to go before I am on my way home. Next month all us crew chiefs are going to have a party that is going to be out of the world. All of us old crew chiefs will be gone home by the 10th of Aug.

I had a big argument this morning with one of the polits. I told him he could

Part Six

shove the mini gun you know where and to make sure it was after he just fired 6,000 rounds so it would be nice and hot. There ain't no need to fire the gun on a G.A.P. but they do it anyway. It is a pain loading 6,000 rounds with only 1,000 round belts of ammo.

Well I am going to go so I can eat lunch and get a few hours sleep. So tell everyone I said hi and will see them soon. Write soon.

Love alway's, Larry

* * *

Camp Evans was one of the largest base camps in the country. Established by the U.S. Marines two years prior, the First Cavalry moved in when the Marines moved north to Quang Tri in early 1968. On the night of May 19, 1968, the ammunition dump at the camp was hit by a couple of NVA rockets, causing a chain reaction of weapons and aircraft fires, and massive explosions. Tents were blown away, bunkers collapsed and the ground shook with fireballs overhead, for hours. Over 10 million rounds of ammunition were destroyed, rendering the First Cavalry combat division ineffective for an entire week until new aircraft and ammo arrived. It was the date of Ho Chi Minh's 78th birthday and undoubtedly a special gift to himself, after years of trying to infiltrate the area. He used our own military strength against us, and it worked. Until we rebuilt, restocked, and plugged all the holes, again.

* * *

17-June-68
Monday night
Dear Mom and Dad,

Hi, just a few lines to say hi and let you know I am still doing okay. Hope everyone at home is fine too. Things are still nice and quiet around here.

I still haven't been doing nothing but laying around all day. The past two days I cleaned up my helicopter so I can take a few pictures of it. Here is a picture of one of the others we have. I don't know who the guy is, but I think it is the crew chief.

I haven't heard from Maryanne lately so I don't know what's going to happen between us. I have been writing her every day so I hope to hear from her soon.

Yesterday was Father's Day and I didn't think of it until now. So tell Dad I said happy late Father's Day.

I haven't really got much to say 'cause I don't do nothing anymore. I am going to town one of these days and pick up some stuff to send home. I know

17. "Shove the Mini-Gun"

you would never wear what I get but at least it is something that came from over here.

By the time you get this letter school should be out and I hope Jo made it.

Well I will close for now cause I can't think of anything else to say. Tell everyone I said hi and will see them soon.

Love always, Larry 49 Days Left

* * *

18-June-68
Monday night

Dear Mom and Dad,

Just received a letter from you and as always was very glad to hear from you. Glad to hear you got to go swimming. It must feel good to swim in a nice clean pool. The only place we got here is a lake. But it still feels good to go swimming there. That's OK about not sending the books. I am getting too short to start a big book anyway.

Now, about this girl Lynn, why didn't you send me her address? If Maryanne ain't got guts enough to tell me she is going out, then I don't think she can be trusted. She told me about that guy Joe, too, and if she is going out with him, then it is OK with me, because I don't care. So how about tell Lynn to write or send me her address. Who know, I may get to like her.

Things are still nice and quiet around here and I still ain't doing nothing but laying around all day. Well only 48 more days now. So be home the 5th to 8th of Aug waiting for my call. Why don't you invite Lynn over on the 8th for supper, then I can get to meet her. I guess you know I got to change my ways alot before I come home. I would hate to act the way I do now at home. I would most likely get locked up.

Well, I will close for now. I got one more letter to get out before I take a shower. So tell everyone I said hi and hope they are fine. See you in no later than 50 days.

Love always, 48 day's

Larry

Tell Lynn I said hi.

* * *

Friday
21-June-68

Dear Mom and Dad,

Just received a letter from you and as always was glad to get it. Hope everyone is still doing fine I am still doing good as ever.

Glad to hear Jo has got a job. I hope she likes it and stays there for a while. Now she will be able to get her a car and you won't have to worry about her using yours.

Part Six

Things got kind of bad around here yesterday. About 4:30 Charlie blew Dong Ha off the map. It was still burning at 8 o'clock this morning. We even got hit last night. That was the first time in weeks. He got just a little too close for my liking's last night. When I heard dirt and stuff hit the tent, I made it for the bunker.

I read a paper that came down from div. today, that said Honia said they could beat us without any outside help. So I don't guess the war will be over for a while. In my point of view, I think they are going to try another Tet Offense. If they do, I hope they wait for 45 1/2 more days before they start.

Have you heard any more about the car? Do you still have the two same cars?

You have really got me wondering about this girl Lynn. You are going to have to tell me more about her.

This morning we had a rifle inspection, which of course I failed. Then I was working on my buddy's helicopter and I found something wrong with it, that may have saved someone's life. Then at 1:00 I had to go to another rifle inspection, which I also failed. I got the Sarge so mad he cleaned it for me and told me to get lost. Now I am sitting out next to my helicopter with a blanket stretched over my head keeping the sun off me. I am supposed to paint two cav. patches on my helicopter, but I told them I won't do it until they get me some spray paint. We are supposed to have some top brass come down today, and the Major told me to act like I was working for a change, so you can see what I am doing now.

Well, that's about it for now, so I guess I will close. Tell everyone I said hi and will see them soon.

Love always, Larry 45 1/2 Days

* * *

North Vietnamese gunners hit Dong Ha, another Marine ammunition supply point, with six 152 mm self-propelled, high explosive howitzer rounds, each strong enough to decimate an armored vehicle. They destroyed all the ammo. Explosions continued throughout the area for hours. In total, over 10,000 tons of ammo and 20 days' worth of supplies were lost in the attack. As he counted down the days to go home in increments of half days now, this would have been too close for comfort for my brother's "short" status, jumpy legs, and shaky hands.

* * *

2-July-68

Dear Mom and Dad,

Received a letter from you or two I should say, one with the two pictures and the other with the paper in it. I haven't wrote in the last week or so

17. "Shove the Mini-Gun"

because I was down at Da Nang having fun. My fun ended the last day, I got throwed in jail.

They sent me to Da Nang to get over my attitude problem, which people seem to think I have. I did have a good time the first four days I was there. I spent two days with Billy. Also two nights. He has only got about 6 more days to go now. He has got a son over here, which he goes to see a lot. The last day I got picked up because I didn't have any orders to be in Da Nang. They took my 38 pistol away from me also. I stayed in jail all night and some sgt. signed for me.

Today I went back down with the major to get my 38 back and couldn't get it. The major just got all kinds of mad. I don't know why, but lately I just can't seem to stay out of trouble. Before I get home, I might be an SP/4 again. Every body is trying to get me busted and the only bad thing about it is, I haven't had time to do anything wrong yet. Today I got jumped on because I had buttons on my shirt undone. I am supposed to take over plt. sgt. in July but the captain said if I don't shape up I will be an SP/4 again.

Not really much going on around here. From what I hear now we are moving south in Sept.

I don't care if you drive my car, but it's going to be hell on gas. Don't forget you have two 4-barrels, which is the same as 8 carburetors. And yes, I will be coming in Newark airport and bring my car. I don't think I sent them pictures last time so I will send them this time plus a few more.

Well, that's about it for now. So, I will close for now. Tell everyone I said hi and will see them soon. 35 days and I leave here.

Love alway's, Larry

* * *

Mama used the back of this letter to practice writing Daddy's name using her own signature. The last page is filled with almost a dozen versions of "Smith, Kenneth V" scattered at all angles. I wonder if she was practicing her forgery skills for a purpose. Perhaps to bail her son out of jail. Perhaps to buy another baby under cover.

* * *

14-July-68

Dear Mom and Dad,

Received your letter about two days ago with the picture of the two cats in it. I don't get much of a chance to write anymore or do anything.

Hope everyone is still fine and doing ok. As for me, I am still doing ok and counting the days. Only 20 more before I get on the big silver bird and 18 before I leave the field and go back to An Khe.

Two nights ago we lost three more men and one helicopter. The ship crashed and exploded right after take off. The best we can tell is the engine

Part Six

blew up. All three guys burnt to death and no one could get close to the ship to try and help them because of the rockets and M60 rounds going off. It was really sickening hearing them screaming and no one could help them. It is one hell of a way to die.

Every one of the crew chiefs except two leave within 25 days, and two nights from now we are going to have the biggest party anyone has ever seen. A lot of the polits are getting us beer and maybe some hard stuff. Right now the guys are having a match fight, throwing lighted matches at each other. It is just a normal night in the tent. Every night we are doing some stupid thing. This tent ain't nothing but a big nut house. Ain't none of us sane anymore.

Well I best be going for now before I get burnt up. So tell everyone I said hi and will be home soon.

Love always, Larry

* * *

Larry never realized the power of his mistaken metaphors. Mama, the master of reading the lines and in between them, would not have missed the irony of his words, or the hidden pain within them. She read more books than ever, and they piled up on the shelf in our den. She had grown cynical of war talk and needed the escape. She retreated to her bedroom often, and I never disturbed her once that door shut at the end of the hall.

Larry rarely shared the names of his fallen friends. When one of the unit's helicopter engines failed on take-off, resulting in a crash right beside landing zone Sharon, Larry heard their screams. One of the three men killed in the crash was Eldin Marion Tapp, and they called him "goop dog" around the base camp. When John McLaughlin, another door gunner, woke up sick on this fateful date, Eldin had volunteered to fill in for him. John later honored his friend with this poem:

> It was the 12th of July 1968
> The morning it was early
> Or the night it was late
> The 12th of July 1968.
> It may have been luck
> Or it may have been fate
> When I survived the 12th of July 1968.
> I was standing there watching
> As the other three died
> On the 12th of July 1968.

17. *"Shove the Mini-Gun"*

> They went down in flames
> One of them in my place
> I know it's a shame
> But I can't see his face.
> But I will never forget Marion Tapp
> Or the date
> The 12th of July 1968.
>
> —John McLaughlin, Jr.

* * *

17-July-68

Dear Mom and Dad,

  Just received a letter from you and as always was glad to hear from you. Well in 20 days from now I will be home.

  I hope the car gets there this month. Has Dad called about it? If it won't be there by the time I get home, cancel it because I don't see any need of it coming any later than August.

  You don't have to fix up the house just because I am coming home. I am only your son, not the president. I will do some painting for you if you want me to, but my hands ain't as steady as they used to be, so I wouldn't be able to paint in hard places.

  I am going to a party in Pennsylvania sometime in Aug. Some of us guys that were together over here (all crew chiefs) are going to get together. We had our party last night, which turned out real good and as usual I had to fly mortar patrol. I had a little trouble making it out to the helicopter but I finally made it. I am glad I didn't have to use the machine gun because I don't think I could of even loaded it right.

  Don't write any letters that will get here after Aug 1st cause I am leaving the field the 2nd. I got two pictures of me having the medals pinned on. I ain't going to send them, just carry them home with me. I was going to buy some stuff to bring home, but they messed up my pay this month and I didn't get paid.

  Well I am going for now, so tell everyone I said hi and will be home soon, real soon.

Love alway's, Larry

* * *

18

"I Blew It by Extending"

He wrote and wrote and wrote. He wrote home, to extended family, to girlfriends, and even to neighbors whose names he didn't remember. The letters had kept him grounded until he could make it back to the states. And like he promised us, he did make it home in August 1968 on the 5th of the month. We welcomed Larry home with open arms and the car of his dreams.

* * *

26-July-68

Dear Mom and Dad,

    Just a few lines to say hi and let you know I am OK. Hope everyone at home is still the same. I haven't heard from you in a few days so I hope everyone is fine. This is going to be my last letter home, it should get there before I do. I should be home in 10 or 11 days from today. I might be home on the 5th but if not, it will be the 6th.

    I will leave V.N. on the 5th and get to Washington on the 5th too. If I get there on the morning of the 5th, I will be home some time that afternoon. If I hadn't of extended I would be home within 5 days from now, but I blew it by extending.

    Well I am going to close for now. I have about 5 more letters to write before I have to go back to work. So tell everyone I said hi and will see them soon.

Love always, Larry

* * *

In twelve months of letters, Larry mentioned a car at least 21 times. The new Charger would welcome him home like nothing else could. Daddy picked him up at the Newark airport in a 1968 Dodge Charger R/T with a 426 Hemi, dual 4 BBL with a 4-speed transmission, dark green top, light yellow/cream exterior, and black leather bucket seats with a console. Just as the brave soldier ordered.

18. "I Blew It by Extending"

My sisters and I baked cookies and helped Mama decorate the house with streamers, balloons, and flags. I lined all my pennies on the front table, so he could see how our bets paid off. He needed to see that I had protected the prized coins, falling far short of filling up my piggy bank, but still worthy of the front table positioning. The silver coins surrounded the copper forces like an army of their own, pulling rank.

When Larry pulled his new Charger into the driveway, he couldn't miss the huge "Welcome Home" banner on the front of our house. It marked the end of his first tour of duty. We were all elated and felt a release of tension that had built up in the house. We were ready to celebrate and spoil him. But nothing felt the same. Nothing would ever be the same.

For the next 30 days of R&R, we didn't see much of my brother. Without crutches or bandages, or physical injuries, we assumed he was "just fine." He slept late and spent his days with friends outside of the house, driving his car as much as possible. When he was home, he was quiet, pensive, and moody. We were told to leave him alone. I yearned for his hugs and wanted to jump on his back, but Mama told me to wait for him to initiate physical contact. I didn't understand and nobody could explain it because they didn't understand either. We used hushed tones. Mama had to wake Larry up using the handle of a broom, so he wouldn't hurt her by accident when he woke up swinging. In his dreams, the enemy remained. He had invisible guns in his arms, prepared to use them.

After a short time at home, Larry's second tour of duty started in September 1968, after he and Barry Brady went to Pennsylvania to attend the wedding of John Stewart. It would be the last time all three men saw each other in person. Our family had another painful goodbye, this time in the driveway. Larry didn't wear a uniform, and we didn't take pictures. You wouldn't know he was a soldier; he hid all signs of it and didn't even take his Army-issued bags. He drove himself to the station, and our father went with him. Larry didn't promise to write this time. He still told us to expect him home in one piece, in a short six months, and he promised to stay safe. He didn't seem as sure this time, and he never promised any letters, pennies or presents for me.

Part Six

No letters arrived. Mama worried during his entire extension, more than ever. She didn't know how he was doing or where he was located, so she couldn't send mail or packages. She made several calls to the Army Headquarters and tried to get a military neighbor's help with some answers. She wore out the kitchen floor some more, dragging the corded phone back and forth. Mama mastered her new habit of twirling and untwirling the phone cord, even with shaky hands that balanced a lit cigarette or glass of tea. She took pills, now. Lots of little pink pills.

We purchased our first artificial Christmas tree in 1968, so we could leave it up and decorated for him. His gifts waited under the tree. Like his place at the dinner table, Mama insisted that everything stay in order and be the same as Christmas Day when Larry got home for good. Daddy tried to convince her to stop worrying, and that "no news is good news" when it came to the U.S. Army.

Larry wouldn't find out for months, but Butch was killed in action 14 days before Larry's last mention of him in May. After arriving in Vietnam in early March, his time in service was cut short during the Battle of Phuoc Yen, near the city of Hue. He served with A Company, 1st Battalion 502nd Airborne Infantry with the 101st Airborne. At the end of the battle, 107 NVA surrendered, marking the largest number surrendering to an American unit of the entire war. Butch and three others were hit by an RPG (rocket-propelled grenade), and he passed away in the helicopter on the way to the hospital. In total, fewer than 10 men were killed in action from A Company, and 33 wounded.

Larry was sick of foreign lands and all he wanted was to be home and done with Vietnam. He altered his leave paperwork and forged an earlier departure date home. Late one night in January 1969, at an hour when the phone didn't usually ring unless there was bad news, Joanna predicted, "That's Larry calling," and she was right. Mama answered before the second ring and Larry said, "Mom, I'm coming home."

Her face softened and her shoulders sank. Tears cascaded down her cheeks. She threw her head back, wiped her eyes, and touched each of us as if to count us like blessings, and went to wake up Daddy

18. "I Blew It by Extending"

with a light skip I had never seen. The whole house exhaled, and even my sisters hugged.

We were told not to question Larry when he got home. Mama knew he would not be ready to talk about things. I don't remember any cookies, or welcome home sign, or reporters. Mama did ask him about letters, thinking the post office might have lost them. Larry lowered his chin. "No, I couldn't write. I tried, so many times, I did. I'm sorry." That's all we ever got about his second tour. There are no stories, medals, letters, slides, or tapes. The first deployment took all he had to give.

Mama made us give Larry extra time alone, so he could unwind, and said he would come around soon, like she told us six months earlier. It wasn't that easy. He clammed up. He never wanted to talk about Vietnam, or much of anything else, ever again. Playing a game, or music, or a ride to the moon was out of the question.

* * *

"Welcome Home" banner makes headlines as Larry ends his first deployment. Left to right: Peggy, Smitty, the family dog, Tracy and Larry's Dodge Charger in the driveway. June 1968, Kendall Park, New Jersey.

Part Six

Larry cut things off with Maryanne soon after returning home, telling us no details. That Lynn girl never panned out; she had been a passing conversation about a neighbor's daughter. One day in April of 1969, two months after his active war service ended, his love life would take a drastic turn. Daddy invited Larry to join him for a beer at the local pub. "Ed and Joe's" on Route 1 was a roadside dive bar close to our neighborhood, where I learned to drink Shirley Temples and shoot pool.

Larry during his second deployment, somewhere in South Vietnam, October 1968 (credit Richard Passer).

I could wiggle on the swiveling bar stool so long as I kept our date a secret from Mama. Daddy was a regular there, and I wanted more than anything to be one, too.

Daddy waited for Larry and Larry's friend Phil to join him. He started up a conversation with a nice young lady at the bar named Marlene Schedeneck after she put quarters on his pool table. By the time she took the first two games, they bet $5 on who would win the next game of 8-ball and became friends. Daddy racked the balls just as Larry arrived.

He asked Marlene, "Do you think this is my son or my brother?" She rolled her eyes, guessing he was his son. Daddy beamed with pride as he introduced him. "This is Larry. Larry, this is Marlene. She's from Edison. He's fresh out of Vietnam, and we're really proud of him."

Daddy gave them a minute to say hello and then added, "Marlene

18. "I Blew It by Extending"

Left to right: Larry in his second deployment when no letters were written, with Richard Leroue, Richard Passer, John McLaughlin, and "Sergeant Pops," October 1968 (credit Richard Passer).

here's a good Catholic girl that cusses like a sailor, and she's damn good at running a pool table." Marlene couldn't take her eyes off the handsome young man as she fumbled her words and scratched on the white ball. Daddy winked at her and smiled that endearing crooked smile of his.

Marlene and Larry dated for seven days. Then they got married a week later after knowing each other for 14 days. They had already decided to live together despite both pairs of old-fashioned parents being opposed. When Marlene's mother suggested they

Part Six

marry instead she didn't think they would go through with it. Before Larry had to leave for Georgia to finish his duty out at Fort Stewart, they went to Edison and sealed the deal in the Middlesex County courthouse.

Because he was under 21 years of age, our parents had to give permission for Larry to get married. The men outnumbered Mama again. But at least this time, signing the papers didn't feel like giving her son permission to die. She agreed, against her better judgment.

On their wedding night, Marlene and Larry stayed at our house, and Mama put Maryanne's 8 × 10 framed portrait on the nightstand beside their bed. She may have signed her approval for the marriage, but that didn't mean she had to like it.

My brother survived the tragedy of the Vietnam War. He got the fast car of his dreams. He met the woman of his heart's desire and married her. He rode off into the sunset in his Dodge Charger, ponytail flying. I would love the story more if Larry's war could end there.

19

I PROMISE YOU

His eyes cannot lie. The pleas in his stare grow weaker, as he is ready to give up. It is your final visit. You tell him everything. "You know I found your buddies, right? So many remember you and gave me precious memories, stories of your time as friends in Vietnam. Barry Brady, John Stewart, Rick Leroue, and your best friend of all, Rich Passer. They all loved you so much and told me stories about serving with you."

You feel a pulse in his hand get stronger. Did he wince? You show him the black and white picture of the eight Cavalry soldiers who were shot down in Happy Valley, and he looks right at it. He doesn't move his eyes off the picture.

"I know you hear me, and I know you know this picture, and remember the story. When I found Rich, we got on the phone together, and he has been looking for you his whole life. He told me everything, Larry. He told me about Charlie. Alvarez." He looks back at you, back at the picture, and back again, with more activity than you've seen in weeks from his tired eyes.

"Charlie didn't suffer, Larry. And he didn't deserve it, just like you didn't. I know the story, about you and Ronnie Dunn in the back seat that day. I know that Charlie Alvarez took the bullet for you. I know how blood destroys magnesium, and how you never stopped doing your job. Even that day and moments after the blood of your friend showered you. You wanted to escort his body home and tell his family the truth. I know that not being able to tell them everything haunted you, so I found them, and they know Charlie's brave story. I told them everything and they told me all about Charlie. They are at peace about his sacrifice, and you should be too.

Part Six

"Let it go. Please let the memories of that day go. Release them. The dark days are long gone, and you did the best you could to help him. You've held it in much too long. Your secret suffering is out, and you know that the truth sets you free. So be free."

Painfully slow, he closes his eyes. In a half an instant, he opens them again and looks at you with half-open eyelids ready to shut down, like the memories that haunt him. Without saying a thing, Larry shows gratitude for your words and softens his gaze in affection.

He's had enough. You've all had enough. His weary eyes rest on pillows of swollen skin beneath them as he sleeps the nights and days away. When he does wake up, his eyes are bloodshot, and his gaze looks resigned. Less manic, more resolved to giving up, but the same message comes across. *Get me out of here.*

On August 5 your brother Larry releases his last tragic breath. It was the same date of his first letter from Vietnam, 33 years prior.

PART SEVEN

20

"Still Have a Long Way to Go"

> Some of the critics viewed Vietnam as a morality play in which the wicked must be punished before the final curtain and where any attempt to salvage self-respect from the outcome compounded the wrong. I viewed it as a genuine tragedy. No one had a monopoly on anguish.—Henry A. Kissinger

Marlene adored Larry and devoted her life to loving him. She saw magic in his eyes and they had a playful, loving relationship. She teased him when he acted goofy, which was often, and called him Baby Huey. Not after the ship, after the cartoon character who kept her laughing as a child. Marlene became a victim to those days of post-combat trauma and supported my brother in the aftermath of his service.

Larry did not have a violent bone in his broken body. However, when he dreamed of his enemies, he woke up swinging, ready to attack. In his mind, he slept in a tree in the Happy Valley, in muddy foxholes, and inside his bloody helicopter while his body lay tossing in their marital bed. Marlene changed many pairs of soaking bedsheets from his night sweats. In the morning, she used a broom handle to nudge him awake, just like Mama warned her to.

They shared a lifetime of love and laughter, despite the challenges. They went on to raise their children in the same home that we grew up in. My parents sold him the house after his days in the service once we moved to North Carolina to live out Daddy's final days. Because he promised Daddy to take care of it, Larry never left that humble family home. He always kept his promises, at least when the world let him.

20. "Still Have a Long Way to Go"

Marlene met some of Larry's Vietnam buddies in the early months of their marriage, including Barry Brady and Rich Passer. Rich visited my brother and his new bride in Georgia where they lived in base housing on Fort Stewart to finish up Larry's military days. Rich was stationed at Hunter Army Airfield in Savannah, Georgia, 40 miles away. Their pranks continued. On one visit, Rich asked Larry if he wanted to try some delicious homemade chicken and handed him a sandwich. Larry took a big bite, before realizing it was a sandwich full of live maggots. After he stopped vomiting, he admitted that Rich got the last laugh.

Rich remembered car engine parts lying in the middle of the compact living room and Larry's ongoing desire to take engines apart and modify them. They could never be fixed enough or fast enough.

Marlene didn't let the boys have all the fun. When she assured the guys she could handle the explosive power of the Charger as well as they could, Rich challenged her to a race. She said, "Let's make it the girls against the guys' race," and she and Rich's wife jumped in the Dodge. Larry and Rich drove Rich's Ford Mustang, and they raced each other on a stretch of road in the back of the Army post. Marlene "charged past" those boys in the Ford, proving her worth behind the wheel. She could hold her own. And she would need those muscles to get through the next several years with my brother. Soon, Rich and Larry lost touch and never reunited.

Many years after the war, Larry collected all his long guns and turned them into the local police department. When Marlene asked him why, he didn't explain. He admitted that he felt safer knowing they were not in his reach. He suffered his truth in silence. He was strong enough to surrender when he needed to.

After a couple decades of hard living and a lifetime of fast driving in muscle cars and Harley motorcycles (at some point he joined the Bandettas biker group), my brother settled down and turned to a life of giving back to his community. As an active member of the VFW Post 9111 and an assistant scoutmaster for over a decade, Larry surrounded himself with service-minded veterans and scouts. He helped boy scouts navigate their place in the troop. In a group setting, he sought out the young boys who didn't seem to fit in or those who sat quietly detached from the others. He related to their struggle and listened well. Larry never missed a meeting, campout, or event and took over leadership of the troops' involvement with the service organization "Order of the Arrow." One of those boy scouts and his father were the only ones to ever see Larry's Army decorations. They were never found in his belongings and were rumored to have been burned. By Larry.

He gave all he had to give. He lived a tough life and died a tough death. It was so unfair. His suffering was our suffering, and it was brutal. I have plenty to blame for his heart being broken in five places. Not just the fault of the military, or mistakes by mankind, or faulty medicine, or the fallacy of anesthesia. The trauma of silence killed my brother day by day. Larry's memorial service was peaceful and simple as he would have wanted. I managed to give his eulogy looking out into the room full of VFW members, Boy Scouts, and troop leaders whom Larry had served with in his final days. My heart swelled seeing the love for my brother in that room and I proudly realized that so many others considered him their hero, too.

* * *

21

In Memory of Charlie

> We who have seen war, will never stop seeing it.
> In the silence of the night,
> we will always hear the screams.
> —Joe Galloway

Charlie Alvarez's story would not have been possible without the blessing of his brother Edward Alvarez and the tales of his friend Holly Tureen. First-hand knowledge of the day's trauma shared by Captain Robert Blackmon, Richard Passer, and Ronnie Dunn (via Greg Bronder) informed the account that follows. Charlie's sacrifice will never be forgotten.

Larry never spoke a word about Friday, February 16, 1968, or anything about the new pilot, Charlie. This single combat mission killed the boy inside my brother. But it should be honored. When the day arrived, it was at the height of the Tet Offensive, and Larry had been flying non-stop. He was exhausted but on deck.

Charles Alvarez arrived in An Khe unannounced in the second week of February 1968. As the company clerk, Greg Bronder kept all records, handled the mail, oriented new soldiers and greeted all incoming officers. He recalls Warrant Officer Alvarez's arrival:

> I was back in An Khe working out of the orderly room again with Wally Miller. It was about February 11th, and I had just come back from my daily mail run to the APO. Miller and I sorted the mail and were getting ready for "beer thirty." The day was warm and sunny and the two of us were the only people back at the "A" battery that day. When I looked out the orderly room front screen door, I saw a Jeep pulling up with two soldiers. When they came into the orderly room, I noticed that one was a private and the other was a warrant officer. The private had a black armband that said something like "Airport Liaison." ... The warrant officer handed me his orders and confirmed that he had been assigned to "A" battery 2/20 and was in the right place.

Part Seven

Bronder welcomed Warrant Officer Charles Alvarez with a handshake, adding his sincere apologies. "I sure am sorry for not picking you up at the airstrip, Sir. We had no notification of your arrival," Bronder explained after checking the paperwork. Enlisted men showed up at all hours and days without warning, but Bronder knew anytime a higher rank was expected to arrive.

"No problem, I'm glad to be here now and ready to go to work." Charlie's smile reassured them he had checked his ego back in the states.

Charles Allen Alvarez, 12-23-46 to 2-16-68 (credit Edward Alvarez).

Bronder continued, "For the next four days, either me or Miller here will drop you off in the morning around 0900 hours. There's a required orientation class for all new personnel in the First Air Cavalry. It's different than all the rest. We will pick you up each day around 1600 hours."

Officer Alvarez smiled, nodded his approval of the plan, respecting the rules of his new unit. Bronder checked the clock on the wall and started packing up his desk, filing away the orders in the file cabinet.

"But for today, Sir, it's beer thirty and we gotta go. If you care for a drink, the Officer's Club is over there," Bronder pointed in the direction where the "brass" gathered before dinner.

"We are going to the EM club for a beer. Chow is at 1730 hours. We will see you then, um, unless you care to grab a beer?" Bronder asked, wanting to give the "FNG" the respect that his pilot wings

21. In Memory of Charlie

earned him, but also offer him the chance to fit in with his guys in the trenches.

Alvarez chose the trenches. Bronder and Miller knew after a couple of beers with Charlie, which he insisted they call him, that the A Battery lucked out in getting a top-notch pilot and an overall good guy. His jolly smile matched his upbeat attitude, and both would be a welcome change in the war-torn base camp.

For the next few days, Bronder drove Charlie to and from the training facility and then to "beer thirty" time before dinner. Evenings were spent with popcorn and a movie on the outdoor screen or playing penny ante poker in the barracks. Bronder and Miller filled Charlie in on all the guys he would be flying with and specifically the crew chiefs who would be crewing his chopper.

"Stewart—He's the tall one, barely fits in the back. Too nice for this war. He does what he's asked and gets along with everyone. Brady—Smart guy. Smart ass, too. Loyal to a fault. A good crew chief that will not let you down. Funny, too. Passer—Jewish kid, knows his ship. And his shit. All the pilots love Richie. He's a jokester. The most experienced here, and always hanging with that Smitty kid. Smitty—the quiet small dude, married to his ship. A bit of a chip on his shoulders. A nice guy who will always have your back and keeps his bird in the air. If he's on the ground, he's writing letters or waiting on mail call."

Crew chiefs grew accustomed to pilots coming and going, sometimes before they could recall their names. Everyone knew Charlie as soon as he arrived and teased him for his untimely name. It was his pearly white smile, framed by warm brown skin tones from his Hispanic heritage, that left an impression on anyone he met. He seemed genuinely happy to be going to combat.

You wouldn't know from the joy Charlie exuded that his young life had been full of tragedy. He grew up in California in a large family of six children. His older brother, Eddie, was closest in age, and they did everything together as children. Eddie and Charlie's old friend Holly still honor his service and sacrifice by sharing his story.

Charlie's mother, Henrietta, was hit by a car in San Diego when Charlie was a young boy and died in Eddie's arms a week later. The family lost the heart of their home, and it changed the course of their lives. Henrietta's sister, Tia Berta, became the legal guardian to Charlie and Eddie, along with brothers David and Danny and sisters Geri, Judy, and Dina. "Aunt Tia" raised 12 children in total, six of her own and six of her sister's children. God bless her.

The blended family spent their younger days in Lakeside, California, at the Cactus Ranch, building trails and forts through cactus plants, and in Lakeside and Santee, where Eddie started primary school. Charlie, a most curious child, insisted that Eddie tell him all about his kindergarten lessons the minute he came home from school. He greeted him with a bounce in his step and plenty of questions.

"What did you do today, Eddie? And then what? Show me how to do that!" Charlie wanted all the details, and Eddie shared what he learned with his precocious little brother to feed his curiosity. Eddie has fond memories of a simple childhood.

"We played a lot of kids' games—Red Rover, Hide and Seek, Cowboys and Indians, Army War Games, and Dirt Clog Fights, stuff like that. It was fun growing up together. We would go to the river in the spring and wade to check out the beavers. Charlie always wanted to go underwater and check out the beaver houses to see if any beavers were home. He craved adventure and wanted answers to endless questions.

"We moved to Grantville, where we played Cowboys and Indians a lot. One time we were practicing being rodeo cowboys and roping steers. Charlie was the header and would rope me over my head, I was the heeler and would rope his ankles. It was my turn to rope, and he jogged slowly past me, and I roped his ankles just as Dad came home and hollered at us. I turned around to address Dad, the rope tightened, and Charlie fell flat on his face. Luckily, he wasn't hurt. Our Dad chewed us both out. I asked Charlie if he was okay, he said yes, and we both laughed about it—needless to say we never played that game again."

Eddie described his brother as "the best of us" Alvarez kids. After high school, the brothers went their own way. Charlie visited his brother at a few fraternity house parties during Eddie's college

21. In Memory of Charlie

days. On one visit after basic training, Charlie told Eddie that what he wanted more than anything was to become a helicopter pilot.

Eddie was proud of his brother joining the Army. When he expressed concern about him going to Vietnam, Charlie assured his brother that he was looking forward to it, if that's where the Army needed him to be. Charlie's oldest brother David had enlisted in the Army when Charlie was young, and Charlie's brother-in-law Charles was a Marine whose service Charlie admired as well. He followed their example and enlisted in the Army.

The young patriot embraced all that being a United States Army Officer meant and he wore the pilot uniform and stripes proudly. Before Charlie left for Vietnam, he told his Aunt Tia that he felt certain he would not be returning. Somehow, he knew his service would begin and end in Vietnam. Charlie Alvarez had arrived in Vietnam two weeks before the Tet attacks and had seen a month of action without any direct battle exposure. Until the day he flew with my brother.

* * *

On Friday morning, Charlie woke early to prepare his gear. As the co-pilot he would be at the controls and in charge of the flight, his first "fire mission" flight in Vietnam. While pilot training looked different with rockets and mortars coming and going, Charlie was ready and prepared for the task. Bronder loaded the gear and baggage into the jeep, drove Charlie to the flight line and waited for his gunship to arrive.

As the Huey approached the landing, Bronder pointed to it and said, "There's your ride Sir, the A Battery flying ship is all yours." With the blades still rotating and dust swirling around them, Bronder loaded the officer's bags onto the ship, and waved it off as it rose back into the air with Charlie at the controls. And Larry right behind him.

Pilots and crew chiefs constantly exchanged flight details and took respectful direction from each other. Pilots realized that a good crew chief held tight reins on the ship's performance and knew the machine better than anyone else in those four seats. Likewise, all crew members appreciated that whoever held the flight controls controlled their destiny and needed to be good at their job and hyper focused on it. Alvarez may have questioned Larry on a maintenance issue or challenged him about the ship's abilities, or Larry could have asked the pilot to back off on the ship if he was running it too hard. Larry often butted heads with the front row of his ship when they thought they knew the ship better than he did. His alliance was to that Huey, first and foremost.

The four-man crew on this day's Huey gunship run included Aircraft Commander Lieutenant (later Captain) Robert Blackmon as the pilot and Warrant Officer (co-pilot) Alvarez in the front seats. Larry and his buddy, door gunner Ronnie Dunn, were strapped loosely in the back, Larry on the left behind Charlie and Ronnie behind the lieutenant in charge.

The day's combat mission: Support infantry units on the ground, engaged in "heavy fighting with a large enemy force" near Quang Tri. It was standard procedure, stuff these boys did on a regular basis without fear or failure. Firepower from Larry's ship would kill some adversaries, and push others away, giving hope to the boots on the ground.

Some of the 48 rockets beneath the soldiers' feet would be released first. Machine gun fire followed from the back seats, either left or right depending on the angle of the plane and the formation of other ships in the force around them. Hostile ground fire reached aircraft units if they flew too low or turned in the wrong direction. To complete the mission on this day in Bong Son (about which Larry complained "this place just ain't for me"), the gunship had to fly beneath the tops of the trees in spurts of aggression. Pilot Alvarez repeated several aerial runs and continued efforts to follow the fundamental rule of combat: complete the mission and exit as soon as possible. Charlie had prepared for this day and was a well-trained pilot as he "rolled in hot" with the rest of the Cavalry.

The UH-1B Huey gunship helicopter, purchased in 1965 by the Army, had logged 1,742 total flight hours to date, many in the previous two weeks. Warrant Officer Charles Alvarez piloted less than two of those hours when the ship lost power. Six shots hit the helicopter. The main rotor blade system suffered severe damage. Charlie

21. In Memory of Charlie

managed to keep the ship in flight as it rocked back and forth. He gained control and began to retreat. Lieutenant Blackmon, known as "Blackie" in the unit, prepared to take over and alerted the team on the radio. They would make one more run and head home while they still had flying power and fuel.

The team took a final dive toward the enemy line, dumping the balance of rockets and simultaneously shooting M-60 machine guns from both sides of the ship. Enemy fire returned with a vengeance with the ship at only 1500 feet. Before the crew could call for a distress signal, a 12.7 mm round ripped through the left windshield. The explosion in the ship caused concussive damage to them all. Intense fire blinded the men and glass shattered and flew in all directions. Deafening sounds consumed their close quarters, rendering sight and hearing useless but for the sounds of a ship in distress. Calls on the radio, screams, gunshots, broken rotors.

Their friendly pilot gave his life, in an instant. Charlie took two bullets—one in the chest and one in the head, killing him on impact. The blood and bones of their brother blanketed the boys in the cabin and every crevice imaginable. The bitter, brutal trauma flooded their senses. There would be no escaping the smells of metal, body odor, human pheromones, blood, and sickness that penetrated the soldiers' olfactory systems. On their skin, their largest organ and primary sensory organ, the temperature, vibrations, pressure, abrasions, and hunks of soft tissue would leave lasting scars. Invisible scars, masking the real pain left in their wake.

My brother died a little bit on February 16, 1968, along with Charlie. Ronnie Dunn told the story to Bronder a couple weeks later: "Blackie is the best fuckin' pilot in Vietnam," Ronnie told Bronder, adding that the flight was just supposed to be a simple clear-out of a suspected VC location.

"I have done these missions at least 50 times and never had a problem," Ronnie said, adding, "We go into our dive and the rockets on both sides are blasting away. I'm firing the shit out of the M-60 and then, out of nowhere, I'm covered in blood, brains, hair, and part of his metal cockpit helmet. Alvarez took a direct hit from a .50 caliber round and it hit him right between the eyes. Although his body

Part Seven

was strapped in, his arms and upper torso fell onto the control panel and the chopper started to free fall. I thought we were going down."

Larry's ship headed into a spin to the left. Blackie screamed over the headset, "Grab him," to pull Charlie's body off the left side controls, so Blackmon could engage his right-side controls. Larry reached from the back seat against the force of gravity, pulling a lever to release Charlie's seat.

Blackmon corrected the aircraft before it crashed. He radioed base camp and reported one man down. Blackmon gathered composure, remembering the men on his ship depending on him to stay alive. There would be no escaping the nauseating reality of losing a team member mid-flight. They couldn't land fast enough. They were lucky to land at all.

As soon as Larry's helicopter arrived on the flight deck, Rich was there to help. Medics removed Charlie's body. Magnesium deteriorates with the introduction of blood, and those ships were made of thin layers of magnesium. To ensure the slightest chance of saving the helicopter, it had to be cleaned right away. It would offer Larry a distraction to his state of shock, giving his hands purpose beyond shaking.

Rich helped Larry clean in silence. It took them hours, working side by side without a word spoken, cleaning the inside of the ship. The shot-up ship went back to work the next day.

Larry asked the Major more than once for approval to escort Charlie to his family back home in California. The brave pilot took a bullet for him, and his family deserved answers. The Army didn't deem it "necessary" and denied Larry's requests.

The A Battery honored Charlie during a memorial service that night, conducted by Chaplain Moore promptly at 1900 hours, in the middle of landing zone Sharon. Days later, General W.C. Westmoreland sent a letter to Charlie's aunt giving his deepest sympathies and heartfelt condolences on behalf of his command. He remarked in the letter that the family may "rest assured that all of us will continue to do our utmost to bring eventual victory so that his sacrifice will not have been in vain."

In the words of U.S. Army Chief of Staff, General Harold K.

21. In Memory of Charlie

Johnson, Charles Alvarez "served his God and his Nation with courage and honor at a time of great need" and left behind a legacy of ultimate sacrifice. Lieutenant General Edgar C. Doleman, Deputy Commander in Chief at Army Pacific Headquarters, sent Charlie's sister Geraldine a letter dated 28 February 1968 extending his personal sympathy.

Major Clarence H. Woliver (the same major who led the search mission in the Happy Valley two months later) extended his sympathy in a letter dated 28 April 1968 to Charlie's aunt and stated that Charles was an "exemplary soldier." His personal property had been collected and forwarded to the family, he assured her.

A couple years after Charlie's death, his older brother David was also killed in action. He died in South Korea while on a last patrol along the DMZ. His Huey crashed on the Kimpa Peninsula when the drive shaft came apart in mid-flight. All crew members perished. David, just 35 years old, had 13 days before his planned retirement. He left behind a wife and seven children.

Prior to his death, Charlie received the National Defense Service Medal, Vietnam Service Medal, Vietnam Campaign Ribbon, Army Aviator Badge, and the Expert Badge with Rifle Bar. Several medals were awarded to Charlie posthumously, including the Bronze Star Medal, Distinguished Flying Cross, Air Medal, and Purple Heart.

Charlie was in the path between Larry and that fateful bullet. Had Charlie not been the brazen warrior who trained to fight and prepared to die—but for the Grace of God—Larry might have taken that shot. If there were a medal for saving my brother, I would hope Charlie is wearing it with pride, and they are enjoying a cold beer together in celebration.

Charles Allen Alvarez never married or had children. His namesake and brave legacy lives on inside his family. Eddie named his first son Charles Allen Alvarez II, and he in turn named his son Charles Allen Alvarez III. They should wear the name with complete pride and honor. Charlie is buried in Ft. Rosecrans National Cemetery in San Diego. If you're in the area, visit Charlie's gravesite at section PS-5, Site 164 or visit his name on the Vietnam Memorial Wall, panel

Part Seven

39E/line 56. Give him your gratitude, and never forget the price he paid for your freedom.

If you see a 1968 penny nearby, you'll know I've been before you.

22

Love Always, Tracy

Today.

Dear Larry,

    I never knew the depth of your love for me until I got your letters. All of them showed me the young boy I never knew and helped me find the other young boys you never forgot. I have so much to thank you for, and only wish I had written this in time.

    My finest gifts have been from you. The Vietnam jacket that I wouldn't take off for days, which gave me first-grade bragging rights. The biggest birthday cake that any 5-year-old deserves. All the doodads for my pink bike. The tarnished St. Christopher charm that showed up in my hands while finishing this book. Your military medals, shiny and new like you would want me to have, arriving at the right time to brighten my world in the middle of a global pandemic and my darkest days. And your precious words, all 37,406 of them. Thank you.

    Because of these gifts, showers of blessings have rained on me. Heartfelt, genuine conversations with Rich Passer, Rick Leroue, Barry Brady, John Stewart, Greg Bronder, Captain Stroud, Colonel Caughron, Jane Jayroe, Captain Blackmon, Lieutenant Hawks, and many others whose lives you touched and many you never met, solidified your brave actions and

Larry served as Assistant Boy Scout Leader for many years. Circa 1999, Kendall Park, New Jersey.

Part Seven

Larry's last family photograph was taken in the same family home where he grew up. Left to right: Michele Smith (Larry's daughter), Larry, Tracy, Marlene Smith (Larry's wife). January 2000. Kendall Park, New Jersey.

Larry and Tracy's last photograph, the day before his heart surgery, January 2000. Kendall Park, New Jersey.

22. Love Always, Tracy

honored your memory. They shared stories and memories, alongside your favorite supporters inside our family that remember your sarcasm and tender heart with fondness. I won't forget the names and stories of those I haven't found. Captain Mills. Warrant Officer Raymond. Ronnie Dunn. Phil Durbin. Your buddy, Rico.

I wish I had been more aware of your love for me and expressed my own more often. I wish I could have helped you fight your demons like you did those bad guys in Vietnam. I wish I could have offered the solutions your body needed to be well. I should have recognized how large your heart was and how badly it needed and deserved mending. If only I knew then what I know now.

You lived through a war filled with epic failures inside our nation's darkest days. You did the right thing day in and day out, earning your place as a First Cavalry trooper. And you took us with you through the journey of your days in uniform, told us the truth even as you figured it out, and kept surprising us with your physical endurance not to mention some savvy and diligent reporting skills. You declared your "Love Always" in each letter and asked for little in return. You spent the rest of your life after the war trying to survive the best you could.

Somewhere along the way in Vietnam, the lines of justice blurred and changed your belief that you could make a difference in the war. You tried, and you did it well. You have never harmed a soul, unless ordered to do so. You epitomized a warrior, and I'm proud to be called your sister. *You* were the special one.

I still wish on chicken bones and taught my children to do the same. I believe in luck, and fate, and destiny existing in the same moment, with you as the biggest testament. Your stories were hard to learn, even harder to tell, but necessary and healing. Your words comforted me. Over and over, I read them, heard you in them, and felt your love get me through the toughest days of my life.

I'm telling your story because you never could. I hope that your lineage of children, grandchildren, and great-grands can better understand and recognize the incredible warrior—and generational trauma—inside their blood. Like you wished in a letter once, my prayer is that none of them or the ones to come ever have to face war like you did.

It's so difficult to say goodbye. Our life was full of goodbyes, ever since that day in Fort Dix. The day the family left New Jersey without you and moved down South. The day in Philly when you told me things about Vietnam for the first time. And in the hours before your heart surgery when you followed me to the car on that freezing January afternoon in early 2000, and gave me your blessings to marry, and one final, warm hug. And every painful hospital visit that same year, until your final surrender.

This is my final goodbye. It is the most important of all. It ends here, with complete healing for us both. The truth has set us free.

Thank you for being a wonderful big brother. Thank you for writing so eloquently and showing me the true meaning of family. Thank you for your honesty about a war that lied to us, even when it didn't serve your best interest to

Scouts to honor late troop leader

By David Weinstein
Staff Writer

Larry R. Smith, a decorated Vietnam War hero and molder of young men through his tireless volunteer efforts with Scouting troops in South Brunswick, died Aug. 5 at Willow Creek Rehabilitation in Somerset. He was 51.

Mr. Smith slipped into a coma following heart bypass surgery in February and never recovered.

Mr. Smith served in Vietnam from 1966 to 1979, earning the Air Medal as a helicopter crew chief for the Army 1st Air Cavalry, twice receiving the Army Commendation Medal for heroism, the Bronze Star and three Purple Hearts.

Born in Whitesville, N.C., Mr. Smith lived in Kendall Park for 36 years. For the last 12 years, Mr. Smith volunteered his time working with the young men of the Cub and Boy Scouts. Mr. Smith was assistant Scout master of Troop 90.

His son, Larry Jr., is expected to receive his Eagle Scout rank in September.

Mr. Smith is survived by his wife, Marlene; two daughters, Cindy Smith of Pinebluff, N.C.; and Michele Smith of Kendall Park; a son, Larry Jr.; three sisters, Tracy Smith of Charlotte, N.C., and Joanne Turner and Peggy Deak of Vass, N.C. and his mother, Bernice Smith, also of Vass.

Mr. Smith was most recently employed by Gemini Trucking and Sales in Edison. He was a member of Veterans of Foreign Wars Post 9111.

His contributions, both to his country and his town, though, will not be forgotten, said long time friend Gary Thomson, Scout master of Troop 90.

Larry R. Smith

"Even after his boy, Larry Jr., made Eagle Scout, Larry kept on going. He was dedicated," he said.

Mr. Thomson recalled Mr. Smith's love of motorcycles, his activeness with the VFW, and his love of Scouting.

But most of all, Mr. Thomson remembered Wednesday, was Mr. Smith's heroism in the Vietnam War.

A memorial service will take place Friday, Aug. 11, beginning at 7 p.m. at the Presbyterian Church of the Sand Hills in Kendall Park.

The service will include prayers offered from members of the Scouting troops with whom Mr. Smith had grown close, as well as from members of Post 9111. The Rev. John H. Maltby, Miller Memorial Presbyterian Church, will preside over the service.

Following the Friday service, friends and family are invited to Post 9111 on Henderson Road, Kendall Park.

In lieu of flowers, contributions should be made in Mr. Smith's memory to Marlene M. Smith.

Larry's obituary in the local newspaper, August 2000.

22. *Love Always, Tracy*

do so. Thank you for your service to our country. Thank you for every penny, even the ones you spent. Rich tells me you spent your days on the ground looking down, to try to find any random coin to send home for my collection. Thank you for never giving up on me or your promises.

Most of all, thank you for your love, still. Your dreams for me were always bigger than your own, so I'm living them large in your memory.

Love Always,

Tracy

P.S. I continue to behave, mostly. And I pick up every penny I spot on the ground.

Index

A Shau Valley 149, 152-153, 181
Air Force 20, 92, 123, 157-158, 160-162, 166-167, 169
Airmobile 12, 27, 28, 29, 86, 124, 155; *see also* Cavalry; First Cavalry
Alvarez, Charles 209, 215-223
ambush 55, 87, 93, 122, 154
ammunition (ammo) 16, 32, 52, 61, 64, 122, 124-125, 150-151, 153, 156 161, 163-164, 167, 195-196, 198
An Khe 11, 30, 52, 58, 68, 99-100, 103, 105, 113, 118, 120, 122, 153, 199, 215
Angelou, Maya 1
ARA (aerial rocket artillery) 12, 20, 46, 60–61, 76, 86, 90, 95, 104, 124, 150, 152, 162–163; *see also* Blue Max

Barlow, Jessie 55
battalion (bty) 60, 95, 141, 152, 157, 162, 183
Blackmon, Lieut. Bob 220–222, 225
Blue Max 12, 95, 150–151, 153–154, 157, 159, 162, 165–167; *see also* ARA
Bong Son 30, 32, 52, 67, 72, 88, 94, 97, 104, 113–114, 121, 220; *see also* Two Bits
Brady, Barry 75, 139, 143, 151, 155, 165, 203, 209, 213, 217, 225
Bronder, Greg 215–217, 219, 221, 225
Bronze Star 94–95, 99, 106, 223
bunker 11, 31, 47, 52, 106, 129, 142, 196, 198

C&C ship 152–153, 159–161
C-rations (rations) 11, 53, 82, 88, 121, 155
Cam Rahn Bay 8–10
Camp Evans 59, 190, 195–196
Caughron, Lt. Col. Kenneth D. 168, 225
Cavalry 52, 115, 122, 154, 162, 173, 209, 216, 220; *see also* airmobile; First Cavalry
Central Highlands 52, 89, 92, 138, 191
Chinook 121
Clark, Paul 55
Cobra 71, 164, 177–178, 183–184, 192
Cronkite, Walter 17, 34, 126

Da Nang 46, 52, 62, 116, 129, 138, 141–145, 149, 157–158, 161, 164–165, 168–169, 177, 190, 199

Dak To 46, 90, 92–95, 119
Daley, Butch (Daniel Wm) 15, 24, 32, 72, 116, 179, 182–183, 204
dead tired 19, 72, 184
DMZ (Demilitarized Military Zone) 52, 55, 62, 65–66, 69, 116, 117, 118, 124, 149, 157, 223
Dodge Charger 79, 82, 94, 104, 127, 129, 176, 182, 186, 202–203, 205, 213
Doleman, Lt. Gen. Edgar C. 223
Donut Dolly 72; *see also* Red Cross
door gunner 9, 12, 27, 51, 61, 70, 151, 154, 162, 165, 200, 220
Dunn, Ronnie 75, 139, 209, 220–222, 225, 228

elephant grass 11–12, 155

F-4 Phantom planes 161–162
First Cavalry (1st Cav) 6, 12, 46, 55, 95, 123, 144, 149, 157, 162, 196, 228; *see also* airmobile; Cavalry
Fort Dix, NJ 7, 23–24, 26–27, 228,
Fort Rucker, AL 7, 24, 123
foxhole 58, 127, 129, 212
friendly fire 93, 121, 142, 159

Gallagher, Johnny 145
Galloway, Joe 215
Gamble, Jane Jayroe 45–51, 55, 116, 225; *see also* Miss America
Germeck, Captain Chuck 151, 154–155, 157, 165
grenade 96, 129, 142, 155–156, 160, 204
gunship 20, 45, 55, 60–61, 86, 93, 150–151, 154, 156, 162–164, 178, 219–220; *see also* Huey; UH-1

H&I (Harassment and Interdiction fire) 121
Happy Valley 148–149, 153–154, 158, 162, 164–165, 209, 212, 223
Hawks, Lieutenant Jim 151, 165, 218
Hembree, James 55
Hill 875 93, 95

231

Index

Ho Chi Minh 136, 176, 196; trail 59, 86, 92, 124, 149
Hong Kong 70, 116
Hope, Bob 71, 105
Howell, SP/4 151, 165
howitzer 98, 198
Hue 116, 122–123, 125–126, 14
Huey 24, 28–29, 61–62, 71, 76, 102, 117, 148, 150–151, 153–154, 156, 159, 162, 164, 167, 177–178, 191, 212, 219–220, 223; *see also* gunship; UH-1

Johnson, Gen. Harold K. 222–223
Johnson, Pres. Lyndon B. 86, 95, 112, 143
Jolly Green 146, 158–165, 168

Karmons, Col. Fred 47, 116
Kennedy John F. 146, 193
Kennedy, Robert, Sr. 143, 146, 193
Khe Sahn 124
KIA (killed in action) 17, 34, 47, 55, 131, 223
King, Martin Luther, Jr. 146
Kissinger, Henry A. 212
Kontum 52, 88–90, 95, 97, 99

Johnson, Carla 169–170 *see also* Oberdier
Johnson, Gen. Harold K. 222–223
Johnson, Pres. Lyndon B. 86, 95, 112, 143

Leroue, Richard (Rick) 151, 154, 156, 164–165, 207, 209, 225
LZ English 46–47, 52
LZ Jane 116
LZ Sharon 47, 152, 164, 190, 200, 222
LZ Tombstone 116
LZ Uplift 47, 51

M-16 9, 121, 125, 129, 153
M-60 28, 53, 61, 90, 121, 125, 130, 150, 153, 200, 221
Marine 15, 65, 92–93, 116, 123–124, 149, 196, 198, 219
McGovern, Sen. George 176
McLaughlin, John 200–201, 207
Mills, Captain 151, 154–155, 157, 159, 162, 165, 169, 225
Miss America 44–47, 49–52, 116; *see also* Gamble, Jane Jayroe
mongoose 62–63
monsoon 44–46, 49, 51, 56, 112, 144, 149, 192
Morford, Loren Lee 55

napalm 93, 157–158, 164
Navy 36, 116, 144, 162
Nixon, Pres. Richard 42

Oberdier, Lyn 158–162, 164, 168–170; *see also* Johnson, Carla
101st Airborne Division 149, 204
173rd Airborne Brigade 92–93
Operation Delaware 149

Passer, Richard 58–59, 63–64, 70, 73, 76, 78, 80, 82, 93–95, 98–99, 102, 105, 116, 127, 140, 151, 165, 193, 206–207, 209, 213, 217, 222, 225, 229
pennies 2, 7, 18, 21–23, 33, 44, 77, 91, 114, 117, 171–172, 177–178, 187, 203, 217, 224, 229
Phillips, Walter Mack 55
Pleiku 157–158, 161, 163–164, 166–168
Purple Heart 53–54, 71–72, 223

Quan Kay 8
Quang Tri 52, 122, 124–126, 143, 150, 152, 177–178, 181, 190, 196, 220
Qui Nhon 47, 62

Raymond, Warrant Officer 151, 165, 225
Reagan, Ronald 86
Red Cross 30, 71–72, 105; *see also* Donut Dolly
Robbins, Billy 15, 27, 101, 145, 147, 193, 199
Robinson, Capt. Winston 55
rotor 19, 54–56, 71, 78, 90, 125, 150, 154, 220–221

Schedeneck, Marlene 206–208, 212–213, 226
Silver Star 94, 168
Sin City 52, 67–68
Singleton, J.D. 55
Skyraider 93, 157–160, 163–164, 166–167, 169, 170
snake 13, 31, 62, 148
South China Sea 32, 52, 121 191
Stewart, John 75, 138–139, 162, 203, 209, 217, 225
Stroud, Tom 158–164, 166–170, 225

Tapp, Eldin Marion 200–201
Tenorio, Sgt. Sam 95
Tet Offensive 122, 124–126, 131, 198, 215, 219, 221
Tolson, Gen. John J. 47, 123
trauma 2, 55, 84, 212, 214, 221; generational 228
Tuy Hoa 69–71, 73
"Two Bits" 47, 51–52, 72, 88, 97, 104–105, 120; *see also* Bong Son

UH-1 29, 71, 76, 150, 220; *see also* gunship; Huey

232

Index

valor 95, 99, 167–168

Westmoreland, Gen. W.C. 86, 222

Wheat, Pryor 55

Woliver, Maj. Clarence H. (Clancy) 162–163, 167, 223

XO (executive officer) 63–64